The Challenges of Cultural Discipleship

The Challenges of Cultural Discipleship

Essays in the Line of Abraham Kuyper

Richard J. Mouw

WILLIAM B. EERDMANS PUBLISHING COMPANY
GRAND RAPIDS, MICHIGAN / CAMBRIDGE, U.K.

Published 2012 by
Wm. B. Eerdmans Publishing Co.
2140 Oak Industrial Drive N.E., Grand Rapids, Michigan 49505 /
P.O. Box 163, Cambridge CB3 9PU U.K.

Printed in the United States of America

17 16 15 14 13 12   7 6 5 4 3 2 1

Library of Congress Cataloging-in-Publication Data

Mouw, Richard J.
   The challenges of cultural discipleship: essays in the line of Abraham Kuyper /
   Richard J. Mouw.
       p.   cm.
   ISBN 978-0-8028-6698-1 (pbk.: alk. paper)
   1. Calvinism. 2. Reformed churches — Doctrines. 3. Kuyper, Abraham, 1837-1920.
   4. Calvin, Jean, 1509-1564.   I. Title.

   BX9410.M68   2012
   230′.42 — dc23

                                                          2011024399

www.eerdmans.com

Contents

Contents

Introduction

The essays in this book form the "back story" of some things I have written in recent decades with the intention of making the ideas associated with a "Kuyperian" perspective accessible to a nonscholarly audience.[1] All the essays here have been published previously, either in scholarly journals or as contributions to books of essays edited by others.

I have been encouraged by several folks to gather these essays together in one book, and I am especially indebted to two of my very talented Ph.D. students at Fuller Seminary, Matt Kaemingk and Cory Willson, who followed through with their urgings by doing some of the early selecting and organizing. I have left most of the essays unchanged from the original published forms, although I have made a few adjustments — such as adding some additional footnotes and providing section headings in those essays where there were none in the original.

In the subtitle I have chosen for this volume, I have characterized my various explorations as being in Kuyper's "line." The "in the line of" expression is a familiar one in Dutch. To say that some presentation is *in de lijn van* some person or school of thought does not necessarily mean that it is intended to express a "party line." The phrase is more typically used to identify a specific strand or school of thought, associated with some im-

---

1. Especially my *Abraham Kuyper: A Short and Personal Introduction* (Grand Rapids: Eerdmans, 2011); also *When the Kings Come Marching In: Isaiah and the New Jerusalem*, rev. ed. (Grand Rapids: Eerdmans, 2004), and *Calvinism in the Las Vegas Airport: Making Connections in Today's World* (Grand Rapids: Zondervan, 2004).

portant leader, within a more general framework — in this case a general Reformed framework — for addressing a particular subject.

The essays in this volume are not meant simply as interpretations or strict applications of Kuyper's thought. On some of the topics I address, I am meaning to expand — and even to correct in several instances — specific ideas that he set forth. Kuyper himself saw the need for a "neo-Calvinism," a reworking of key concepts in John Calvin's system of thought for new challenges and contexts. For similar reasons some of us think of ourselves as engaged in an ongoing cooperative — to use Vincent Bacote's happy phrase[2] — "neo-Kuyperian" project. But we still look to Kuyper for guidance and inspiration.

Those of us who work "in the line of Kuyper" are aware of other "lines," and we are convinced that Kuyper offered some themes and concepts that provide a compelling alternative to other overall schemes for dealing with key questions of church and culture. We may not want to draw the lines as sharply as Kuyper did between a Reformed perspective and, say, a Catholic or an Anabaptist outlook. But we do see some important differences at work.

At a few points in these pages I pay attention to some of those important differences as they show up even within Dutch Calvinism, in both the Netherlands and North America. For me, it is helpful to see how Kuyper was interacting with these other "lines" on topics of debate that recur frequently in that particular theological environment. For those who might want some help in navigating that territory, I have provided a brief appendix at the end, with some explanations of labels and names. But, for the most part, my own interests are focused on exploring and developing the Kuyperian perspective for some key topics bearing on a broad Christian engagement with the challenges of cultural discipleship.

One particular essay — the final one in this volume, but the earliest one written — is especially outdated, but I have fought the temptation to add anything to it in the light of further developments. For me, to rework it would be like photo-shopping a beloved snapshot from the past. In 1985, during the months just before I departed from the Calvin College Philosophy Department to join the faculty at Fuller Theological Seminary, I did considerable research and reflection for the essay, "Dutch Calvinist Philosophical Influences in North America." I wrote it as a loving tribute to the

2. Vincent Bacote, *The Spirit in Public Theology: Appropriating the Legacy of Abraham Kuyper* (Grand Rapids: Baker Academic, 2005), 155-56.

philosophy department — and to the college of which it is a part — where I had taught for the previous seventeen years.

Then, on the day the moving van departed for the West Coast, my wife and son dropped me off at the Grand Rapids airport, where I began a trip to Amsterdam while they drove to California. During the next week I presented the paper at the Vrije Universiteit, the school founded by Abraham Kuyper, as a participant in a consultation on the influences of Dutch Calvinist thought in various parts of the world. Then, having made my own interim "summing up" on Dutch soil, I flew to Los Angeles, where Phyllis and Dirk picked me up after their cross-country drive. Thus I began a new stage of my intellectual and spiritual journey, taking my Kuyperian convictions with me into the cultural and theological environs of California, hoping to work there on the project I describe at the end of that essay: articulating a neo-Calvinist perspective that will "continue to grow as an indigenous, ecumenically enriched activity, in which the ideas and insights of nineteenth-century Holland are appropriated and recontextualized" for new challenges in Christian thought and service.

Many good things have happened at Calvin College — and in the larger world of Kuyperian scholarship — since I wrote that essay. But what has not changed is my deep gratitude for the wonderful years I spent in a community where Kuyper's great manifesto, that no "square inch in the whole domain of our human existence" lies outside of the sovereign rule of Jesus Christ, is taken with utmost seriousness. For that, and for all in which I have also been privileged to participate since then at Fuller Seminary — I am eternally grateful.

Calvin's Legacy for Public Theology

In discussing the role of the ideal legislator in book 2 of his *Social Contract,* Jean-Jacques Rousseau paid tribute in a footnote to the Protestant Reformer who had dominated public life in the city of Geneva two centuries earlier: "Those who only consider Calvin as a theologian do not understand the extent of his genius. The drawing up of our wise edicts, in which he played a large part, does him as much honor as his *Institutes.* Whatever revolution time may bring in our cult, as long as love of the homeland and liberty is not extinguished among us, the memory of that great man will never cease to be blessed."[1]

Rousseau does not offer any examples of the sort of wise edicts he has in mind, but he does eventually make it clear why he is not enthusiastic about the substance of Calvin's theology. When he gets around to discussing the role of religion in public life further on in his treatise, he singles out, without mentioning the Reformer by name, the kind of theology for which Calvin was known as posing a serious danger to the very fabric of civil society. Theological intolerance, Rousseau argues, is inextricably linked to civil intolerance. The believer in an intolerant God will be obliged to hate those whom God hates. "It is impossible to live in peace with people whom one believes are damned. . . . Wherever

---

1. Jean-Jacques Rousseau, *On the Social Contract, with Geneva Manuscript and Political Economy,* ed. Roger D. Masters, trans. Judith R. Masters (New York: St. Martin's Press, 1978), 68-69, starred footnote.

This essay previously appeared in *Political Theology* 10, no. 3 (2009). It is printed here with permission.

theological intolerance exists, it is impossible for it not to have some civil effect."[2]

Rousseau would have had no difficulty bringing forth examples of the actual results of Calvin's theological intolerance for political life. Calvin's well-known complicity in the burning of Servetus is an obvious case in point. And, if anything, the Calvinist attitude on such matters had hardened in a place like Scotland in the years following the Reformation era. The Presbyterian "Covenanter" James Guthrie, in his 1651 pamphlet *The Causes of God's Wrath against Scotland*, offered just the kind of sentiment Rousseau was worried about when he wrote: "we judge it but the effect of wisdom of the flesh and to smell rankly of a carnal politic spirit to halve and divide the things of God for making peace amongst men."[3]

There is no reason to question, however, the sincerity of Rousseau's explicit praise for Calvin's impact on life in Geneva. The best way of reading that accolade in conjunction with his condemnation of a theological intolerance is to take Rousseau as expressing a genuine ambivalence about the overall merits of Calvin's contribution to an understanding of a flourishing civil society. Furthermore, his concern about a Calvinist type of theological intolerance points to an important area of exploration that goes beyond a focus specifically on Calvin's views on political life in particular — a topic, to be sure, that deserves much detailed attention. Rousseau's observation about a theology's "civil effect" highlights a concern that has been receiving considerable theological attention in recent decades, particularly in that area of discussion that has come to be known as "public theology."

Theology and Civil Society

Public theology as an identifiable theological subdiscipline addresses an agenda that overlaps with those associated with some other rubrics that have been given much attention in the past century, such as "Christian social ethics," "political theology," and "church and society." While these other subdisciplines are still very much alive, public theologians have wanted to explore questions about "public" life that are not adequately addressed simply by focusing on "ethical," "political," or "church-and-state" topics.

2. Rousseau, *Social Contract*, 131.

3. James Guthrie, *Causes of God's Wrath against Scotland*, quoted by J. D. Douglas, *Light in the North: The Story of the Scottish Covenanters* (Grand Rapids: Eerdmans, 1964), 74.

This expanded theological focus takes up the concern expressed by some social scientists, that the identification of the public with the political tends to focus too exclusively on the relationship of the individual to the state in exploring normative questions about societal life, ignoring thereby the significant role that "mediating structures" can play — neighborhood organizations, youth clubs, service groups, churches, and families themselves — in creating a buffer zone between the state and the individual.[4] This broad "middle" area of social interaction, characterized by a variety of associational groupings, is what constitutes much of civil society, and a healthy public life will encourage the flourishing of these entities. Conversely, as Robert Putnam has made the case in his much-discussed *Bowling Alone,* the decline in these associational patterns means a loss of the "social capital" that plays a crucial role in the character formation that is in turn necessary for effective citizenship.[5]

These same issues have been taken up in the public theology discussions. Special attention has been given to the ways in which Christian theology and spirituality can contribute to the flourishing of civil society in this broader sense. In this context, Rousseau's concern about a theological intolerance has special poignancy. What is the "civil effect" of a theology like John Calvin's?

"Two Calvins"

Rousseau's ambivalence about Calvin's contribution is certainly understandable, since even those who have strong sympathies for the basics of Calvin's theology have to deal with some obvious tensions in his thought. Indeed, one of Calvin's mostly sympathetic biographers, William Bouwsma, sees the tensions in the Reformer's theology as stemming from conflicts deep in his psyche — so deep in fact that Bouwsma resorts to positing "two Calvins, coexisting uncomfortably within the same historical personage."

One of those Calvins is "the philosophical Calvin" who, "as a rationalist and a schoolman of the high Scholastic tradition," favored a "static or-

---

4. Peter Berger, *Facing Up to Modernity: Excursions in Society, Politics, and Religion* (New York: Basic Books, 1977), 140.

5. Robert Putnam, *Bowling Alone: The Collapse and Revival of American Community* (New York: Simon and Schuster, 2000).

thodoxy" and "craved desperately for intelligibility, order, certainty. Distrusting freedom, he struggled to control both himself and the world." The second John Calvin, though, "was a rhetorician and a humanist" who "was flexible to the point of opportunism, and a revolutionary in spite of himself." This was a Calvin who "was inclined to celebrate the paradoxes and mystery at the heart of existence."[6]

It is easy to see something like these two Calvins at work in, for example, the Reformer's struggles with the topic of Christian obedience to government. In his commentary on the classic "powers that be" passage in Romans 13, he comes down unambiguously on the side of unfailing submission to political authorities, allowing no room for legitimate political resistance, even in the case of unjust rulers. What are Christian citizens to do, he asks, when confronted with magistrates who "degenerate" from the proper use of power? Even in these difficult situations, Calvin insists, "the obedience due to princes ought to be rendered to them. For since a wicked prince is the Lord's scourge to punish the sins of the people, let us remember, that it happens through our fault that this excellent blessing of God is turned into a curse."[7] Thus, it is the apostle's teaching "that we ought to obey kings and governors, whoever they may be, not because we are constrained, but because it is a service acceptable to God."[8]

This counsel stands in rather stark contrast, though, to the position he sets forth in the last section of the *Institutes* where, while pointing his readers to "that obedience which we have shown to be due the authority of rulers," he nonetheless acknowledges that "we are always to make this exception," namely, "that such obedience is never to lead us away from obedience to him, to whose will the desires of all kings ought to be subject, to whose decrees all their commands ought to yield, to whose majesty their scepters ought to be submitted." Christian citizens must never forget that it is "the King of Kings, who, when he has opened his sacred mouth, must alone be heard, before all and above all men." If earthly rulers "command anything against him, let it go unesteemed."[9]

6. William Bouwsma, *John Calvin: A Sixteenth Century Portrait* (New York: Oxford University Press, 1988), 230-31.

7. John Calvin, *Commentary on Romans,* http://www.ccel.org/ccel/calvin/calcom38 .xvii.ii.html.

8. Calvin, *Commentary on Romans,* http://www.ccel.org/ccel/calvin/calcom38.xvii.iii .html.

9. John Calvin, *Institutes of the Christian Religion,* trans. Ford Lewis Battles, ed. John T. McNeill, 2 vols. (Philadelphia: Westminster, 1960), 2.4.20, p. 32.

More directly relevant for his views on civil society is the tension that characterizes Calvin's diverse assessments of the cultural insights of the unregenerate mind. On the one hand, his own studies in classical thought had given him a sense of his intellectual debt to several pagan thinkers, especially Seneca. This debt led him to point to "a universal apprehension of reason and understanding [that] is by nature implanted in men," which, "because it is bestowed indiscriminately upon pious and impious, . . . is rightly counted among natural gifts"; indeed, says Calvin, every human being ought to recognize this implanted rational nature as a "peculiar grace of God."[10] Moreover, when we observe this gift at work in "secular writers," Calvin advises, we should

> let that admirable light of truth shining in them teach us that the mind of man, though fallen and perverted from its wholeness, is nevertheless clothed and ornamented with God's excellent gifts. If we regard the Spirit of God as the sole fountain of truth, we shall neither reject the truth itself, nor despise it where it shall appear, unless we wish to dishonor the Spirit of God. . . . Those men whom Scripture [1 Cor. 2:14] calls "natural men" were, indeed, sharp and penetrating in their investigation of inferior things. Let us, accordingly, learn by their example how many gifts the Lord left to human nature even after it was despoiled of its true good.[11]

In spite of such praise, Calvin could also speak very negatively about the products of the unregenerate mind. When Calvin credits the unredeemed with some grasp of the principles of civic fairness, for example, he quickly adds that even when the human mind follows after truth, "it limps and staggers" in doing so.[12] In the lives of unbelievers, he says, the civic "virtues are so sullied that before God they lose all favor," so that anything in them "that appears praiseworthy must be considered worthless."[13] And while he acknowledges that "some sparks still gleam" in the non-Christian mind, that light is nonetheless "choked with dense ignorance, so that it cannot come forth effectively."[14]

Given these two different emphases in Calvin's assessments of "the

10. Calvin, *Institutes* 2.3.3, p. 292.
11. Calvin, *Institutes* 2.2.15, pp. 273-75.
12. Calvin, *Institutes* 2.2.13, pp. 272-73.
13. Calvin, *Institutes* 2.3.4, p. 294.
14. Calvin, *Institutes* 2.2.12, pp. 270-71.

natural man," it should not surprise us that when Karl Barth and Emil Brunner debated the question of natural theology in the 1930s, each accused the other of betraying the basic aims of Reformation thought. On the one hand, Barth insisted that fidelity to the Reformation necessitated a firm rejection of natural theology as such, while Brunner issued a more modest call for "our generation to find the way back to a true *theologia naturalis*."[15] And each of them, in making their case, appealed to the authority of John Calvin, quoting passages that reinforced their respective positions — with Brunner insisting that his more favorable assessment of "the natural mind" was the dominant viewpoint in Calvin's writings, and Barth responding that we should not allow "that little corner which has been left uncovered in Calvin's treatment" to lure us down a dangerous path.[16]

Are we simply left with the "two Calvins," then, resigning ourselves to debates between parties who choose from what are finally contradictory patterns in the Reformer's thinking about important matters? Further on we will point to one creative effort to construct a public theology that draws on both of these strands. But for a beginning, it is instructive to single out a few themes in Calvin's thought — however they might be reconciled with other elements in his theology — that do contribute to the task of public theology.

Theology and "Collectivities"

In his study of Scottish Enlightenment thought, Richard Sher observes that some of the concepts that figured prominently in the exploration of societal phenomena were based directly — for all the secularized language in which they were couched — on "Calvinist foundations." Specifically, Sher cites the Calvinist insistence "that human beings constitute integral parts of the particular societies in which they live and cannot be studied apart from them; that God frequently uses people (or peoples) for divine purposes that remain unknown to them, such as punishing the sinful and rewarding the righteous (the famous concept of 'unintended conse-

---

15. Emil Brunner, "Nature and Grace: A Contribution to the Discussion with Karl Barth," in Emil Brunner and Karl Barth, *Natural Theology,* trans. Peter Fraenkel (London: Centenary Press, 1946), 59.

16. Barth, "NO!" in Barth and Brunner, *Natural Theology,* 103.

quences'); and that the study of collectivities — nations, tribes, and the like — is rich with moral and religious significance."[17]

Sher identifies an important feature of Calvin's theology here: the attention given to collective social entities. He also rightly connects this focus to the strong Calvinist emphasis on divine providence. In one sense, of course, providence is surrounded by mystery in the Calvinist scheme — which means that the Calvinist will always nurture a degree of pious agnosticism about what God is really doing in the "macro-" movements of history. God "orders and executes his work in the most excellent and just manner even when the devil and wicked men act unjustly," says one of the sixteenth-century Calvinist confessions; "[a]nd as to what he doth surpassing human understanding we will not curiously inquire into it further than our capacity will admit of," being content "with the greatest humility and reverence [to] adore the righteous judgments of God which are hid from us."[18]

Calvin would certainly endorse that pious affirmation regarding the ways of providence. But he would also insist that we not decide too quickly what is being "hid from us" as "surpassing human understanding." Calvin was an astute student of collective entities. He had strong ideas about how a government ought to conduct itself in a variety of areas. And he exerted his influence as a church leader in a variety of areas of Genevan life: sewage systems, the treatment of refugees, medical care, the concerns of the poor, family patterns, entertainment activities, education, and so on. It was precisely this broad area of societal address that led Andre Bieler to write about Calvin's "social humanism."[19]

Furthermore, while Rousseau was certainly correct in attributing a fair measure of both theological and civic intolerance to Calvin, as we have seen, there are elements in Calvin's thought that clearly point toward an appreciation of the cultural contributions of unbelievers. And Calvin did devote some attention to the theological foundations for such a posture. His probings in the direction of a natural law perspective, as developed by some of his theological heirs, have recently been given sustained exposi-

17. R. B. Sher, *Church and University in the Scottish Enlightenment: The Moderate Literati of Edinburgh* (Princeton: Princeton University Press, 1985), 43.

18. Belgic Confession, article 13, in Philip Schaff, ed., *The Creeds of Christendom, with a History and Critical Notes,* vol. 3 (Grand Rapids: Baker, 1996), 396-97.

19. Andre Bieler, *The Social Humanism of John Calvin* (Richmond: John Knox, 1964); for a more expanded treatment of the subjects treated in Bieler's small book, see W. Fred Graham, *The Constructive Revolutionary: John Calvin and His Socio-Economic Impact* (Richmond: John Knox, 1971).

tion by Stephen Grabill.[20] But Calvin also explored other ways of accounting for human commonness — as residing in a shared human *sensus divinitatis* and a *semen religionis,* as well as a shared access to general revelation — all of which serve in his mind at least to remind the unregenerate of some of the basic demands for righteous living.

None of this amounts, of course, to a robust theology of civil society. Much of that task has to consist — as is evident in those who make a case for Calvin as a resource for a theology of cultural life — of looking for underlying patterns in how Calvin addressed the social, educational, and economic issues of his day.[21] One obvious and highly significant pattern in this regard is Calvin's insistence, in contrast to the thought of both Luther and the Anabaptists, on the strong continuity between ancient Israel and the Christian church. This insistence, grounded in his affirmation of the "third use of the law," which portrayed the Decalogue as a continuing norm for interactions in the public arena,[22] meant that Calvin was disposed to look for extensive guidance for the Christian community in the Old Testament's deliverances on social, economic, and legal matters. Calvin even took this to the point of arguing that the "form" of Israel's politics, which he saw as featuring an "aristocracy bordering on democracy," continues to be the preferred structure of political life.[23]

Later Influences

John Calvin's theological interest in political topics was passed on to many of his spiritual heirs; indeed, it often came to dominate their lives. This was certainly true in Scotland where, as J. D. Douglas put it in his study of the Scot-

---

20. Stephen J. Grabill, *Rediscovering the Natural Law in Reformed Theological Ethics* (Grand Rapids: Eerdmans, 2006), 187.

21. The literature that probes for these patterns is voluminous. In addition to Bieler, *The Social Humanism of John Calvin,* Graham, *The Constructive Revolutionary,* and Henry Van Til, *The Calvinistic Concept of Culture* (Grand Rapids: Baker Academic, 1959), chapter 7, some more recent efforts can be found in David W. Hall, *The Legacy of John Calvin* (Phillipsburg, N.J.: P&R Publishing, 2008), 11-41, and in the essays on topics dealing with Calvin's views in these areas in Donald McKim, ed., *The Cambridge Companion to John Calvin* (Cambridge: Cambridge University Press, 2004), and Edward Dommen and James D. Bratt, eds., *John Calvin Rediscovered: The Impact of His Social and Economic Thought* (Louisville: Westminster John Knox, 2007).

22. Calvin, *Institutes* 2.7.12, pp. 360-61.

23. Calvin, *Institutes* 4.20.8, p. 1493.

tish "covenanting" movement, the "None but Christ saves" theme of the Scottish Calvinists in the sixteenth century came to be largely replaced in the seventeenth by the "None but Christ reigns" rallying cry.[24] The Presbyterian struggle often took the form of bloody battles for political control; but the period of this struggle also produced some major works in political theology, with perhaps the most influential being Samuel Rutherford's 1644 *Lex, Rex*.[25]

While the Scottish Presbyterians and the Puritans also paid some attention to broader questions regarding civil society, those matters were given special attention by early Calvinists in the Netherlands, especially in the influential work of Johannes Althusius, who in the seventeenth century explicitly addressed the ways in which political authority could nurture a vital public arena in which a variety of private associations might flourish.[26] This broader agenda was in turn taken up as a sustained theological project in the nineteenth century by the "neo-Calvinist" movement initiated by the Dutch statesman-theologian Abraham Kuyper.

Like the Scottish Covenanter theology, Kuyper's theological reflections were forged in the context of practical involvement in public life. But Kuyper's public career ranged over an unusually wide variety of involvements in civil society. He founded and edited two newspapers, established a major university where he also taught theology, led a significant ecclesiastical schism that resulted in a new Dutch Reformed denomination, and birthed a political party that he then represented in parliament, eventually serving a term as prime minister of the Netherlands.[27]

"Neo-Calvinism" and the Cultural Spheres

The "neo" part of the "neo-Calvinist" label signals a significant departure from Calvin himself on a key point, as well as an expansion of the Calvinist agenda on some other related matters. The departure from Calvin had to

24. Douglas, *Light in the North*, 13.

25. Samuel Rutherford, *Lex Rex: The Law and the Prince; A Dispute for the Just Prerogative of King and People* (London: John Field, 1644).

26. For an excellent account of Althusius's contribution to the development of Calvinist thought on this subject, see Frederick Carney, "Associational Thought in Early Calvinism," in *Voluntary Associations: A Study of Groups in Free Societies*, ed. D. B. Robertson (Richmond: John Knox, 1966), 39-53.

27. For a more expanded biographical sketch of Kuyper's career, see Peter S. Heslam, *Creating a Christian Worldview: Abraham Kuyper's Lectures on Calvinism* (Grand Rapids: Eerdmans, 1998), 27-56.

do with the way in which the Reformer had understood the proper arrangement between church and state. In his 1898 Stone Lectures at Princeton Seminary, Kuyper was quite candid on this subject, citing examples of what he saw as the intolerant behavior of Calvin and many of those who followed in his train: Calvin's sending of Servetus to the stake, the Scottish Presbyterians' treatment of Independents, centuries-long restrictions on Catholic worship and practice in the Netherlands — and all of this stemming, Kuyper argued, from "the unanimous and uniform advice of Calvin and his epigones, who demanded intervention of the government in the matter of religion."[28]

While Kuyper saw this past pattern of intolerance as deeply regrettable, he insisted that it was not essential to the Calvinist perspective. "[T]he underlying characteristic of Calvinism must be sought," he argued, "not in what it has adopted from the past, but what it has newly created."[29] And this new creation is to be found in Calvinism's consistent defense of "liberty of conscience" along with an advocacy of an ecclesiology "in which in principle the *visible unity* is discarded." The persecutions conducted by the Church of Rome "issued from the identification of the visible with the invisible Church, and from *this* dangerous line Calvin departed." The Reformer was certainly convinced that his own confessional position was the true one, but he also knew this truth "may never be imposed by force upon other people."[30] It was only a matter of time, Kuyper argued, until the broader view of liberty implicit in this insight would come to a fuller expression in the Calvinist movement. And for Kuyper this meant the recognition that the most consistent way for the state to preserve the liberty of conscience was to encourage the flourishing of associations in a variety of cultural spheres.

"Multiformity" was a favorite term of Kuyper's, and he applied it to a number of areas of collective life. His rejection of a visible ecclesiastical unity meant that he advocated a multiform church — a variety of denominations that would have equal status in the eyes of the state. But he also extended the multiformity concept to the broader cultural arena, espousing an associational diversity that approximates present-day explorations of a diverse civil society. For Kuyper, though, the encouragement of a variety of mediating structures was not a mere pragmatic strategy for avoiding stat-

28. Abraham Kuyper, *Lectures on Calvinism: Six Lectures Delivered at Princeton University under Auspices of the L. P. Stone Foundation* (Grand Rapids: Eerdmans, 1931), 99.

29. Kuyper, *Lectures on Calvinism,* 102.

30. Kuyper, *Lectures on Calvinism,* 102-3.

ism and individualism. Because God built the basic patterns of associational interaction — family, art, commerce, worship, recreation, and the like — into the design of creation as such, these cultural spheres do not exist merely by the permission of the state or of any other human authority. Each sphere has its own God-ordained function in God's purposes for the world. Kuyper's elaboration on these matters is what constituted his doctrine of "sphere sovereignty."[31]

At the heart of the neo-Calvinist perspective on cultural multiformity is an insistence that the redemption accomplished by Christ is not only about the salvation of individuals — it is the reclaiming of the whole creation. The flourishing of a rich and complex cultural life was a key element in God's creating purposes, as evidenced by the command of Genesis 1 to "fill the earth," which the neo-Calvinist movement sees as a "cultural mandate" given to humankind. And the results of human cultural activity will be cleansed and gathered in at the end of history as we know it. Thus, the eschaton, according to Kuyper's younger colleague Herman Bavinck, "will be rich and glorious beyond all description. We expect a new heaven, a new earth, a new humanity, a renewed universe, a constantly progressing and undisturbed unfoldment." The cultural development of human history, says Bavinck, "has value in itself. It will continue to exert its influence also in the coming dispensation, and it will continue to furnish material for the exaltation and glorification of God by a redeemed humanity."[32]

The neo-Calvinist insistence that God's renewing purposes aim at the reclaiming of the whole creation allowed for a significant role for the cultural contributions of the nonelect in their understanding of the divine scheme. Kuyper treated this subject at length in developing his doctrine of "common grace" — a nonsalvific attitude of divine favor that allows for the nonelect to contribute to the positive formation of culture.

Unlike Calvin, who, as we saw earlier, also acknowledged the positive contributions of "the natural man," Kuyper goes beyond the bare affirmation of the reality of these contributions to view them in the context of a larger theology in which cultural development plays a significant role. To be sure, he also emphasizes the pervasive effects of the Fall, a theme that

31. For a critical examination of Kuyper's sphere sovereignty doctrine in relation to contemporary discussions, see my "Some Reflections on Sphere Sovereignty," in *Religion, Pluralism, and Public Life: Abraham Kuyper's Legacy for the Twenty-First Century,* ed. Luis Lugo (Grand Rapids: Eerdmans, 2000), 87-109.

32. Herman Bavinck, *The Doctrine of God,* trans. William Hendriksen (Grand Rapids: Eerdmans, 1951), 392-93.

for Kuyper is given expression in his doctrine of "the antithesis": unredeemed cultural activity is directed by a spirit of rebellion, which stands in contrast to those God-honoring patterns to which the redeemed are called. But Kuyper's common grace doctrine spells out the ways in which the rebellious motives of the unredeemed are curbed, and even on occasion guided in a direction that serves God's cultural goals. Thus he can acknowledge the Spirit's workings in the broad human community "wherever civic virtue, a sense of domesticity, natural love, the practice of human virtue, the improvement of the public conscience, integrity, mutual loyalty among people, and a feeling for piety leaven life."[33]

Oppression or Liberation?

None of this, however, would suffice to calm Rousseau's worries about the negative effects for civil society that a Calvinist theological perspective is capable of perpetrating. Nor would a present-day sympathizer with Rousseau have too far to look for an actual case study. The architects and enforcers of the deep injustices of South African apartheid not only professed a Calvinist theology, they often made their case for the segregationist civil order by appealing directly to tenets associated with Kuyperian neo-Calvinism.

Not all claims about an actual link of Afrikaner ideology to Calvin's own thought hold up under careful scrutiny. In his otherwise excellent study of Afrikaner civil religion, for example, T. Dunbar Moodie argues that the Afrikaner sense of being given a special divine mission draws directly on Calvin's teaching that a postbiblical national people can be given "chosen nation" status in the divine economy. Thus, says Moodie, Calvin "insisted on a distinction between the individual's 'special call' to salvation and the 'intermediate election' of an ethnic group called by God to fulfill His special purposes."[34]

Moodie is only partly right. Calvin did think that a specific ethnic group could receive a special divine assignment. But it is clear from the context of the passages cited by Moodie that Calvin was referring only to

33. Abraham Kuyper, "Common Grace," in *Abraham Kuyper: A Centennial Reader*, ed. James D. Bratt (Grand Rapids: Eerdmans, 1998), 181.

34. T. Dunbar Moodie, *The Rise of Afrikanerdom: Power, Apartheid, and the Afrikaner Civil Religion* (Berkeley: University of California Press, 1975), 26.

the election of Old Testament Israel, by way of explaining the sense in which Israel as a corporate people could be elected even though not every individual citizen of Israel was elected to eternal salvation.[35] But this particular "intermediate election" of an ethnic group was, for Calvin, not a repeatable phenomenon. To be sure, Calvin intended that a parallel distinction could be applied to the New Testament church: the visible church as a whole is an elect community, even though not every member of the church is necessarily elected in the individual sense. But there is nothing in any of this to indicate that Calvin thought postbiblical national or ethnic entities could be beneficiaries of a corporate election.

Unfortunately, however, more can be said for the claim of Kuyperian influence on apartheid ideology — although even here the charge cannot be made without some important qualifications. The actual influence is due to at least two features of Kuyper's thought. One is the racist tone that characterizes many of his comments about the indigenous culture of the African continent — a region from which, as he put it, "[n]o impulse for any higher life has ever gone forth."[36] Ironically, he believed the solution to what he saw as a lack of cultural development lay primarily in the encouragement of racial intermarriage. "It is noteworthy," he argued, "that the process of human development steadily proceeds with those groups whose historic circumstance is not isolation but the commingling of blood." So just as the quality of plant life is raised by "the crossing of different breeds," cultural progress can be facilitated by "the union of natural powers, [presently] divided among different tribes."[37] The Afrikaners who drew on Kuyper's thought, however, chose to emphasize his overall racist attitude, without adopting his prescribed remedy.

The second serious Kuyperian defect that influenced apartheid thinking was his imprecision in spelling out his understanding of what constitutes a cultural "sphere." In his Stone Lectures, for example, when arguing on the limits that must be imposed upon state interference in the basic cultural spheres, he offers this list: "Neither the life of science nor of art, nor of agriculture, nor of industry, nor of commerce, nor of navigation, nor of the family, nor of human relationship may be coerced to suit itself to the grace of government."[38]

---

35. Calvin, *Institutes* 3.21.5-7, pp. 926-31.
36. Kuyper, *Lectures on Calvinism*, 35.
37. Kuyper, *Lectures on Calvinism*, 35-36.
38. Kuyper, *Lectures on Calvinism*, 96-97.

A list like that raises the question of what Kuyper believes is a basic cultural "sphere."[39] Why, for example, are navigation and agriculture spheres in the same basic sense as, say, art and family? To be sure, nothing in that imprecision leads directly to the imposition of racial segregation, but the very fact of the unclarity can at least explain the basic move that the Afrikaners made: the designation of race as a Kuyperian sphere. In that scheme, then, it was not simply that commerce as such was a sphere, but that the insistence upon a rigid distinction between black commercial establishments and white ones was also seen as a way of avoiding — to use the title of one of Kuyper's well-known essays — "the blurring of the boundaries."[40]

There is another Kuyperian side to the apartheid story, however. In detailing the role of Kuyper's thought in the racial struggle, the black South African theologian Russel Botman notes that "Kuyper has had an oppressive influence and also a liberative influence on South Africa."[41] While "Afrikaner-Dutch Kuyperianism had used the negative aspects of Kuyper," Botman observes, "it was the task of Black Kuyperianism to select the positive aspects and present their theological relevance to South Africa."[42] In this regard, Botman cites the example of another black theologian, Allan Boesak, who appealed to Kuyper in support of the struggle for racial justice: "We believe passionately with Abraham Kuyper that there is not a single inch of life that does not fall under the lordship of Christ. . . . Here the Reformed tradition comes so close to the African idea of the wholeness of life that these two should combine to renew the thrust that was brought to Christian life by the followers of Calvin."[43] Thus, says Botman, we must simply acknowledge that "[t]he real Kuyper was both these things: a praiseworthy Reformed theologian who, regrettably, held to the potentially oppressive core value of separateness."[44]

39. I discuss this question in more detail in my "Some Reflections on Sphere Sovereignty," 87-109.

40. Abraham Kuyper, "The Blurring of the Boundaries," in *Abraham Kuyper: A Centennial Reader*, 363-402.

41. H. Russel Botman, "Is Blood Thicker Than Justice? The Legacy of Abraham Kuyper for Southern Africa," in *Religion, Pluralism, and Public Life*, 343.

42. Botman, "Is Blood Thicker?" 344.

43. Allan Boesak, *Black and Reformed: Apartheid, Liberation, and the Calvinist Tradition* (New York: Orbis, 1884), 87; quoted by Botman, "Is Blood Thicker?" 344.

44. Botman, "Is Blood Thicker?" 354.

An Ongoing Resource

It is not insignificant that the South African struggle reveals the reality of "two Kuypers," just as others have seen the origins of a Reformed theology of public life as requiring the recognition of "two Calvins." This means that the ongoing efforts to draw upon the heritage of John Calvin for an understanding of civil society must be careful to take the point of departure from "the good Calvin." And as "the good Kuyper" saw it, the place to begin is in Calvin's bold declaration of "the dogma of *God's Sovereignty*."[45] By building on that doctrine, and expanding its application, it is possible to follow Kuyper's kind of program for attempting to understand the relevance of the affirmation of divine sovereignty, not only for the life and mission of the church and the authority of the state, but also for the broader ranges of societal life.[46]

It is significant that these broader societal ranges are being carefully examined today in many quarters and from diverse perspectives, by both social scientists and popular commentators who are deeply concerned to promote a healthier civil society. It is a good thing that theologians participate in this conversation. To be sure, a public theology grounded in the Christian tradition will want to proceed with the awareness that a true and lasting public life will arrive only with the eschaton. But for those who embrace a partially realized eschatology, it is not unrealistic to expect signs of renewal in the present — first fruits of the end-time that can embolden us to join others in the larger human quest for a flourishing public life. And at least some of us will find John Calvin, along with those past disciples of his who have developed his insights about public life, to be important guides as we continue in that quest.

45. Kuyper *Lectures on Calvinism*, 58, emphasis Kuyper's.
46. Kuyper, *Lectures on Calvinism*, 79.

Culture, Church, and Civil Society:
Abraham Kuyper for a New Century

In an essay offering a Jewish assessment of Karl Barth's contribution to "divine command" ethics, Rabbi David Novak expresses some puzzlement about why Barth was so negative about natural law thinking. He sees Barth as a lot like some prominent Jewish thinkers, teachers who advocate a "retreat into sectarian enclaves, where [people of faith] can live more consistently and continually according to the direct commandments of God."[1] Novak rejects that kind of approach. And having pointed to what he sees as an important weakness in Barth's perspective, Novak suggests a remedy that should gladden the hearts of at least some Reformed Christians. Expressing the wish that Barth "had been more of a Calvinist in his treatment of law," Novak offers, in a footnote, some examples of people whose writings he wishes Barth had read with an openness to learning from their views. And at the beginning of his list is "the Dutch Calvinist theologian/ statesman Abraham Kuyper."[2]

As someone who does his theological scholarship, as the Dutch would say, "in the line of Kuyper," I take much delight in that counsel to Barth. To be sure, in the same breath in which Novak commends Kuyper's thought he also observes that Kuyper "was certainly not in Karl Barth's theological league." But this is, of course, a legitimate assessment. When it comes to

1. David Novak, *Talking with Christians: Musings of a Jewish Theologian* (Grand Rapids: Eerdmans, 2005), 143.

2. Novak, *Talking with Christians*, 144 n. 44.

This essay — Princeton Seminary's 2007 Kuyper Prize Lecture — originally appeared in *Princeton Seminary Bulletin* 28, no. 1 (2007). It is printed here with permission.

sheer sustained scholarly theological brilliance, Barth was clearly in a league of his own.

There are other theological leagues, however, and if we were to do our ranking with reference to a very broad range of roles and activities, Kuyper would stand out as a giant in the league we have come to think of as public theology. Much of Kuyper's theological output was produced on the run. His theological probings were never far removed from his public commitments as the founder of two newspapers, a university, a political party, and a denomination. In addition, he regularly wrote articles for his newspapers, while also leading his party both as a member of the Dutch parliament and, for a few years, as prime minister, as well as actively participating in the denominational controversies in the Dutch Reformed churches.

And even when Kuyper sat back and engaged in systematic theological reflection, his thoughts were never far removed from his public roles. It has often been noted by scholars who have studied his parliamentary career,[3] for example, that two key themes he held in tension within his theological system — the radical antithesis between Christian and non-Christian thought on the one hand, and the reality of common grace on the other — played an important role in his political leadership: when Kuyper wanted to rally the Calvinist troops to support an unpopular partisan effort he would preach antithesis, but when the opportunity arose to forge a strategic alliance with another party on a given issue he would remind his followers that God often works mysteriously in the hearts of the unregenerate to restrain their sinful tendencies.

My guess is that Kuyper's common grace preachments are the kind of thing that led Rabbi Novak to suggest that Karl Barth might have profitably interacted with Kuyper's thought. And while I take delight in that piece of counsel, I have my doubts whether Karl Barth would actually have gotten much help from Kuyper on the topic of natural law in particular. Kuyper's understanding of God's lawful ordering of the universe was of a very dynamic sort. As Kuyper's younger colleague Herman Bavinck put the view: "God does not stand outside of nature and is not excluded from it by a hedge of laws but is present in it and sustains it by the word of his power."[4] Kuyper's God is ever present to his creation, a cosmic legislator

---

3. See, e.g., James D. Bratt, *Dutch Calvinism in Modern America: A History of a Conservative Subculture* (Grand Rapids: Eerdmans, 1984), 19-20.

4. Herman Bavinck, *Reformed Dogmatics*, vol. 1, *Prolegomena*, trans. John Vriend (Grand Rapids: Baker Academic, 2003), 370.

whose law "lays full claim, not only to the believer (as though less were required from the unbeliever), but to every human being and to all human relationships."[5]

While these emphases are clearly grounded in a robust theology of creation, they are also linked to a theology of redemption that features the notion, to use the apt phrase that Albert Wolters chose for the title of his book setting forth the Kuyperian perspective, of "creation regained."[6] One of Kuyper's images for Christ's redemptive mission is as a kind of cleaning operation. "Verily," he says, "Christ has swept away the dust with which man's sinful limitations had covered up this world-order, and has made it glitter again in its original brilliancy."[7]

Kuyper included the full range of cultural reality within the scope of this cleaning operation. In what follows I want to sketch out some thoughts about how Kuyper's perspective on these matters, appropriately recontextualized, can speak to some key issues in the twenty-first century, with special reference to the relationship between church and public life in North America. And I am not going to avoid putting my case in quite personal terms. I discovered Kuyper in the 1960s when I was struggling with fundamental tensions between my evangelical pietism and what I had come to see as the nonnegotiable biblical mandate actively to work for justice and peace in the larger human community. Kuyper helped me, more than any other thinker, to see the profound connection between the atoning work of the loving Savior who is my "only comfort in life and death" and that Savior's kingly rule over all spheres of human interaction. That very personal impact has led me to think long and hard over several decades now about what must go into the project that I like to think of — borrowing an image from Vatican II — as a neo-Calvinist *aggiornamento*, a Kuyperian updating.

Createdness and Fallenness

There are some basics, of course, that do not need significant updating, especially the foundational redemption-as-restoration theme that led

---

5. Abraham Kuyper, *Lectures on Calvinism* (Grand Rapids: Eerdmans, 1931), 71-72.
6. Albert M. Wolters, *Creation Regained: Biblical Basics for a Reformational Worldview* (Grand Rapids: Eerdmans, 1985).
7. Kuyper, *Lectures on Calvinism*, 71-72.

Kuyper to focus on providing guidance for Christians in their everyday cultural involvement to a degree matched by few other theologians. This focus, in turn, emerged from a markedly different theological impulse than we find in those Christian thinkers today who depict the workings of present-day culture primarily, if not exclusively, in terms of fallenness. Here is a story that illustrates my own appropriation of the Kuyperian impulse.

During the 1970s, I attended a gathering of folks who were focusing on "radical discipleship," and one of the speakers kept describing the United States as given over to "the way of death." His primary example, of course, was the war being waged in Vietnam, which we all agreed needed to be opposed. He formulated his case theologically by citing William Stringfellow's argument, quite popular at the time, that the United States was the present-day manifestation of the biblical portrayal of fallen Babylon.[8] As I listened, I was struck by the gap between this unqualified rhetorical depiction of the American political system as given over to death dealing and my own experience that very week of accompanying our son on his way to school. He had just started kindergarten, and his daily walk to school followed a path through many blocks in the inner city. As I took the journey with him, I was especially aware, as a parent concerned for the safety of our son, of the places where there were traffic lights and stop signs. Approaching the school, I overheard two teachers mention a fire-safety inspection that the city had conducted the day before. Later, as I drove during the noon hour to the campus where I was teaching, I passed another school where a uniformed crossing guard was taking children by the hand to lead them across the street.

These phenomena all struck me as life-promoting services provided by the government, for which I as a parent was deeply grateful. In the light of those services, the unqualified rhetorical depiction of "the American system" as given over to "a way of death" struck me as rooted in, among things, a theological myopia. My uneasiness with that kind of perspective was grounded in what I am presenting here as a very basic Kuyperian impulse.

The late Mennonite theologian John Howard Yoder once captured the impulse quite nicely when, during one of our public Anabaptist-Calvinist debates in the 1970s, someone in the audience asked him if he could put in simple terms what he saw as the basic issue of disagreement between his

---

8. Cf. William Stringfellow, *An Ethics for Christians and Other Aliens in a Strange Land* (Waco, Tex.: Word, 1973).

views and mine. Here is how he answered: on questions of culture, he observed, "Mouw wants to say, 'Fallen, but *created*,' and I want to say, 'Created, but *fallen*.'"

That was a helpful way of putting the differences, including the element of ambivalence in each case. We Kuyperians do pay considerable attention to fallenness — at least we ought to — but our basic Kuyperian impulse is to look for signs that God has not given up, even in the midst of a fallen world, on restoring the purposes that were at work in God's initial creating activity. This calls for Christians, then, actively to work together as agents of this restorative program that encompasses the whole range of cultural involvement. Indeed, it is no rare thing in those circles where Kuyper's name is still revered, for laypeople to credit Kuyper's influence in their understanding of what it means to serve the Lord in the insurance business or journalism, or as a state legislator or in the teaching of English literature. Even when these folks may not know much about the technical details of Kuyper's theological system, they are quick to quote at least some version of his bold manifesto, set forth toward the end of his inaugural address at the founding of the Vrije Universiteit: "There is not a square inch in the whole domain of our human existence over which Christ, who is sovereign over all, does not cry: 'Mine!'"[9]

But what about the other impulse, the one expressed by Yoder's created-but-fallen emphasis? As articulated more recently by Stanley Hauerwas and William Willimon in their influential book *Resident Aliens: Life in the Christian Colony*, this impulse means that while this is still in some profound sense "our Father's world," our collective fallenness has nonetheless so pervaded the original creation that there is no clear basis for looking outside of the church for signs of God's restorative activity. For Hauerwas and Willimon, the Way of Jesus embodies economic, political, and social norms that are so antithetical to the patterns of collective life in the larger human culture that Christians are required, in effect, to create an alternative "public," embodied within the life of the Christian community. They even wonder whether Christians can legitimately use terms like "justice" and "peace" in addressing issues of public policy, since that assumes that Christians share a common core of meaning with non-Christians in using that kind of language. Because only the biblical witness to Jesus' ministry "gives content to our faith," they argue, it is questionable whether

9. Abraham Kuyper, "Sphere Sovereignty," in *Abraham Kuyper: A Centennial Reader*, ed. James D. Bratt (Grand Rapids: Eerdmans, 1998), 488.

such terms can have meaning "apart from the life and death of Jesus of Nazareth."[10]

But here too there is an element of ambivalence. Hauerwas has actually been taken to task by people who have drawn inspiration from his writings but who worry about what they see as a lack of consistency in his formulations. The philosopher Robert Brimlow has been particularly outspoken on this. He complains that while "the vast majority of Hauerwas's formulations are correct and contain blessed insights," Hauerwas seems inclined to take away with one hand what he has offered in the other, as when he insists that he has "no interest in legitimating and/or recommending a withdrawal of Christians or the Church from social or political affairs. I simply want them to be there as Christians and as Church." This is a concession that Brimlow labels "ridiculous," given what he admires as the main thrust of Hauerwas's theological ethics.[11]

While I see Hauerwas's ambivalence as a healthy groping for the kind of larger vision that Kuyper's perspective in fact provides, I can also express a qualified Kuyperian appreciation for a rigorous opposition to the dominant patterns of present-day culture. The firm Anabaptist-type "Nein!" is mindful of some very dangerous collective tendencies in our fallen world, pointing us to times in human history when those tendencies ran wild. This is evident, for example, in the "post-Christendom" and "post-Constantinian" rhetoric that has become quite popular these days, which has certainly made us aware of the ways in which the church-state and church-culture arrangements of the past often promoted a perverse merging of civic and Christian identity that led the believing community into sinful cultural compromises. The users of this rhetoric also rightly point us to the horrors of the Nazi terror, a time when established churches openly cooperated with programs of unspeakable evil. And in reminding us of these historical examples, they also rightly celebrate those followers of Jesus Christ who in those circumstances were willing to risk all to "follow the Lamb wherever he goes" (Rev. 14:4). These are crucial lessons that we ignore at our eternal peril.

But we also run spiritual risks if we fail to align ourselves with God's positive purposes in the world. No theologian, for example, has done more

10. Stanley Hauerwas and William Willimon, *Resident Aliens: Life in the Christian Colony* (Nashville: Abingdon, 1989), 23.

11. Robert W. Brimlow, "Solomon's Porch: The Church as Sectarian Ghetto," in *The Church as Counterculture*, ed. Michael L. Budde and Robert W. Brimlow (Albany: State University of New York Press, 2000), 113.

in recent years to urge us to take seriously our "post-Christendom" missional location than the late Lesslie Newbigin. Yet Newbigin also calls for care in assessing the errors of Constantinianism. "Much has been written," he notes, "about the harm done to the cause of the gospel when Constantine accepted baptism, and it is not difficult to expatiate on this theme"; there is no question, says Newbigin, that the church has regularly fallen "into the temptation of worldly power." But should we conclude from this that the proper alternative was for the church simply to "have . . . washed its hands of responsibility for the political order?" Do we really think, Newbigin asks, that the cause of the gospel would have been better served "if the church had refused all political responsibility, if there had never been a 'Christian' Europe?"[12] The fact is, he observes, that the Constantinian project had its origins in a creative response to a significant cultural challenge. There was in Constantine's day, he says, a spiritual crisis in the larger culture, and people "turned to the church as the one society that could hold a disintegrating world together." And for all the mistakes that were made along the way, it was nonetheless a good thing that the church actively took up this challenge.[13]

Divine Ordering

Like Newbigin, Kuyper was well aware of the dangers of Constantinianism. When he delivered his Stone Lectures at Princeton in 1898, he explicitly lamented Calvinism's historic role in promoting strong ties between church and state. Indeed, his repudiation of this Calvinist history is one of the reasons why those of us who follow him in these matters choose to call ourselves "neo-Calvinists." But neither was Kuyper willing to give up on Christian involvement in the political structures of the larger culture. Indeed, he insisted that Calvinism contained within its own theological system the capacity to liberate itself from the defects that had long been associated with Constantinian arrangements.[14]

This is one of those areas where we see Kuyper's conviction at work regarding the culturally restorative aspects of redemption. Even politics

12. Lesslie Newbigin, *Foolishness to the Greeks: The Gospel and Western Culture* (Grand Rapids: Eerdmans, 1986), 100-101.

13. Newbigin, *Foolishness to the Greeks,* 100-101.

14. Kuyper, *Lectures on Calvinism,* 99-100.

— often depicted by theologians as a purely postlapsarian remedial re-sponse to human rebellion — is grounded for Kuyper in God's original creating purposes. While he insisted that the basic social unit in God's de-sign was the family, he argued that even in the pre-Fall condition the need would have developed for groups of family, seeking "a higher unity," to engage in collective decision-making. This need would have given rise to a sinless pattern of government that "would have *internally* . . . ruled reg-ularly, directly and harmoniously in the hearts of all men," but which would also have had to function *"externally"* in the form of some sort of "hierarchy."[15]

The fact that Kuyper, as a child of his day, also assumed that this prelapsarian hierarchical pattern would have been "patriarchal" in nature should not divert our attention from his basic point, namely, that even in a sinless social setting some sort of collective decision-making would be necessary for the harmonious ordering of human affairs. In a sinless world where complex activities take place, rules and regulations would have an important function. Even totally benevolent, God-glorifying human be-ings would have to decide which side of the road to drive on, and would have to stipulate when individuals who wanted to practice playing their tu-bas could do so without unnecessarily disturbing the nap times of children who lived in the same subsection of the Garden. It is this same kind of or-dering/regulating function that also promotes flourishing under present sinful conditions by setting up traffic signals and hiring school crossing guards.

Things get especially interesting in Kuyper, of course, when he dis-cusses what God actually wants to get *ordered* by government, a subject he develops at length in setting forth his theory of "sphere sovereignty." This theory has much to offer to contemporary discussions of civil society, but not without some serious reworking in the light of present-day conditions.

Foundational to the requisite reworking is, as I see it, the preservation of two key Kuyperian themes. One is Kuyper's insistence that God has pro-grammed the creation to display a marvelously complex diversity, includ-ing a complex array of spheres of human interaction. The other is the ne-cessity, especially under sinful conditions, that we be diligent in maintaining clarity about the differences among these diverse cultural spheres. The titles of two of Kuyper's essays bear witness to the importance he attributed to both themes. One title is "Uniformity: The Curse of Mod-

---

15. Kuyper, *Lectures on Calvinism*, 92f.

ern Life," and the other, "The Blurring of the Boundaries."[16] I will reflect briefly on each of these themes.

"Many-ness"

Multiformity — a favorite term of Kuyper's — was in his view necessary for created life to flourish in a "fresh and vigorous" manner.[17] Referring to the biblical account of creation, Kuyper notes that the Lord willed "[t]hat all life should multiply 'after its kind.'" That the Genesis writer employed this phrase specifically with reference to animal life does not deter Kuyper from making a more general application. "[E]very domain of nature," he says, displays an "infinite diversity, an inexhaustible profusion of variations." And this many-ness also rules the world of humanity, which "undulates and teems" with the same sort of diversity, bestowed upon our collective existence by a "generous God who from the riches of his glory distributed gifts, powers, aptitude, and talents to each according to his divine will."[18]

Kuyper's sense that God loves many-ness also informs his sphere sovereignty doctrine. A healthy God-honoring culture, Kuyper insists, will be characterized by many-ness, plurality. His views here comport well with those of recent commentators on civil society who call for the nurturing of diverse "mediating structures" — neighborhood clubs, service organizations, athletic leagues, religious bodies, and so on — that can constitute a social identity-nurturing interactive arena between the individual and the state, thus serving as a buffer zone to safeguard against both individualism and statism.

For Kuyper, though, advocacy for a plurality of cultural engagement requires a theological underpinning. Mediating structures are not merely to be valued for their functions of shaping character and curbing the powers of the state. God built these patterns of associational diversity into the very fabric of creation. Families, schools, and businesses do not exist by the permission of governments or churchly authorities — Kuyper was equally critical of totalitarian states and politically powerful churches. God has or-

---

16. Both essays are included in *Abraham Kuyper:* "Uniformity: The Curse of Modern Life," 19-44, and "The Blurring of the Boundaries," 363-402.

17. Kuyper, "Uniformity," 25.

18. Kuyper, "Uniformity," 34.

dained the plurality of spheres, and no human power has the right to inhibit their proper functioning.

This leads immediately to the second crucial theme: the importance of maintaining clarity about the boundaries that define the unique character of each sphere. Consider, for example, a woman and a man who are related in three different ways. She is the young man's mother. She is also an elder in the church where their family worships. And she is the academic dean at the university where he serves on the faculty. Suppose, though, that he commits a serious crime — using, for example, a university computer for illicit sexual purposes. As his dean she will be required to fire him. As his church elder she might even participate in a decision to excommunicate him. But as his mother she continues to love him as a member of the family. In each case her authority role is different, as is also the basis for her acceptance of him within each relationship. In the university she judges his fitness to remain a member of the community by some straightforwardly formal standards of performance. In the church, she also enforces certain norms, but here with a pastoral openness to repentance and restoration. In the family, the ties go much deeper — so much so that the bond is not easily broken by either bad performance or unrepentant sin. In short, families are families; churches are churches; and the academy is the academy. Suppose, for example, the young man was to complain to his mother: "How can you fire me from my teaching job? I'm your *son!*" This would be a clear case of blurring the boundaries of the spheres.

So far, so good. This theme, as I have said, is for me a nonnegotiable Kuyperian emphasis. There is a problem today, though, in following Kuyper too closely in the way he spelled out the practical implications of this theme. Again, I must offer a personal example.

During many visits to mainland China over the past decade, I have discussed with church, seminary, and government leaders some pressing cultural challenges being faced in changing urban communities: especially a rising divorce rate, new patterns of intergenerational conflict, and an increase in the number of suicides. Much of this seems to be a result of a breakdown of traditional kinship systems because of increasing social mobility and the reconfiguring of urban neighborhoods. The supportive infrastructure provided in the past by stable extended families has been deteriorating.

My recommendation, which has been met with considerable agreement, is that the Christian community in China would do well to place a special emphasis right now on the biblical image of the church as the family of God. I must confess that there was a time in my life when I would have resisted such a recommendation on Kuyperian grounds. As my example of the mother and son illustrates, the ecclesial bond is different from the familial bond. Churches are churches; they are not families. Each mode of association has its own place in the divine ordering of human life. So, as I have been strongly inclined to argue in the past, we ought not to get carried away with "church as family" language. There may be something interesting about it as a metaphor, but it is *only* a metaphor. Families are families, and churches are churches. What God hath put asunder let no human being try to put together.

I think differently these days. In the China case, for example, I think it is important for the church to take on some of the functions of the family. To be sure, I still see my views on the subject as fundamentally Kuyperian, in this sense: Kuyper was right in his insistence that families are different from churches. Each occupies an important place in the array of God-ordained spheres of interaction. The problem, of course, is that in many situations one of those spheres becomes severely weakened. As a Kuyperian, I want to be very clear about what is lost when things are not going the way God intended in a particular sphere. And having identified the missing functions, we must do one of two things. Either we repair that sphere in the light of our understanding of God's creating intentions. Or, when that is not immediately feasible, we look for ways in which some other sphere can compensate for the loss by taking on additional cultural "work." In China — and indeed in our own culture — I believe it is important for the church to provide some infrastructural support for cultural "shrinkage" in the sphere of family life. But again: this compensatory strategy can be seen as a way of honoring Kuyper's insistence that we be clear about the differences between family and church in the divine design.

Shrinking Spheres

Other aspects of Kuyper's views about family also need rethinking. In his day, for example, Dutch families tended to be associated with rather stable confessional or ideological communities. While Kuyper certainly considered his version of Calvinism the most robust of the perspectives that competed in Dutch culture, he also attributed a fairly high degree of coherence to the prominent alternatives of his day — Roman Catholicism and socialism, for example. Thus the "pillarization" pattern of Dutch life

— strongly influenced by Kuyper — in which various "thick" worldview-ish pillars generated their own school systems, labor unions, art guilds, and farming organizations.

Things are very different in our day. We have been experiencing not just a thinning out, but in fact a kind of slicing up, of worldviews. The leader of an evangelical campus ministry told me a few years ago that in past decades evangelicals often employed an apologetic approach that emphasized the coherence of a Christian view of reality that could answer more questions adequately than other worldviews. But today's students, he reported, don't seem to put much stock in coherence and consistency. They think nothing of participating in an evangelical Bible study on Wednesday night and then engaging in a New Age meditation group on Thursday night, while spending their daily jogging time listening to a taped reading of *The Celestine Prophecy,* followed by a yoga session — without any sense that there is anything inappropriate about moving in and out of these very different perspectives on reality.

This differs significantly from nineteenth-century Dutch society, where one could count on relatively stable "pillar" communities. And even where we *can* identify long-standing "pillars" in American life today — for example, Judaism, Roman Catholicism, Lutheranism, and Islam — we still must take into account the greatly increased mobility *between* these pillars. People change religious affiliations frequently in our culture — thus the phenomenon of "church shopping." Families think nothing of moving from a Presbyterian church to, say, a Nazarene congregation — while also sending the occasional contribution to a Southern Baptist TV preacher and enrolling their children in a Christian school sponsored by Pentecostals.

A parallel issue has to do with Kuyper's insistence on the primacy of the family in God's creating purposes. In the "pillarized" system of educational pluralism that he did so much to establish in the Netherlands, for example, much emphasis was placed on parental choice. In our culture, however, many children live in single-parent or blended families, with increasing numbers even moving back and forth between two or more family units. Kuyper's scheme is not easily transposed onto this context.

Here too, though, the solution is not to abandon Kuyperianism, but rather to focus on the more fundamental issues through Kuyperian lenses. Not only are we experiencing sphere shrinkage, we are also experiencing worldview fragmentation. The necessary remedies, then, will require both sphere repair and worldview nurturing. These in turn require patient work within civil society, in a variety of spheres, including an address to issues in public policy, a focus on various vocations, specific kinds of marriages, family counseling, and so on. And all of that requires new, concerted educational strategies on liberal arts and seminary campuses, as well as in think tanks and parachurch ministries. And in churches. Especially in churches — a topic to which I now want to give special attention as I draw to a close.

The Church's Role

In a conversation I had with Craig Dykstra[19] a few years ago, he told me about the three questions he wished every seminary would be clear about when it prepared its funding proposal to the Lilly Endowment. I now regularly cite these questions at Fuller Seminary, not simply out of fund-raising motives, but because they strike me as extremely insightful questions. The first and most important one is this: What is God doing in the world? Then, secondly: What must the church be like in order to align itself with what God is doing in the world? And then this third question: What do theological schools need to be like in order to equip the church to align itself with what God is doing in the world?

As a Kuyperian, however, I do privately sneak a few subsidiary thoughts into the Dykstra scheme. I want also to know how God's people, beyond the boundaries of church life, can align themselves with God's purposes in various spheres of cultural activity. And then I am forced to think about how churches can best equip God's people for that broader involvement — and, of course, how theological schools, in turn, can equip the church for that cultural equipping.

This line of thinking has forced me to give some thought to how we might have to update Kuyper's views about the church in particular. I am convinced that the church today must take on some additional functions precisely because of the cultural factors I have already pointed to: when, say, the familial sphere has been weakened, the church must compensate for that weakness, at least as a temporary remedial strategy. And much the same holds for other spheres: when, say, labor or politics or art or business cannot draw on the more robust worldviews and confessional identities that once pervaded the culture, the church needs to make a special effort to

19. Vice president for religion, the Lilly Endowment.

focus on areas of concern that are not, strictly speaking, items in its original sphere-portfolio.

Kuyper's views about the role of the church in culture were grounded in his conviction that the real problem in the long-standing Christendom arrangement was not simply that the church was too closely allied with the state; the real problem was with the underlying ecclesiology that informed that alliance. For too long Christians had operated, he said, on the assumption "that the Church of Christ on earth could express itself only in one form and as one institution." It was necessary, then, to "break that one Church into fragments," acknowledging "that the Church of Christ can reveal itself in many forms, in different countries; nay, even in the same country, in a multiplicity of institutions." He saw it as a strength of the kind of Calvinism he espoused that it had "ruptured the unity of the Church," by encouraging "a rich variety of all manner of church formations."[20] For all the problems caused by a divided Christianity, he argued, it was necessary for the vitality of religious life in particular and society in general for a variety of churches to conduct their respective ministries, as he put it, "from their own strength on the voluntary principle."[21]

There is much wisdom in this. But that it was obviously motivated in part by Kuyper's fear of a too-powerful church was made clear in his choice to give the name "Free" *(Vrije)* to the university he founded, thus symbolizing its autonomy, not only from the state, but also from ecclesiastical control. And this same worry about undue ecclesiastical power took on a practical urgency in the early 1890s, during the merger negotiations between Kuyper's orthodox party, having recently departed from the larger Dutch Reformed Church *(Nederlandse Hervormde Kerk),* and a group that had split from that larger body earlier in the century. A key point of contention between the two groups had to do with the sphere to which theological education belongs.[22] Kuyper and his followers saw the university as the proper home for theologians, where they could carry on their "scientific" work free from churchly control, whereas the earlier dissenters had maintained a theological school whose faculty was appointed and directly supervised by the church.

In the end, the two sides forged a compromise, allowing for a choice

20. Kuyper, *Lectures on Calvinism,* 101.
21. Kuyper, *Lectures on Calvinism,* 64-65, 106.
22. I discuss this dispute in more detail in my essay "The Seminary, the Church, and the Academy," later in this volume.

between the two modes. But the tensions continued. It is difficult today to understand the depth of the disagreement. I see no real problem in the notion of theologians on a university faculty doing their rigorous scholarship for the sake of the church and its mission. Nor do I see any confusion in the idea of an ecclesiastically monitored seminary faculty whose teaching and research are viewed as an extension of the church's *catechesis* — albeit of a sort that takes the norms of the academy with utmost seriousness.

I strongly suspect that Kuyper's opposition to an ecclesially sponsored theological school was basically rooted in an ambivalence he felt toward the church as such. He was certainly a deeply devoted servant of the church. Yet he also wanted very much to keep it in its place — to be sure that it pursued a mission that was "after its own kind." And of all the modes of cultural interaction, he was especially worried about the dangers that both a strong state and a strong church posed to the effective flourishing of the other spheres.

The sort of stifling control exercised by the church over other spheres that Kuyper worried about is not really a serious threat today. To be sure, it is common to hear complaints from social commentators about the dangers posed by present-day "theocrats." But to the degree that there is anything to this worry, it is not really about ecclesial control. Take an obvious case of someone in North American public life who is often labeled a "theocrat," the "televangelist" Pat Robertson. The fact is that Robertson does not even function presently as an official clergyman. Early on he was ordained in a local Baptist congregation, but he long ago ceased to maintain his ministerial credentials. To the degree that Robertson poses any sort of "theocratic" threat to American culture, it is not from any sort of ecclesiastical power base, but rather in his role as political leader, journalist, and educator, which is to say that in his cultural presence — his formal combination of "sphere roles," as it were — he is more like Abraham Kuyper than like, say, the stated clerk of the Presbyterian denomination to which I belong.

The truth is that what Kuyper understood to be the churchly sphere is remarkably weak today. In Protestantism at least, ecclesial credentials are not the route to cultural influence. With the possible exception of a few Southern Baptist officials, those religious leaders whose voices are taken seriously on questions of public policy typically do not do so because of their churchly connections. What church ever authorized Charles Colson to speak out on public policy? Or Jim Wallis? Or James Dobson? Or Jesse Jackson?

30

Spiritual Resources

In calling for a more central role for the church than Kuyper was willing to tolerate, I don't think I am actually proposing a major revision in the basics of neo-Calvinism. I share Kuyper's worries about a church that fixes its gaze too intently on the specifics of public policy or cultural practice. For Kuyper that kind of address was the job of the Christian political party, the Christian labor union, the Christian farmers group, the Christian artists guild, and so on. And I agree with that conception of the proper pattern for the Christian distribution of labor.

The problem is that it is not so among us. We do not have the kind of sphere-specific associations that can provide a robust "thick" address to complex issues. Not that the solution, then, is for the church to begin offering that kind of address. But where Kuyper wanted the church completely to keep hands off the Christian groups in other spheres, this is a time for the churches to take on an intentional transspherical nurturing role. This will require the kinds of ecclesiological emphases Max Stackhouse commended when he outlined a strategy wherein "local congregations will be more important than the national bodies" and where "fixed confessional and doctrinal statements will become less important than the quests for a personal faith lived out in a series of inspiring communities, all governed by a generous and truly catholic worldview."[23]

Geerhardus Vos, who represented the neo-Calvinist perspective on the Princeton Seminary faculty for just a year short of four decades, echoed Kuyper's worries about the dangers of undue ecclesiastical influence over Christian activity in the other spheres. The goals of God's kingdom are not served, Vos warned, "by making human life in all its spheres subject to the visible church." We must "separate between the visible church and such things as the Christian state, Christian art, Christian science, etc." These various modes of interaction can flourish, Vos insisted, only if they stand not under, but alongside of, the visible church, drawing — just as the visible church must also do — directly from "the regenerated life of the invisible church."[24]

But again, the problem today is the inability of most Christians to

23. Hak Joon Lee, "On Being Reformed: An Interview with Max Stackhouse," *Perspectives: A Journal of Reformed Thought* (Web site), October 2005, http://www.rca.org/page.aspx?pid=3080.

24. Geerhardus Vos, *The Teaching of Jesus concerning the Kingdom of God and the Church* (Eugene, Oreg.: Wipf and Stock, 1998), 164-65.

know how rightly to draw on the spiritual resources available for kingdom service in the diverse spheres of cultural life. In an informal discussion among a group of Kuyperians a few years ago, someone remarked that while the Netherlands is in a "post-Kuyper phase," North America may presently be "pre-Kuyper." I hope so. If that is the case, however, we neo-Calvinists must take the "pre" part of that very seriously, and engage in the necessary preparatory work. And I am convinced that much of this work right now must have the character of spiritual formation, of a sort that takes place in local congregations that serve, in Ronald Thiemann's apt phrasing, as "'schools of public virtue,' communities that seek to form the kind of character necessary for public life."[25] In some insightful reflections that he recently published, Al Wolters suggested that a neo-Calvinism that is well equipped for our present situation will have to be undergirded by a deep piety that draws on various spiritual disciplines, including those, for example, from both Ignatian and Pentecostal resources.[26] I agree whole-heartedly. And I think that Kuyper, if he were aware of our present-day context, would concur. After all, the Kuyper who has inspired many of us with his profound insights into the proper contours of public discipleship also wrote many meditations about the spiritual life, published under the general title *Nabij God te Zijn*, "to be near unto God."[27] The connection for him was very clear: we cannot properly participate in those cultural spheres that stand *coram deo*, directly before the face of God, unless we too cultivate a very personal experience of the divine presence. In this twenty-first century, it is important to be especially clear about the connection between the "every square inch" of cultural engagement and a sense of nearness to God that must necessarily be grounded in the worshiping and nurturing life of the local church.

25. Ronald Thiemann, *Constructing Public Theology: The Church in a Pluralistic Culture* (Louisville: Westminster John Knox, 1991), 43.

26. Albert M. Wolters, "What Is to Be Done . . . toward a Neocalvinist Agenda?" *Comment: Public Theology for the Common Good*, October 14, 2005, http://www.cardus.ca/comment/article/282/.

27. Abraham Kuyper, *To Be Near unto God*, trans. John Hendrick De Vries (Grand Rapids: Baker, 1979).

Some Reflections on Sphere Sovereignty

During the years when I regularly taught a course in social and political philosophy at Calvin College, I required my students to read substantial portions of Abraham Kuyper's 1898 Stone Lectures. In my class discussions I focused especially on his lecture "Calvinism and Politics," spending considerable time talking about his theory of "sphere sovereignty." There was one student, however, who apparently paid no attention to what went on in this part of the course. But this did not keep him from offering a rather bold account of what he imagined Kuyper might say on the subject. In response to a question on the final exam that invited students to reflect critically on a major theme in Kuyper's social thought, this young man gave a summary of what he took to be Kuyper's espousal of "spear sovereignty." As a Calvinist, this student opined, Kuyper believed that governments have the power of the sword. Sinful people will never do anything good unless they have a spear aimed at them, he argued. So Kuyper believed that human society can be held together only by the fear of punishment. Thus, in a sinful world the governmental spear must be sovereign.

Needless to say, the student's brief account of the nature of political authority bore some clear traces of Calvinist influence. Romans 13 has been a key text for the followers of John Calvin in their portrayal of the role of government — to the point that a slightly expanded paraphrase of

---

This essay previously appeared in *Princeton Seminary Bulletin* 19, no. 2 (1998): 160-82, and was also published in *Religion, Pluralism, and the Public Life: Abraham Kuyper's Legacy for the Twenty-First Century*, ed. Luis E. Lugo (Grand Rapids: Eerdmans, 2000), 87-109. It is printed here with permission.

that biblical passage has sometimes sufficed as a way of stating *the* Christian perspective on political life. But in drawing this summary out of his Calvinist memory bank, the student failed to capture even a few of the basic nuances of Kuyperian social thought. And I do want to emphasize the word "social." In his use of the sphere sovereignty motif, Kuyper was more interested in viewing governmental authority against the larger tapestry of human interaction than he was in providing a detailed theory of the proper functionings of government.

The need to keep government in its proper place is a topic that Kuyper addressed with considerable passion in his Stone Lecture on politics. The creation order, he argued, displays a rich variety of societal spheres. Since all these spheres have the same origin in "the divine mandate," political authority must respect that each of the other spheres has its own integrity. "Neither the life of science nor of art, nor of agriculture, nor of industry, nor of commerce, nor of navigation, nor of the family, nor of human relationship may be coerced to suit itself to the grace of government," said Kuyper. "The State may never become an octopus, which stifles the whole of life." Then, abruptly switching metaphors, he continued: political government "must occupy its own place, on its own root, among all the other trees of the forest, and thus it has to honor and maintain every form of life which grows independently in its own sacred autonomy."[1]

Much in just these few lines suggests clear links to themes that loom large in our contemporary discussions about societal health. It is important to acknowledge these links and to recognize the common ground that Kuyper shares with those who have been thinking much in recent years about "the good society." But Kuyper's sphere sovereignty perspective cannot simply be subsumed under the categories that dominate our present-day discussions, and it is a good thing to be clear about why this is so if we are to make proper use of Kuyper's societal vision in our contemporary context. As Jacob Klapwijk has insisted, while Kuyper's sphere sovereignty concept "deserves a new chance in our time," this requires subjecting Kuyper's "bits and pieces" to considerable refinement in the light of contemporary questions and concerns.[2]

I will not provide all that necessary clarification here, but I do hope to contribute something to that larger project. In what follows, I will briefly

1. Abraham Kuyper, *Lectures on Calvinism* (Grand Rapids: Eerdmans, 1931), 96-97.
2. Jacob Klapwijk, "The Struggle for a Christian Philosophy: Another Look at Dooyeweerd," *Reformed Journal,* February 1980, 15.

discuss the relationship of Kuyper's idea of sphere sovereignty to three themes that have been given much attention in recent years, and which seem to have some connections to the sphere sovereignty notion: the insistence in some quarters on minimal government; the strong interest these days in mediating structures; and a renewed emphasis in contemporary Christian thought on the Roman Catholic idea of subsidiarity. Then I will look at some of the broad theological-philosophical commitments that were at work, as I see it, in Kuyper's strong advocacy of the sphere sovereignty conception. In all this, I will focus especially on how these commitments can help Christians today who are interested in developing the kind of overall perspective on societal life that Kuyper pointed us to in his preachments about sphere sovereignty.

Government Intervention

Consider, first, the contemporary version of the desire to limit the role of government. At first glance Kuyper would seem to be a strong ally in this cause. In the remarks I have just quoted from his Stone Lecture on politics, for example, he is obviously concerned to keep the government from undue intrusion in the affairs of the other spheres. But the key term here is "undue." Having used the metaphors of the tree whose roots spread too far and the grasping octopus, Kuyper quickly goes on to ask: "Does this mean that the government has no right *whatever* of interference in these autonomous spheres of life?" And his answer is: "Not at all." Government, he explains, has a "threefold right and duty": first, to adjudicate disputes between spheres, "compel[ling] mutual regard for the boundary-lines of each"; second, to defend the weak against the strong within each sphere; and third, to exercise the coercive power necessary to guarantee that citizens "bear *personal* and *financial* burdens for the maintenance of the natural unity of the State."[3]

Kuyper's three qualifications are significant. They not only suggest what governments *may* do, but they also point to some governmental *duties*. And in this regard Kuyper does actually work with a kind of "spear sovereignty" notion. Government has a special role to play among the spheres, seeing to it that the relationships among and within the spheres are properly ordered. And this ordering function is an active one. Indeed,

3. Kuyper, *Lectures on Calvinism*, 97.

one can make room — given the way Kuyper actually states his three qualifications — for a fairly energetic interventionist pattern for governments.

The first function that Kuyper mentions in specifying government's
"threefold right and duty" is the adjudication of *inter*sphere boundary disputes. Obvious examples here would be an "adult" bookstore attempting
to set up shop and display its wares on a street heavily traveled by school-
children, or a religious group wanting to use a public university meeting
room to engage in worship activities. But other, more subtle claims of alleged boundary violation could also be considered. Suppose, for example,
that parents want limits placed on TV advertising of fast-food products,
on the grounds that such messages invade the home with propagandizing
on behalf of poor nutrition, or that homosexual organizations claim that
churches use their theology regarding sexuality to promote discriminatory
attitudes toward gays and lesbians. Nothing in Kuyper's formulation tells
us *how* the government ought to decide such cases, but he does seem to
imply that the government could have a proper adjudicatory role to play in
these kinds of situations.

The second qualification has to do with *intra*sphere conflict: government is obliged to protect the weak from the strong within each sphere.
Here again, there are obvious cases: governments may, for example, inter-
vene in families where spouse abuse or child abuse occurs, or in manufac-
turing plants where there are oppressive workplace conditions. But this
qualification can also be interpreted to include less overt patterns of per-
ceived harm, of the sort frequently associated these days with the more
subtle varieties of alleged "sexual harassment."

Kuyper's third qualification has to do with what we might think of as
*trans*spherical patterns. His concern here can be illustrated with a simple
example: roads. Thoroughfares are used to conduct the affairs of many
spheres. Families pile into their vans to head for picnics. Heads of state
travel to ceremonies in motorcades. Business leaders take cabs to meetings. Players on sports teams are bused to the stadium. Roads serve all the
spheres, and everyone, regardless of status in a particular sphere, has an
interest in the maintenance of appropriate patterns of transport. It is the
task of the state to see to it that we all do our part to maintain a good road
system.

While Kuyper did want to keep the state in its place, government does
have a right and duty to reach *from* that place into the other spheres, regulating inter-, intra-, and transspherical patterns. One can surely raise questions about how often and how far a government may reach in pursuing

these obligations. Those are good and important questions. But they are not to be decided simply by pointing to the fact of sphere sovereignty, as Kuyper employs that idea with reference to the proper patterns of political authority.

Kuyperian Spheres

A number of North American social critics have emphasized in recent years the important role that "mediating structures" play in providing a buffer zone between the individual and the state. Peter Berger put the case clearly when he argued that the "megastructures" of societal life cannot work for human flourishing without assistance from other collective entities. States and corporations need to look "below" themselves for "moral sustenance," providing room for the significant influence of those "living subcultures from which people derive meaning and identity."[4] Such entities protect us from the all-encompassing tendencies of the state on the one hand and an isolated individualism on the other.

On one level this comports well with some of Kuyper's practical concerns. But Kuyper also wants to highlight themes that are not touched on in many of the present-day discussions of mediating structures. For one thing, Kuyper is not merely interested in strengthening mediating structures; he also wants to understand that these so-called mediating structures are themselves organizational manifestations of more basic spheres of interaction. For him it is important to see the ways in which, say, familial relations are very different from ecclesial ones, or how artistic activity differs from scientific investigation. Kuyper focuses on the reality of a variety of societal entities that are "below" the state, not primarily because they can play an important role in curbing the power of government, but because they also display diverse patterns of human interaction that are important elements in God's structuring of the creation. Whether it is good to have Rotary Clubs and Parent-Teacher Associations is not as important to Kuyper as whether art and religion and business and family life are granted their allotted place in the God-ordained scheme of things.

To be sure, Kuyper was never very precise as to what counted as a

<hr />

4. Peter Berger, "In Praise of Particularity: The Concept of Mediating Structures," in his *Facing Up to Modernity: Excursions in Society, Politics, and Religion* (New York: Basic Books, 1977), 140.

creational "sphere." The passage quoted above from the Stone Lectures shows his lack of precision. It isn't clear, for example, how navigation and agriculture deserve a separate status as distinct creational spheres in the same sense as science, art, commerce, industry, the family, and "human relationship" (by which he probably had in mind marriage and friendship) qualify. One sphere seems to differ from another in Kuyper's view by virtue of the spheres' different "points." As Gordon Spykman summarized the Kuyperian conception: "Each sphere has its own identity, its own unique task, its own God-given prerogatives. On each God has conferred its own peculiar right of existence and reason for existence."[5] The point of doing art is to display aesthetic excellence, while the point of science — a term Kuyper uses broadly to cover all orderly intellectual investigation — is to advance the cause of knowledge. Economic activity aims at stewardship. Politics aims at justice.

Corresponding to these different "points" is a diversity of authority patterns. The way a parent exercises authority over a child should be different from the way a legislator exercises authority over constituents, or a professor over students, or a coach over team players. This means too that the skills associated with a specific mode of authority do not automatically transfer to other spheres. Someone might be a good parent but a poor politician or bishop. Again, it was more important for Kuyper that this diversity be recognized and respected than that particular organizational structures serve the practical function of curbing tendencies toward statism.

Sphere Sovereignty and Subsidiarity

The idea of sphere sovereignty is often mentioned in the same breath with the Roman Catholic principle of subsidiarity. Nelson Gonzalez makes the equation in a recent article, when he refers to "*subsidiarity* or *sphere sovereignty,* as known in the Reformed tradition," as a "foundational Christian Democratic principle." And as Gonzalez states the principle, the link is, for practical purposes, a helpful one. "Because politics is for the good of the person," he explains, "the state should never do for 'mediating structures,'

5. Gordon J. Spykman, "Sphere Sovereignty in Calvin and the Calvinist Tradition," in *Exploring the Heritage of John Calvin,* ed. David E. Holwerda (Grand Rapids: Baker, 1976), 167.

such as churches, neighborhoods, families, and schools, what they can do for themselves."[6]

All things considered, though, the relationship between subsidiarity and sphere sovereignty is not an exact fit. For one thing, Calvinist commentators often emphasize the fact that while Roman Catholics sometimes use the principle of subsidiarity to defend decentralized patterns *within* a given sphere, Kuyper appealed to sphere sovereignty only as a way of clarifying the differences *among* spheres. While this is a helpful observation for illustrating the lack of a perfect fit, it is not necessary to make too much of it. In his study of the use of subsidiarity in Catholic ecclesiology, Ad Leys provides examples of ways in which the principle has been employed by Catholics to lay out the proper relations between the papacy and the episcopacy.[7] Even though Kuyper did not intend sphere sovereignty to make a parallel point about Protestant church life, he did in fact harbor strong anti-"hierarchical" sentiments in his understanding of the relationship of local churches to broader ecclesiastical bodies;[8] and he even referred, in his Stone Lecture on politics, to "the social life of cities and villages" as forming "a separate sphere of existence . . . and which therefore must be autonomous."[9] While Kuyper's "localist" sympathies do not, strictly speaking, follow from his notion of sphere sovereignty, it is difficult to think that there is no spillover from his prescriptions about intersphere relations to his views on intrasphere patterns.

More interesting is the fact that some Kuyperians have insisted that the apparent commonalities between sphere sovereignty and subsidiarity mask very deep philosophical differences. That is certainly the way Herman Dooyeweerd views the relationship. He sees the Roman Catholic view as a hierarchical scheme in which the state is "the totality of natural society,"[10] with the church representing an even higher manifestation "of

6. Nelson R. Gonzalez, "The European Christian Democratic Tradition: A Neglected Font of Political Wisdom," *Regeneration Quarterly,* Summer 1996, 30.

7. Ad Leys, *Ecclesiological Impacts of the Principle of Subsidiarity,* trans. A. van Santvoord (Kampen: Kok, 1995).

8. For an account of Kuyper's views in this area, see Cornelis Veenhof, "Church Polity in 1886 and 1944," in *Seeking Our Brothers in the Light: A Plea for Reformed Ecumenicity,* ed. Theodore Plantinga (Neerlandia, Alberta: Inheritance Publications, 1992).

9. Kuyper, *Lectures on Calvinism,* 96.

10. Herman Dooyeweerd, *Roots of Western Culture: Pagan, Secular, and Christian Options,* ed. Mark Vander Vennen and Bernard Zylstra, trans. John Kraay (Toronto: Wedge, 1979), 127.

christian society in its supranatural perfection." In such a view, as Dooyeweerd describes it, communities such as family, university, and corporation are lower parts of these higher organic unities: families are organically subordinate to the state, and the state to the church. The principle of subsidiarity, then, serves only as a kind of pragmatic limitation on the real authority of church and state, dictating that whenever possible the lower entities should be allowed to function without interference from higher authorities. By way of contrast, Dooyeweerd insists, sphere sovereignty does not merely prescribe a practical "hands-off" policy; rather, the boundaries that separate the spheres are a part of the very nature of things. Neither the state nor the church has any business viewing the other spheres as somehow "under" it. Kuyper's scheme places "the different spheres of life alongside each other," finding their unity not in some "higher" visible community but in the ordering of a creation that is ruled by God.[11]

I am not concerned here to defend the details of Dooyeweerd's interpretation of the deeper intentions of subsidiarity thinking. My own sense is that his way of drawing the contrast is a bit too stark.[12] But his critique does give clear expression to the way in which Kuyper and his followers have wanted to emphasize the fact that each of the created spheres has its own integrity, with its own unique mandate from the Creator — an emphasis not usually found in Roman Catholic expositions of subsidiarity. To use a favorite phrase of Kuyper's, each sphere exists *coram deo,* standing in an unmediated relationship to the rule of God.

Created Culture

These brief observations on the differences between Kuyper's perspective and some kindred themes in more recent Christian social thought are meant to emphasize the fact that Kuyper was not motivated by exactly the same concerns as those contemporary thinkers who, in Klapwijk's words, "prefer to explain the diversity of social structures as a purely pragmatic

11. Dooyeweerd, *Roots of Western Culture,* 129.

12. For a more nuanced Kuyperian critique than Dooyeweerd's, with suggestions for reformulating the principle of subsidiarity in less "hierarchical" terms, see Jonathan Chaplin, "Subsidiarity as a Political Norm," in *Political Theory and Christian Vision: Essays in Memory of Bernard Zylstra,* ed. Jonathan Chaplin and Paul Marshall (Lanham, Md.: University Press of America, 1994), 81-100.

outcome of historical evolution or as a functional decentralization of the authority of the state."[13] Kuyper was guided by some very basic philosophical-theological commitments that he considered to be "principal" in character. In briefly examining a few of these key commitments here, I am interested not only in the way they functioned in shaping Kuyper's thought, but also in their contemporary relevance. Kuyper obviously took these matters seriously. But why should we? Is the larger perspective that shaped his "sphere sovereignty" program still a viable way of viewing things in our own cultural context?

I begin with Kuyper's strong emphasis on culture as an integral dimension of the original creation. Without paying attention to this theme, it is impossible to understand his views about how the spheres relate to each other. I have already noted, for example, that while he surely wanted to keep the state in its place, he also wanted the proper role of other spheres of human interaction to be recognized and honored. This in turn presupposed a larger perspective, one he considered to be a profoundly biblical vision of societal life. And as Kuyper set forth his understanding of that perspective, he gave a central emphasis to the ordered creation as the fundamental context for grasping the proper "place" of any given sphere.

In the Kuyperian scheme, God invested the original creation with complex cultural potential, which human beings were then expected to actualize. In a classic statement of this perspective, aptly entitled *The Calvinistic Concept of Culture,* Henry Van Til explained the Kuyperian understanding of the "cultural mandate" in Genesis 1 by arguing that the Creator's initial assignment to the first human pair — the directive to "fill the earth" (Gen. 1:28) — featured God's deep interest in the cultural development of the creation. God placed Adam and Eve, Van Til observed, into a "primary environment" — a garden containing plant and animal life — with the expectation that they would impose upon this raw nature a "secondary environment," a cultural one. By shaping artifacts and instituting patterns of interaction, created humanity would bring out creation's rich cultural potential, thus displaying God's multifaceted design — aesthetic, familial, economic, political, and so on — for the created order.[14] This cultural mandate is an expression of God's own investment in cultural formation, and it has in no way been canceled by the introduction of sin into the creation. Indeed, our sinfulness inevitably manifests itself in cultural

13. Klapwijk, "The Struggle," 13.

14. Henry R. Van Til, *The Calvinistic Concept of Culture* (Grand Rapids: Baker, 1959), 7.

terms: as a result of the Fall, cultural obedience was replaced by cultural disobedience, resulting in a distortion of the cultural activity for which we were created. To be redeemed from sin, then, is to be restored to the patterns of obedient cultural formation for which we were created.

This restorative motif looms large in the way Kuyper describes Christ's redemptive mission:

> Can we imagine that at one time God willed to rule things in a certain moral order, but that now, in Christ, He wills to rule it otherwise? As though He were not the Eternal, the Unchangeable, Who, from the very hour of creation, even unto all eternity, had willed, wills, and shall will and maintain, one and the same firm moral world-order! Verily Christ has swept away the dust with which man's sinful limitations had covered up this world-order, and has made it glitter again in its original brilliancy. . . . [T]he world-order remains just what it was from the beginning. It lays full claim, not only to the believer (as though less were required from the unbeliever), but to every human being and to all human relationships.[15]

Note that what is restored here, in Kuyper's way of stating the case, is a "world-order." God did not just invest the creation with cultural potentials and leave it up to creatures to do what they will in actualizing those potentials. Our cultural activity, in both its obedient and disobedient forms, occurs within a creation that is *ordered* culturally, in at least two senses: God created a macro-ordering of diverse spheres of cultural interaction, and he gave to each of the individual spheres its own unique internal orderedness. The fulfillment of the cultural mandate, then, requires the discovery and implementation of God's complex ordering design, both among and within the spheres.

In placing such a strong emphasis on order, Kuyper was exhibiting some rather basic Calvinist instincts. Sheldon Wolin has observed that Calvin was unique among the sixteenth-century Protestant Reformers in insisting that societal life was divinely ordered. On Wolin's reading of Reformation thought, both Luther and the Anabaptists believed in a divinely ordered cosmos, but they saw extra-ecclesial social reality "as a dark, disordered mass trembling on the brink of anarchy and seemingly outside the beneficent order of God." In contrast, says Wolin, John Calvin insisted on

15. Kuyper, *Lectures on Calvinism,* 71-72.

reconciling "Christian cosmology" with "Christian sociology" by portraying all of social reality as under the ordering rule of God.[16] Wolin may be overstating the case, but he is right at least about some overall emphases. Calvin and his followers have typically given more attention than other Protestants to the fact of a divinely instituted social order. And Kuyper clearly stands in this tradition, emphasizing with other Calvinists the "spear sovereignty" role of the state in ordering the rest of society.

This ordering task is not, however, *simply* a function of the "spear" of Romans 13:4. As Kuyper portrays the ordering role of government, it is more than a postlapsarian coercive necessity. What we experience as the state under fallen conditions is a manifestation of something that was already implicit in the original creation design. Even if the Fall had not occurred, Kuyper argues in his Stone Lecture on politics, there would have developed a need for government — not in the form of coercive nation-states, but as "one organic world-empire, with God as its King; exactly what is prophesied for the future which awaits us, when all sin shall have disappeared."[17] Here government is not fundamentally a remedial response to human perversity, but a natural provision for the regulating — the ordering — of the complexity of created cultural life.

This idea that politics, as well as the diversity of other cultural spheres, is a part of the original creation design is obviously basic to Kuyper's thought. But what are the *grounds* for believing in such a thing? While Kuyper and his followers say surprisingly little on this topic, choosing for the most part to explicate rather than provide a rationale for their scheme, there are occasional references to what they apparently view as a biblical grounding for the sphere sovereignty idea. Writings on sphere sovereignty often contain allusions to the descriptions in the Genesis story of plants and animals being created "after their own kind." Kuyper's colleague Herman Bavinck sprinkles his account of sphere sovereignty with these references.

> Everything was created with its own nature and is based upon ordinances appointed by God for it. Sun and moon and stars have their own peculiar tasks; plants and animals and man have their own distinct natures. . . . Every creature received its own nature and its own existence,

16. Sheldon Wolin, *Politics and Vision: Continuity and Innovation in Western Political Thought* (Boston: Little, Brown, 1960), 180.

17. Kuyper, *Lectures on Calvinism*, 92.

> its own life and its own law of life . . . so all creatures carried in their own nature the principles and laws of their own development. . . . As creatures were given their own peculiar natures along with differences among them, so there are also differences in the laws by which they act and in the relationships which they sustain to each other.[18]

These comments illustrate the way in which Kuyperians often move rather quickly from relatively straightforward paraphrases of biblical references to the creation of plants, animals, and celestial bodies to more general comments about the larger patterns of created reality. For example, at one point Bavinck refers to Psalm 148:6, where God is described as having "fixed [the] bounds" of various celestial bodies and angelic beings. Bavinck uses this to make the more general point that "God gave to all creatures a certain order, a law which they do not violate." Then he quickly moves into an even more robust invocation of sphere sovereignty, observing that all creatures as such "differ in the area of both physical things and psychic things, in the intellectual and ethical realms, in the family and in society, in science and in art, in the domain of earth and in the domain of heaven."[19]

Kuyper himself provides the outline of an even larger rationale for sphere sovereignty, when he poses the question in his address at the founding of the Vrije Universiteit, "whether 'sphere sovereignty' is derived from the heart of Scripture and from the treasure of the Reformed life." Kuyper explains what gave rise to this conception in his thinking:

> Should anyone ask whether "sphere sovereignty" is really derived from the heart of Scripture and the treasury of Reformed life, I would entreat him first of all to plumb the depths of the organic *faith principle* in Scripture, further to note Hebron's tribal law for David's coronation, to notice Elijah's resistance to Ahab's tyranny, the disciples' refusal to yield to Jerusalem's police regulations, and, not least, to listen to their Lord's maxim concerning what is God's and what is Caesar's. As to Reformed life, don't you know about Calvin's "lesser magistrates"? Isn't sphere sovereignty the basis for the entire presbyterian church order? Did not almost all Reformed nations incline toward a confederate form of gov-

18. Herman Bavinck, *Gereformeerde Dogmatiek* (Kampen: Kok, 1928), various sections, as translated and quoted by Spykman, "Sphere Sovereignty," 179-82.
19. Bavinck, in Spykman, "Sphere Sovereignty," 180.

ernment? Are not civil liberties most luxuriantly developed in Reformed lands? Can it be denied that domestic peace, decentralization, and municipal autonomy are best guaranteed even today among the heirs of Calvin?[20]

Without examining in detail the biblical and historical examples that Kuyper cites here, it is at least obvious that they all, in one way or another, illustrate the separation of powers.

Is any of this convincing as a rationale for sphere sovereignty? In one sense it obviously is not. It is one thing to note, in the spirit of Kuyper's list of examples, that God saw to it that the separate offices of prophet, priest, and king were distinguished in the life of ancient Israel, or that presbyterian polity assigns different functions to pastors, elders, and deacons. But it is another thing to insist that God shaped the world in such a way that, say, universities would have different creational mandates than churches. Similarly, Bavinck's comments about creation contain some significant "leaps": he begins with rather straightforward paraphrases of biblical references to the peculiar natures and boundaries of specific created entities, moving from there to more general statements about a lawful order that those specific creatures must obey, and then to an even more general account of the lawful ordering of a variety of creational spheres.

What about this? At least two things can be said in defense of what Kuyper and Bavinck are doing. One is that they are engaged in the very kind of intellectual activity that gives life to much good theological reflection. They are going beyond the explicit statements of Scripture to explore larger patterns of coherence that can shed light on the *patterns* of biblically based thought. The second is that there is a "fit" of sorts between the actual biblical passages they allude to and the more speculative claims they make. For example, Bavinck is referring to biblical instances that do in fact focus on the ways in which God shapes and governs the creation, using those references to talk about even more general ways in which God structures and orders created life. Much the same can be said for the way Kuyper moves from actual biblical examples of the separation of powers to more general claims about God's desire to draw clear lines of separation among the societal spheres. In one sense the leap is significant. But Kuyper is, as it were, asking us to consider the possibility that these particular examples illus-

---

20. Kuyper, "Sphere Sovereignty," in *Abraham Kuyper: A Centennial Reader,* ed. James D. Bratt (Grand Rapids: Eerdmans, 1998), 480-81.

trate a more general divine interest in the separation of powers, by viewing these separations as built into the very fabric of creation itself.

Needless to say, Kuyper is also moving much beyond the actual biblical data in setting forth his views about the ways in which the cultural spheres as such are somehow "contained" within the original creation. His even-if-the-Fall-had-not-occurred type of hypotheses will strike some as highly speculative. And in an important sense they are. For those of us, though, who find biblically based imaginative proposals to be useful theological exercises, this is not necessarily a bad thing. There is a helpful parallel to be drawn here to the ways in which some historians use counterfactual claims to explore what has recently been labeled "virtual history": they ask, for example, what if Lee had won the Battle of Gettysburg or what if Charles I had refused to negotiate with the Scottish Covenanters in 1639?[21] As J. M. Roberts has argued, in spite of the objections of skeptics, "the fiction that things could have been otherwise often seems in some sense to illuminate what actually happened"; while contrary-to-fact conditionals can obviously "be clumsily or implausibly made," they can also "do positive good in the hands of good teachers."[22]

Kuyper seems to be a reliable teacher in this regard. In his speculations about creation, he uses the counterfactual as a means of conceptual clarification. When he argues, for example, that politics was a part of the original creation, he means to isolate those dimensions of political life that are not merely contingent on human perversity. This allows him to point to the need for the regulation of group activities even when it is not necessary to reinforce such regulative activity with coercive threats. To offer an effective rebuttal to this line of argument, it is not sufficient simply to reject his use of the counterfactual as such; rather, it is necessary to show that there is something conceptually implausible about what his use of the counterfactual is meant to illustrate, namely, the idea of a prelapsarian political order.

Creational Diversity

We must highlight Kuyper's emphasis on cultural diversity if we are to be clear about why his thought does not match up exactly with those contem-

21. See J. M. Roberts, "Putting the *What If?* in History," *Times Literary Supplement,* no. 4922 (August 1, 1997): 6.
22. Roberts, "Putting," 6.

porary thinkers who are primarily concerned about the ways in which the state in particular tends to overextend its authority. As we have seen, the case for mediating structures is often put in terms of the need to avoid an inflated state on the one hand and an inflated individual on the other. To guard against the twin dangers of statism and individualism, the argument goes, we need strong nonpolitical communal entities.

While Kuyper would be sympathetic to the specific concerns here, he also warned against the dangers of inflating any one of these mediating structures, political or otherwise. He was especially vocal about the dangers of an overextended church. For Kuyper, the mandate given to the institutional church — local congregations and the broader ecclesial assemblies — had to do primarily with such activities as worship, catechesis, and evangelism. Churches were not to take on functions that were appropriate to other spheres. Here is how one of his American disciples, Princeton Seminary theologian Geerhardus Vos, put the Kuyperian point:

> There is a sphere of science, a sphere of art, a sphere of family life and of the state, a sphere of commerce and industry. Whenever one of these spheres comes under the controlling influence of the principle of divine supremacy and glory, and this outwardly reveals itself, there we can truly say that the kingdom of God has become manifest. . . . [Jesus'] doctrine of the kingdom was founded on such a profound and broad conviction of the absolute supremacy of God in all things, that he could not but look upon every normal and legitimate province of human life as intended to form part of God's kingdom. . . . [But] it was not his intention that this result should be reached by making human life in all its spheres subject to the visible church. . . . [W]hat is true of the relation between church and state, may also be applied to the relation between the visible church and the various other branches into which the organic life of humanity divides itself.[23]

The worries that Vos expresses here about an overextended church loomed large in Kuyper's thought. Much of his practical activity as a public figure concentrated on opposing two very basic patterns of cultural hegemony: statism, which tries to invest political government with the right to direct all of cultural life to its own purposes, and the kind of ecclesiasticism typi-

---

23. Geerhardus Vos, *The Kingdom and the Church* (Grand Rapids: Eerdmans, 1951), 87-89, quoted in Spykman, "Sphere Sovereignty," 176-77.

fied in his mind by much of medieval life, where the church went beyond its proper authority in imposing its influence on family life, art, business, and politics.

Kuyper's choice of the name for the university he founded, the Vrije Universiteit, is an important example in this regard. The *vrijheid* of his university was meant to be a freedom from both governmental and ecclesial control. Each of these three entities — state, church, and university — belongs to a different sphere: the state as a political body exists to guarantee the distinctness of diverse sphere boundaries; the church is meant to provide a context for preaching, the sacraments, and the fostering of spiritual nurture; the university sponsors scientific activity, in the broad sense of science as the business of disciplined intellectual investigation. Each of these spheres has its own unique set of functions and norms — what goes into good government is not the same as what makes for good preaching or good scholarship. The Christian university, then, must avoid being controlled by government. But it must also stand apart from the direct influence of ecclesiastical authority. For Kuyper this meant that the university should be governed by an association *(vereniging)* of persons whose sole purpose is to see to it that a specific kind of confessionally guided science is allowed to flourish.

In assessing the contemporary relevance of Kuyper's strong insistence on the need to respect the boundaries between various spheres, it is more important, I think, to pay attention to the general contours of his thought than to get caught up with his specific views about how the boundaries are to be drawn in practice. There is some irony in this assessment, since Kuyper's actual references to sphere sovereignty are more often than not to be found in contexts where he is insisting that a recognition of the diversity of spheres is the only way to avoid very practical confusions in societal life. Nonetheless, we do him no favors by focusing too much on his own practical applications for the purposes of evaluating his overall scheme.

I offer one quick example as a case in point. During the early 1890s Kuyper got caught up in a rather intense debate over the appropriate sphere-setting for theological education. It is not necessary here to set out the historical specifics of this debate — which had to do with the merger negotiations between two Dutch Reformed denominations.[24] The question being debated posed a simple choice: Should the education of clergy

---

24. The details can be found in Hendrik Bouma, *Secession, Doleantie, and Union: 1834-1892*, trans. Theodore Plantinga (Neerlandia, Alberta: Inheritance Publications, 1995).

take place in a church-controlled theological school or in a theology department housed in a "free" university? As might be expected, Kuyper argued passionately for the latter option. He was opposed with equal passion, however, by supporters of ecclesiastical sponsorship. In the final analysis the two sides agreed to a compromise: the newly merged denomination would have two tracks for theological education, one in a church-controlled school and the other in a university setting.

It is important to see why Kuyper could not win this argument simply by appealing to sphere sovereignty. He could certainly insist that theology is a science in his broad sense of the term, and that it therefore deserves departmental embodiment in a Christian university. But that was not at issue in the debate. The important question for his opponents was whether the theology department of a freestanding university was the right sort of context for preparing people for parish ministries. And Kuyper's opponents could point out that the sphere sovereignty scheme does allow for education to take place in various spheres. Kuyper himself argued strenuously that, in contrast to the university, the education of children was primarily a parental responsibility — thus the strong emphasis in many Dutch Calvinist communities, both in the Netherlands and in North America, on the need for "parent-controlled" Christian schools. Kuyper would also concede that there are patterns of educational activities that are important to other spheres: management training, education of artists by artists, and so on.

More specific to the debate about clergy education is the fact that the church too has a form of education in which it properly engages, namely, catechesis. Kuyper would certainly acknowledge this. What his opponents in the debate over theological education were arguing in effect was that the training of clergy was an important extension of the church's catechetical mandate. Since the argument, then, is one formulated *within* the framework of sphere sovereignty, Kuyper had no decisive response to offer.

Does this mean, then, that the sphere sovereignty idea is not very helpful in deciding practical disputes like this one? Maybe not in *deciding* them, but it certainly provides much help by way of *informing* the debate. It is important, for example, to be clear about the ways in which education occurs in some contexts as a means of supporting a larger sphere mandate (as in management training), in contrast to the way in which education should be pursued in that "scientific" sphere where disciplined intellectual inquiry is itself the primary "business" of that area of human interaction.

The Merits of the Kuyperian Project

Why follow Kuyper in his deep concern for drawing clear boundary lines among cultural spheres? Is it really all that good a thing to want to keep everything in its place in this manner?

An answer of sorts is suggested by the Scottish theologian James Hutton MacKay, in an observation about Dutch habits of mind that he offered in Glasgow in 1911. Having recently completed a pastoral tour of duty in the Netherlands, MacKay delivered a series of lectures on nineteenth-century Dutch religious thought, and he used Kuyper as an example of what he saw as a typical Dutch fascination with the setting of boundaries. The Dutch mind, said MacKay, is fond of making distinctions: "'We are a people of dykes and dams,' a Dutch writer said recently, 'both as to our land and our mental life.' And Dr. Kuyper's often-quoted saying about the danger of 'blurring the boundary lines' is characteristically Dutch. . . . [And] much, I believe, can be learned from a people who have a remarkable gift of making distinctions, wrought into their nature, possibly, by many centuries of unrelaxing toil in making and holding that distinction between land and sea, which to them is a matter of life and death."[25] MacKay is suggesting that even if Kuyper's habits of mind reflect a more general pattern in the Dutch way of viewing things — one that might require, say, a "geo-intellectual" explanation[26] — it is still possible that "much . . . can be learned" by paying attention to this deep interest in boundary setting.

Of course, the willingness to learn from Kuyper requires certain dispositions. One is the disposition to see *culture as woven into the original creation*. While legitimate criticisms can be lodged against the way in which H. Richard Niebuhr sorts out the various "Christ and culture" options in his classic book on that topic, he is right to point to the fact that Christians can all read the same Bible and yet come away with rather different assessments of what God's basic intentions are with respect to the various manifestations of human cultural activity. And Niebuhr speaks well for those of us who subscribe to the "transformationalist" option when he identifies that position with the conviction that while culture as

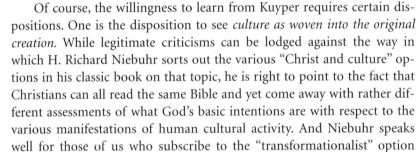

---

25. James Hutton MacKay, *Religious Thought in Holland during the Nineteenth Century* (New York: Hodder and Stoughton, 1911), 10.

26. I discuss this possibility in a little more detail in my "Dutch Calvinist Philosophical Influences in North America," *Calvin Theological Journal* 24, no. 1 (April 1989): 93-94.

we experience it under present conditions is corrupt, it is "corrupted order rather than order for corruption . . . it is evil as perversion, and not as badness of being."[27] Furthermore, if God had something much better in mind for the complex patterns of culture — familial, economic, recreational, ecclesial, political — than what we presently encounter, it is incumbent on us to get as much clarity as we can about the boundaries God wants us to respect.

In saying this, I must emphasize again that it does not matter much whether Kuyper himself got all the spheres exactly right. Indeed, I am not even convinced that we ought to hold on too tightly to the idea of sphere as such. As I have argued elsewhere,[28] Kuyper's scheme, and Herman Dooyeweerd's rather elaborate refinement of it, basically offers us a kind of *hermeneutic for modal discernment* for our attempts to understand the complexities of cultural life. Dooyeweerd helped to improve the Kuyperian case by substituting the language of "modes" for Kuyper's "sphere" talk. When we put too much emphasis on "spheres," we are tempted to view the creation as containing spaces or "slots" that need to be filled with various kinds of institutions and associations. A more modal conception, on the other hand, allows us to look for aspects and patterns that may in fact be configured in a number of possible combinations.

An example will help to clarify my meaning here. If we apply Kuyper's views very strictly, say, to the phenomenon of the "family business" — for example, a dry-cleaning establishment owned and operated by members of a single family — we would have to view such a social entity with suspicion: families are families and businesses are businesses, and it is not good to mix the two spheres. I see no need to follow him consistently on such a matter. But where the Kuyperian scheme *is* still helpful — and very much so, I want to argue — is in "reading" the family business phenomenon. Such an entity is indeed a combination of at least two different modes of cultural association: family and business. While the two modes may be combined, they should not be confused. It is good for participants in a family business to be very clear about the differences between familial and business relations.

Another disposition that is required looks kindly on the idea of *created*

27. H. Richard Niebuhr, *Christ and Culture* (New York: Harper and Row, 1951), 194.

28. See my "On Creation's 'Several Parts': Modal Diversity in Dooyeweerd's Social Thought," in *Christian Philosophy at the Close of the Twentieth Century: Assessment and Perspective,* ed. Sander Griffioen and Bert M. Balk (Kampen: Uitgeverij Kok, 1995), 180-82.

diversity. Roger Henderson has rightly described the Kuyperian movement as having a strong fascination with "the radical diversity of creation."[29] Kuyper's God has a distinct bias in favor of diversity in the creation. As we have seen, it is precisely the emphasis in Genesis on the proliferation of "kinds" in the animal and vegetative realms that Kuyper builds upon in making his case for a divinely ordained diversity of spheres of cultural activity. To accept Kuyper's sphere sovereignty scheme, then, is to possess a rather complex framework for discerning boundary lines and making distinctions.

The need for maintaining clear boundaries is not obvious to everyone these days, and very often the resistance to boundary maintenance is an expression of dissatisfaction with the fact of cultural diversity. One does not have to shop very far in the marketplace of contemporary ideas to find people who celebrate the blurring of boundaries and the breaking down of barriers that have long separated various spheres of interaction and inquiry. An obvious example is found in popular New Age teachings, which herald the appearance of an "emergent culture" where new syntheses are replacing older polarities between magic and science, East and West, nature and technology, women and men, folk teachings and scholarship, "primitive" and "advanced."[30] An interest in boundary blurring between spheres can also be seen in a more mainstream — including mainstream Christian — fondness for borrowing the motifs and concepts of one sphere for use in another: as in the church as "family" and management "teams."

How these contemporary boundary blurrings are to be evaluated from Kuyper's perspective is a large and important topic. Three observations will have to suffice here. The first is, both Kuyper's sphere sovereignty scheme and more recent celebrations of mergings and syntheses are expressions of a shared concern about the increasing threat of *fragmentation* in the patterns of human interaction. Some defenders of the starker versions of "postmodern" thought are willing, of course, to embrace the fragmentation, even to the point of cultivating what Iban Hassan describes as "an epistemological obsession with fragments" as a necessary means of avoiding "the tyranny of wholes."[31] For those who are not attracted to this

29. R. D. Henderson, "Illuminating Law: The Construction of Herman Dooyeweerd's Philosophy, 1918-1928" (Ph.D. diss., Vrije Universiteit, 1994), 128.

30. This perspective is set forth in detail in Marilyn Ferguson, *The Aquarian Conspiracy: Personal and Social Transformation in the 1980s* (Los Angeles: T. P. Tarcher, 1980), a book often described as "the bible of the New Age movement."

31. Quoted by Richard J. Bernstein, *The New Constellation* (Cambridge: MIT Press, 1992), 199.

option, however, the search for new *connections between* the various spheres is an important project.

The desire to find intersphere connections is not a bad thing from a Kuyperian perspective. Indeed, some Kuyperians have suggested that it is necessary to emphasize a kind of "sphere universality" to balance out the possible fragmenting tendencies of the sphere sovereignty idea.[32] But in the final analysis Kuyper was not as interested in looking for the connecting principles *within* the creation as he was in emphasizing the fact that the spheres are ultimately coordinated and linked by virtue of their mutual relationship to the transcendent will of the Creator.

Second, while Kuyper and his followers are quite willing to allow for transspherical commonalities and applications, they also find it necessary to warn against the very real dangers of sphere confusion. For Kuyper the most basic confusion of all is the failure to keep clear about the boundary that separates the infinite being of the creation Creator from the finite creation; the title of an essay he published in English in 1893 is instructive in this regard: "Pantheism's Destruction of Boundaries."[33] Original sin stems from this fundamental confusion: "and you will be like God, knowing good and evil" (Gen. 3:5). Kuyper's followers, especially those who developed his views in more systematic-philosophical terms, have expended much energy sorting out, and warning against, the various "reductionisms" that result from forming idolatrous attachments to this or that aspect of created reality. But we need not put the case in those harsh terms. We can simply employ the sphere sovereignty scheme to point to the dangers that lurk wherever people borrow too heavily from one sphere in spelling out the proper patterns of interaction in another sphere.

Take the application of familial concepts to the church. In his illuminating study of the rise of Methodism in America, Gregory Schneider shows how the nineteenth-century Methodists increasingly "domesticated" their understanding of the life and calling of the Christian community, focusing on "the image of home: the secluded and affectionate domestic circle constrained by the self-effacing love of the mother." The Methodist church "housed the family of God. The outlooks and sentiments they learned as members of the spiritual family disposed them to

32. See Spykman, "Sphere Sovereignty," 168, and L. Kalsbeek, *Contours of a Christian Philosophy: An Introduction to Herman Dooyeweerd's Thought* (Toronto: Wedge, 1975), chapter 13.

33. Abraham Kuyper, "Pantheism's Destruction of Boundaries," *Methodist Review* 53 (July 1893): 520-35; (September 1893): 762-78.

evolve a vision of domesticity and increasingly to identify their literal families and home circles with the idea of the spiritual family."[34] As the Methodist movement grew, however, many of its functions increasingly required the skills associated with managerial expertise. It was difficult, argues Schneider, for Methodists to integrate these functions into their theological understanding of the church, since they were operating with a bifurcated view of ecclesial life: "domestic piety and bureaucratic enterprise" seemed irreconcilable.[35]

From a sphere sovereignty perspective, it is important to emphasize that churches are neither families nor businesses, even though there may be important links between churchly functions and things that happen in these other spheres. If the unique calling of the church is, say, to promote the proper patterns of the worship and service of the God of the Bible, then both the more intimate dimensions of churchly fellowship and the managerial functions of the churchly structures are to be integrated with a view to fulfilling that larger mandate. When a clear focus on the unique patterns of ecclesial reality is not maintained, there is a constant danger that the church will borrow too heavily from other spheres for its understanding of its life and mission, thereby suffering from the distortions that these borrowings will inevitably effect.

Third, while good reasons can be offered for insisting within the Kuyperian framework that boundary lines should be carefully monitored, it is nonetheless necessary to avoid drawing too many boundaries. Not all diversity ought to be viewed as a good thing. The ways in which the Kuyperian scheme was used in the development of South African apartheid ideology raises necessary warning signals in this regard. Building on Kuyper's ideas, some influential Afrikaner thinkers extended the notion of separate cultural spheres to the need for separate *ethnic cultures*.[36] Needless to say, it is not difficult to show how this extension was not entailed by Kuyper's actual formulations of the sphere sovereignty idea. But given the ways in which Kuyper himself was able to move quite freely among different contexts of boundary drawings — from the Creator-creature boundary, to the boundaries between animal "kinds," to the boundaries that sep-

---

34. A. Gregory Schneider, *The Way of the Cross Leads Home: The Domestication of American Methodism* (Bloomington: Indiana University Press, 1993), 196.

35. Schneider, *The Way*, 205-7.

36. The story of how Kuyper's views were used in this manner is told in detail by T. Dunbar Moodie, *The Rise of Afrikanerdom: Power, Apartheid, and the Afrikaner Civil Religion* (Los Angeles: University of California Press, 1975), 153-74, 215-33.

arate cultural spheres — careful attention must be given to the proper and improper patterns of boundary setting.

A final disposition is rooted in an optimism about *our ability to discern the proper contours of created culture.* Many Kuyperians express their optimism on this point in bold and sweeping terms. Here, for example, is Gordon Spykman on the subject:

> The writings of the Old and New Testaments are the "spectacles" through which we seek to discern the meaning of our lives within God's creation. As our window on God's world, the Bible calls us to bow obediently to the full authority of God's Word for all of life. It leads us to recognize the normativity of God's revelation in creation, the creation ordinances by which God from the beginning structured the life of His creation. For creation is a cosmos (a richly diversified, yet coherently unified whole), not a chaos. Though the structures of creation have fallen under sin, God still upholds them by His Word and redeems them in Jesus Christ. Scripture, serving as a pair of glasses, opens our eyes to the norms of these creation-redemption ordinances as they hold continuously for the full range of our societal life.[37]

For those of us in the Kuyperian tradition, the terminology employed here comes easily. And we should not too quickly abandon these phrases, since they serve as necessary reminders of the robustness of the vision that has shaped our ways of thinking about culture. But we also realize — or we ought to realize — that this is not the way to make our case to the larger community, even the larger Christian community. Our contemporary context requires a more modest and tentative presentation.

Here, as I see it, is how such a presentation should go. First, we should work with the realization that the Kuyperian scheme is not a mere summary of what the Bible explicitly "teaches." Spykman's formulations make that clear with his references (borrowed from Calvin's *Institutes*) to the Bible as "spectacles" through which we look at created reality. But we must go a step further, to admit that it is not always easy to see, or even to know enough to look for, creation's "normativity," simply by studying the Bible and then turning to the observation of our lived-in world. The fact that some of us have learned to probe created reality for "ordinances" has much to do with a company of gifted instructors — Calvin, Kuyper, Bavinck,

37. Spykman, "Sphere Sovereignty," 164.

Dooyeweerd, and others — who taught us to pay attention to specific passages of the Scriptures, and to use the themes and motifs and hints that we find there to organize our understanding of the larger picture that we see being sketched out in the Word.

In explaining this process to others, we need to be clear about the fact that we have been captivated by a very imaginative way of charting out God's designs in the revealed drama of creation, fall, redemption, and eschaton. And when we encounter disagreement and dissent, as we surely will, we cannot fall back on pronouncements. Rather, we must explain as best we can why we are deeply convinced that all of this is, while surely a speculative exercise, the product of <u>sanctified imaginations.</u>

In a very important sense, however, the merits of the Kuyperian scheme will be seen most clearly in the ways it sensitizes us to important questions that arise in the ways we wrestle with the very real quandaries and challenges of our complex lives. Defenders of the sphere sovereignty perspective need to engage in the kind of critical probing that Jean Bethke Elshtain exemplifies in discussing an actual case where familial imagery is applied to an area that is not literally "family." Referring to Mario Cuomo's reference, in his address to the 1984 Democratic National Convention, to the United States as a family, she acknowledges that the motive at work in this sort of comment can be a laudable one. But she also points to the dangers of this way of characterizing political life: "Let's grant the decent intent behind the turn to familial metaphors. But to call a modern nation-state a family, in the interest of connecting us to one another, should be faulted because it too easily transforms citizens into Big Children. Government, in this scenario, becomes a benevolent, sometimes chiding caretaker and protector."[38] Elshtain is making a simple but important conceptual observation here: as helpful as it might be in some respects to liken our roles as citizens to familial relations, there are very significant ways in which nation-states are *not* families; and to confuse the two can be very dangerous. This is a case in point for the kind of probing that Kuyperians must regularly pursue. When people apply the concepts of one mode of cultural life to another one, what is going on? What gives these references the feel of plausibility? What are the dangers that lurk beneath the surface?

We do not do justice to Kuyper, of course, if we commend his perspective only for its pragmatic value in dealing with critical social challenges.

---

38. Jean Bethke Elshtain, "Mario Cuomo Isn't Your Daddy," *New Oxford Review*, December 1996, 26.

He did, after all, insist that his own practical proposals were shaped by "principial" convictions, by a "world and life view" that was grounded in biblical teaching. This bigger picture, so important to Kuyper, has not lost its power, even in the very different societal context in which many of us continue to think about what we have learned from him. To find ways of showing not only that the Kuyperian hermeneutic of modal discernment can help us to ask good practical questions, but also how its pragmatic value is integrally connected to a larger vision of God's creating and redeeming purposes — this is for some of us a crucial challenge in our contemporary surroundings, one that also calls for the gift of discernment in large measure.

Modal Diversity in Dooyeweerd's Social Thought

In his recent book on Berkeley's intellectual development, David Berman places a strong emphasis on the impact of Bishop Berkeley's Christian convictions on his philosophical thought: "Probably no major philosopher of the past three hundred years has assigned such a central and operative role to God in his system. . . . [Berkeley's] conviction of the existence and presence of God seems to have been unusually powerful."[1]

Berman's treatment is an important corrective to the views of those who see Bishop Berkeley as a mere transition figure between Locke and Hume; on such a minimalist reading of Berkeley's role, Berkeley anticipated Hume by offering a critique of Locke's material substratum, but he attempted to forestall Humean skepticism by positing a God, of the *deus ex machina* variety, whose existence guarantees some sort of "objective" reality. Berman portrays Berkeley — and convincingly so — as a much more subtle thinker than this, and one whose philosophical probings were characterized by a pervasive "theocentric force."[2]

Berkeley's God-centered philosophy was a systematic attempt to answer some very basic epistemological and metaphysical questions in a manner that does justice to the power of the biblical God. Berkeley's God

1. David Berman, *George Berkeley: Idealism and the Man* (Oxford: Clarendon, 1994), 52-53.

2. Berman, *George Berkeley,* 54.

This essay previously appeared in *Christian Philosophy at the Close of the Twentieth Century,* ed. Sander Griffioen and Bert M. Balk (Kampen: Kok, 1995), 175-83. It is printed here with permission.

is ever-present in a very *immediate* way: he constantly delivers sensory data to our finite minds, and he infuses these data collectively with the requisite coherence and consistency — in my experience of touching my coffee cup, for example, God not only gives me the appropriate visual and tactile sensations, but he does so in such a way that I accept these distinct sensations as being an experience *of* one and the same cup.

In his own peculiar way, then, Berkeley's God is an extremely busy deity. Berman is right to describe the bishop as having assigned a very "central and operative role to God in his system." But, for all that, God's role in Berkeley's world is rather "thin," in a way that roles can *be* both pervasive and thin: think, for example, of a play in which the central character is always busily on stage, but where neither the character himself, nor the plot of the play, is well developed.

Berkeley does not develop God's character or the divine plot to any significant degree in his philosophical system. In fact, he even seems on occasion to celebrate this lack of development. In the *Three Dialogues* he has Philonous observe that while some thinkers have "proved beyond all controversy, from the beauty and usefulness of the several parts of the creation, that it was the workmanship of God," there is nonetheless a certain advantage to a system in which "the being of God" is "necessarily inferred from the bare *existence* of the sensible world."[3] The problem is, of course, that Berkeley's whole system seems to feature a God who is busily maintaining the "bare existence" of that which is empirically given. Little attention is paid to the way God has invested his purposes in "the beauty and usefulness of the several parts of the creation."

To say that Herman Dooyeweerd's philosophy, in contrast to Berkeley's, features a strong emphasis on creation's "several parts" is surely an understatement. As Roger Henderson has noted, Dooyeweerd's thought is permeated with a neo-Calvinist fascination with "the radical diversity of creation,"[4] an emphasis that is spelled out in an elaborate portrayal of the character of God's intentions in the cosmic drama. In this sense, Dooyeweerd's system can be viewed as providing, in a very different way than Berkeley's does, "theocentric force" to philosophical investigation.

Dooyeweerd's neo-Calvinist philosophy thus serves as an important

3. George Berkeley, *Three Dialogues between Hylas and Philonous,* ed. C. M. Turbayne (New York: Bobbs-Merrill, 1954), 56.
4. Roger D. Henderson, "Illuminating Law: The Construction of Herman Dooyeweerd's Philosophy, 1918-1928" (Ph.D. diss., Vrije Universiteit, 1994), 128.

corrective to the kind of Christian thinking that focuses primarily on God's maintenance of the "bare existence" of the creation. Berkeley's thin portrayal of God's dealings with the world fosters a kind of God-centeredness that generates very little beyond the mere acknowledgment of God's supreme "existence and presence." It is very different in Dooyeweerd's scheme: while Dooyeweerd certainly sees God as the sovereign sustainer of the "bare existence" of our world of experience, he is far more interested in the ways in which God displays his broader creating and redeeming purposes in a richly diverse created order.

Calvinism itself has often had a thin, Berkeleyan-type fixation with a God who is totally absorbed in managing the "bare existence" of the world. In the traditional Calvinist celebration of divine sovereignty, God is seen as having a very active and central role in the governance of all that exists. But there is often little interest in an active discerning of God's creating purposes. The title of Berkeley's little-known treatise in moral and political thought, *Passive Obedience,* could serve as the organizing motif for a not uncommon line of argument among Calvinists: God controls all things; nothing happens without his sovereign consent; when things do happen that we cannot understand, it is not our task to inquire into God's secret purposes; we must be content to bow in humble submission to the will of the One who keeps his own counsel.

We can find this line of argument in article 13 ("The Doctrine of God's Providence") of the Belgic Confession. But, of course, the confession goes on to remind us that we must be "content to be Christ's disciples, so as to learn only what he shows us in his Word, without going beyond those limits." And this is precisely where the neo-Calvinist wants to argue that a passive submission to empirical reality in its "bare existence" is not the normative Christian posture. To "be Christ's disciples" is to explore all that the inscripturated Word teaches us regarding "the beauty and usefulness of the several parts of the creation."

Calvinism and Social Institutions

When Calvinists have allowed their minds to roam beyond a mere focus on "bare existence," they have often had very profound things to say about social institutions. The historian Richard Sher has argued, in his study of Scottish Enlightenment thought, that some of the concepts that figured prominently in the study of society during the Scottish Enlightenment were based directly — for all the secularized language in which they were couched — on "Calvinist foundations." Specifically, Sher points to the Calvinist insistence "that human beings constitute integral parts of the particular societies in which they live and cannot be studied apart from them; that God frequently uses people (or peoples) for divine purposes that remain unknown to them, such as punishing the sinful and rewarding the righteous (the famous concept of 'unintended consequences'); and that the study of collectivities — nations, tribes, and the like — is rich with moral and religious significance."[5]

This last Calvinist emphasis mentioned by Sher is the point worth underscoring for our present purposes. The Calvinist insistence on the rich moral and religious significance of the collective patterns of human interaction is an insight that is elaborated at length in Dooyeweerd's treatment of societal institutions.

One of Dooyeweerd's most significant contributions to Christian philosophy is his stubborn insistence that we are moved in our theoretical explorations by primordial *religious* impulses. His use of "religious" here points to the reality of those fundamental trustings that serve as "the deepest driving forces"[6] that inspire and shape all that we do, including all our theoretical doings.

Many contemporary postmodernist thinkers concur with part of what Dooyeweerd argues. In his rejection of the neutrality of reasoning, his thought is more "contemporary" now than it was in his own lifetime. The failure of the Enlightenment project is being boldly proclaimed today. The notion that there is a "universal reason" that can itself generate norms that are binding across cultures and nationalities is treated with much disdain.

But Dooyeweerd's analysis of the religious character of our fundamental motivations challenges postmodern accounts of what *does* give direction to nonneutral theoretical thought. Postmodernists insist that Enlightenment-type celebrations of universal reason always in fact mask a desire to exercise power. Of course, Dooyeweerd would agree that the way a person or community forms its fundamental trustings may mean that a given theoretical project may *be* motivated by power. But this is only one of the ways in which we can give direction to theoretical activity. For

5. Richard B. Sher, *Church and University in the Scottish Enlightenment: The Moderate Literati of Edinburgh* (Princeton: Princeton University Press, 1985), 43.

6. Herman Dooyeweerd, *Roots of Western Culture: Pagan, Secular, and Christian Options,* trans. J. Kraay (Toronto: Wedge, 1979), 9.

Dooyeweerd, it is important to distinguish between the idolatrous and the faithful in sorting out our basic trustings. To recontextualize his account of the religious character of theoretical activity is an important task for contemporary neo-Calvinist philosophy.

The postmodernist enterprise is dedicated to exposing the ways in which our hegemonic designs are camouflaged by allegedly "neutral" theoretical systems. Iban Hassan speaks for many contemporary intellectuals when he describes our present situation as the following:

> an antinomian moment that assumes a vast unmaking of the Western mind — what Michel Foucault might call postmodern *epistēmē*. I say "unmaking" though other terms are now *de rigueur*: for instance, deconstruction, decentering, disappearance, demystification, discontinuity, *différance*, dispersion, etc. Such terms express an ontological rejection of the traditional full subject, the *cogito* of Western philosophy. They express, too, an epistemological obsession with fragments, and a corresponding ideological commitment to minorities in politics, sex and language. To think well, to feel well, to act well, to read well according to this *epistēmē* of unmaking, is to refuse the tyranny of wholes: totalization in human endeavour is potentially totalitarian.[7]

Here it is taken for granted that power is what motivates all narratives that purport to provide some unifying features to human interaction. To reject this "tyranny of wholes" is necessarily to be caught up in "an epistemological obsession with fragments, and a corresponding ideological commitment to minorities in politics, sex and language." This epistemological obsession is not aimed at eliminating the power motif; it perpetuates it, albeit by fragmentation. Political, sexual, and linguistic minorities are encouraged to reject totalizing tyrannies in favor of the exercise of power over their own patterns of social interaction.

Jeffrey Stout has characterized this situation as one for which the biblical image of "Babel" can serve as "a trope." Stout focuses specifically on the fragmentation of our moral discourse, but his observations apply equally well to the broader "multiculturalist" context: "Three specters haunt the philosophy of moral diversity — skepticism, nihilism and relativism. Each, in its own way, involves loss of confidence in our ordinary

7. Quoted in Richard Bernstein, *The New Constellation: The Ethical-Political Horizons of Modernity/Postmodernity* (Boston: MIT Press, 1992), 199.

talk of moral truth and justification, and each can have worrisome effects on how we live our lives."[8]

Assessing Diversity

What does the neo-Calvinist perspective on social institutions have to say to our present-day "Babel" crisis?

In *Pluralisms and Horizons,* Sander Griffioen and I distinguished three kinds of pluralities that must be taken into account in understanding the diversity that presently characterizes human societal interaction: the diversity of religious directions; the diversity of associational patterns — families, businesses, churches, teams, states, etc. — and the diversity of characteristics that we loosely refer to as cultural — race, ethnicity, gender, geography.[9]

The first of these pluralities, directional diversity, is not a part of the Creator's original design for the world. It results from our sinful rebellion. But the two other kinds of pluralities — associational and contextual — are, Griffioen and I argued in our book, positive dimensions of God's creating purposes. In claiming a creational status of associational diversity we are on solid Dooyeweerdian ground. As Griffioen has pointed out elsewhere,[10] however, the status of contextual diversity is not as clearly spelled out in Dooyeweerd's system.

This lack of clarity about contextual diversity in Dooyeweerd's scheme has evoked criticism from people who are generally sympathetic to his overall project. The main critical concerns are set forth in Griffioen's aforementioned paper. They focus primarily on Dooyeweerd's views of the historical process of structural differentiation. Griffioen mentions C. T. McIntire's criticism of Dooyeweerd's "Eurocentric" bias: Dooyeweerd, McIntire points out, assumed the normative character of the kind of structural differentiation experienced in Western societies. This bias accounts, in turn, for Dooyeweerd's assumption, also mentioned by Griffioen, that

8. Jeffrey Stout, *Ethics after Babel: The Languages of Morals and Their Discontents* (Boston: Beacon Press, 1988), 3.

9. Richard J. Mouw and Sander Griffioen, *Pluralisms and Horizons* (Grand Rapids: Eerdmans, 1993), passim.

10. Sander Griffioen, "The Relevance of Dooyeweerd's Theory of Social Institutions," in *Christian Philosophy at the Close of the Twentieth Century,* ed. Sander Griffioen and Bert M. Balk (Kampen: Kok, 1995), 139-58.

"blood bound" collectivities are bound to disappear as structural differentiation develops. Since, for example, tribes are structurally undifferentiated entities, they will gradually dissolve as their various functions — juridical, familial, economic, aesthetic, cultic — separate out in the course of historical development.

Griffioen softens these criticisms of Dooyeweerd by pointing out that Dooyeweerd never emphasized differentiation without also insisting on the importance of integration. I would like to soften them further by giving a slightly more detailed defense — even though, like McIntire and Griffioen, I do see some weaknesses in Dooyeweerd's account on this score.

Dooyeweerdian Discernment

The charge of "Eurocentricism" against Dooyeweerd has a convincing ring to it. The experience of institutional differentiation does seem to be especially tied to the North Atlantic cultures. Many of us take it for granted, for example, that when Abraham Kuyper gave up his ministerial credentials as he embarked upon his political career, he was demonstrating an appropriate sense of differentiation. He knew that political leadership differs from ecclesial leadership; the two spheres operate in accordance with different norms, appropriate to their respective places in the creational scheme.

But why assume that Kuyper was being clearer about the character of public leadership than, say, *the Reverend* Martin Luther King, or *the Reverend* Jesse Jackson, or *Archbishop* Tutu, or *Father* Jean-Bertrand Aristide? Isn't there something to be said for more "holistic" voices — words uttered by leaders who refuse to be segmented into a "religious" or a "political" role, but who insist on addressing the larger issues of *public* life?

Or take the lessons that many in the Western business community have been encouraged to learn from Japanese corporations in recent years. The Japanese firm, they have been told, has never completely divorced economic production from kinship patterns. How should we respond to this observation? Should we insist that, instead of our learning *from* the Japanese, they must be encouraged to learn from *us* about Western-style differentiation?

Again, I think this concern about a "Eurocentric" bias has some legitimacy. But I do not think it necessitates our abandoning the *framework* that informs Dooyeweerd's views about differentiation. I have found it most helpful to see Dooyeweerd as providing us with what we might think of as a *hermeneutic for modal discernment* for our attempts to understand the patterns of social interaction. One significant way in which Dooyeweerd improved on Kuyper's very rough insights regarding sphere sovereignty was by substituting the language of "modes" for Kuyper's "sphere" terminology. To talk about God's interest in "spheres" tempts us to think of creation as containing spaces or "slots" that need to be filled with very specific kinds of associational *entities*. A focus on "modes," in contrast, allows us to concentrate, in less "reifying" ways, on *aspects* of associational interaction — on patterns that may be instantiated in a variety of different institutional structures and configurations — and even in a variety of combinations.

To be sure, Dooyeweerd did have very strong notions about what kinds of institutional entities or arrangements best embody these creational modes of interaction. And in setting forth these notions, he makes it clear that he thinks institutional differentiation is a very good thing. Thus, it seems obvious that Dooyeweerd would not look kindly on, say, a pattern of public leadership in which ecclesial and political roles are not clearly differentiated.

What I am suggesting, though, is that we can distance ourselves from this Dooyeweerdian fondness for concrete differentiation while still making good use of Dooyeweerd's modal scheme. For example, Dooyeweerd was obviously convinced that tribes would wither away in the historical process. Suppose, though, that he was wrong in making this historical prophecy. The Dooyeweerdian scheme is still helpful — significantly helpful, I think — in ascertaining what a tribe *is*. Using his framework as a hermeneutic for modal discernment, we can be clear about the fact that the tribe functions in multiple *ways:* familially, economically, politically, ecclesially, etc. In this way, Dooyeweerd helps us to see, not how *many* institutions there will be in a fully actualized social setting, but how to *read* whatever kinds of institutions we do happen upon.

I do not mean, however, completely to discredit Dooyeweerd's actual views about historical development. It seems clear to me that, once we have learned to utilize Dooyeweerd's scheme as a hermeneutic for modal discernment, we will want to be at least somewhat skeptical about attempts to move from more to less differentiated associational arrangements, or even attempts to hang on to purportedly undifferentiated institutions in a world characterized by a high awareness of differentiation.

This is a large topic, and I can only hint at some issues here by offering some highly speculative comments. But let us briefly consider contemporary "blood bound" associational entities. I am inclined to think that any advocacy of such structures in the late twentieth century is most accurately labeled as "neo-": neo-tribalism, neo-nationalism, neo-ethnicism.

Let me explain this suggestion in terms that seem in the Dooyeweerdian spirit, if not the letter. Blood ties have served in the past to cement associational patterns that were not yet differentiated, and whose specific modal norms were not therefore fully distinguished. As historical differentiation does occur, human beings attend in a more focused way on the specifically political, economic, ecclesial, etc., modes of association, with the result that such things as kinship bonds and charismatic authority diminish in their associational force. Once this historical process is set in motion, no attempt to retard it, by either returning to or maintaining the older undifferentiated patterns, can be fully effective. This is not to say that those modes that have been concretely differentiated cannot be recombined to form new configurations. It may be, for example, that the American "megachurch" is a reconfiguring of modes that results in an institution that approximates the cathedrals of earlier centuries. But it will inevitably be a *neo*-cathedral: we can *name* the modes (ecclesial, educational, aesthetic, economic) that it combines in a way that our forebears could not.

Recent history provides impressive evidence, however, that at least some "neo-" movements actually mask very different sorts of dynamics than might be inferred from surface appearances. Michael Ignatieff has argued this persuasively with reference to the Bosnian crisis. Ignatieff warns us not to be taken in by the "false narratives" that tell of "the resurfacing of ancient hatreds" between ethnic or religious groups in Bosnia. The real forces at work are external to the Bosnian context: neighboring expansionist states that have exploited rather ordinary cultural differences within Bosnia, "redefining them as essential, pure, and indissoluble signs of national identity."[11] None of this proves, of course, the impossibility of a revival or survival of "pure" forms of older "blood bound" modes of social cohesiveness. Nonetheless, we are at least on safe ground, I think, if we learn a healthy skepticism from Dooyeweerd about the seeming persistence of such associational ties.

---

11. Michael Ignatieff, "Homage to Bosnia," *New York Review of Books,* April 21, 1994, 3-6.

"Blood Bound" Yearnings

But I now offer an even more highly speculative suggestion. It may be that the reason why "blood bound" modes of association continue to be attractive in our contemporary cultures — even if they can never be revived in their naive purity — is that they are anticipations, albeit often highly distorted ones, of a way of relating to each other that we yearn for now but can only realize in the eschaton. It is, after all, the blood-bought victory of the Lamb of God that will actualize a new kind of unity among those who have been gathered from many tribes and tongues and peoples and nations of the earth (Rev. 5:9-10). It may be that this gospel promise reaches deeper into the human experience than we have sometimes thought: that the concrete patterns of "blood bound" association are disappearing, not because they are mere outmoded fragments of a past consciousness, but because they are faint foreshadowings of an associational bonding that will only be realized when the Lamb's victory is fully manifest.

But that day is not yet here. And so in the meantime we are pilgrims who, as Sander Griffioen reminds us, both laugh and weep as we nurture hopes that are "irrelevantly relevant" to contemporary collective life. The tone of Griffioen's reminder in this regard suggests the need for neo-Calvinism to devote more attention to the *virtues,* the qualities of Christian character, that are appropriate to our involvement in social institutions. Here we reformational scholars would do well to learn some lessons from the Lutheran side of the Reformation. As Harro Hopfl has argued,[12] while Calvin fostered a systematic interest in the public-institutional ordering of life, Luther was far more interested in the character of the public leader and in the spiritual manner of the Christian's involvement in the public arena. Luther's characterization of the calling of the Christian prince is especially poignant: the prince must be spiritually vigilant, he warns, if he wants to guarantee that "his condition will be outwardly and inwardly right, pleasing to God and men." And in doing so, Luther quickly adds, the prince "must anticipate a great deal of envy and suffering. As illustrious a man as this will soon feel the cross lying on his neck."[13]

Those of us in the Dutch Calvinist tradition live with memories of some of our spiritual ancestors who once thought it important to describe

---

12. Harro Hopfl, *Luther and Calvin on Secular Authority* (Cambridge: Cambridge University Press, 1991), xiii-xiv.

13. Hopfl, *Luther and Calvin,* 41.

themselves as members of "the churches under the cross." Perhaps it is time for us to revive that category of self-understanding, applying it this time to our broader responsibilities in the public square: as people called to live out our patterns of social interaction *under the cross* — a place, a mode of life, where our tears and laughter inevitably mingle as we wait for a much more profound experience of the richness of a creation for which neo-Calvinism taught us to yearn.

Law, Covenant, and Moral Commonalities: Some Neo-Calvinist Explorations

In his 2006 study of the role of natural law thinking in the Calvinist ethical tradition, Stephen J. Grabill calls for — even in the very title he chooses for his book — a "rediscovery" of the notion of natural law on the part of Reformed ethicists. Grabill argues that John Calvin and other sixteenth-century Reformers carried earlier natural law themes over, with some modifications, into their theologies, a practice that was continued by seventeenth-century Reformed scholastic theologians. Natural law thinking fell on hard times in the eighteenth century, though, due to the influence of various strands of philosophical rationalism. But the real blow to the idea came in the twentieth century, when Karl Barth and others firmly rejected the notion of natural law because it was fundamentally incompatible with certain key themes in Reformed theology.

Grabill's call for a rediscovery of the natural law tradition by Reformed theology is guided by some important concerns. He rightly observes that the desire by many Reformed thinkers to make "a clean and total break with Rome" has disposed them to refuse to engage in a "substantive investigation of continuities and discontinuities" of Reformed thought with medieval formulations on this subject. He also rightly sees this as an unfortunate habit of mind, in the light of the possible benefits today of exploring "the catholicity of Protestant doctrinal formulations in relation to the broader and older Christian traditions of the

This essay previously appeared in *Public Theology for a Global Society,* ed. Dierdre King Hainsworth and Scott R. Paeth (Grand Rapids: Eerdmans, 2010), 103-20. It is printed here with permission.

West and the East."[1] This legitimate desire to explore catholicity is especially important in our present context, where so much of what is associated with the "postmodern" fosters a suspicion toward the sorts of "metanarratives" that posit a shared human nature that allows for moral commonalities and continuities across cultural divides.

What Reformed thinkers have to ask, though, is whether natural law doctrine in particular provides the best theological framework for promoting these important theological and moral continuities. Reformed theology has other available resources for reinforcing the notion of a shared human nature with underlying moral commonalities. The contemporary theological-ethical exploration of moral commonalities does not require an exclusive focus on the natural law tradition. And I want to argue here that this is a good thing. While a firm rejection of everything associated with natural law thinking may not be the right strategy for contemporary Reformed thought, we must still acknowledge — more than Grabill seems willing to do — that thinkers in the tradition that draws heavily on the insights of the Calvinist Reformation have legitimate reasons for, at best, a genuine ambivalence about natural law ethics, so much so that they have good reasons for exploring other theological motifs in attempting to make room in Reformed thought for a robust understanding of a shared human moral awareness.

Avoiding the "Nein!"

In his fascinating study of the virtue theories developed by French women thinkers in the last half of the seventeenth century, the Jesuit philosopher John J. Conley observes that whatever their particular ecclesial-confessional affiliation, these women emphasized the radical "specificity of Christian ethics." Conley offers examples of their condemnation of those "vain virtues" that are attractive to "a corrupt human nature," by way of expositing their view that Christian ethics should take "Christ's act of redemption" as its starting point, in contrast to the notion that the Christian understanding of the moral life should "be understood as an expansion or a deepening of a generic moral project."[2]

The women whose views Conley describes would fit well in a promi-

---

1. Stephen J. Grabill, *Rediscovering the Natural Law in Reformed Theological Ethics* (Grand Rapids: Eerdmans, 2006), 187.

2. John J. Conley, *The Suspicion of Virtue: Women Philosophers in Neoclassical France* (Ithaca, N.Y.: Cornell University Press, 2002), 164-65.

nent contemporary school of thought in Christian ethics. Stanley Hauerwas, like his Mennonite mentor John Howard Yoder, has popularized the view that the Way of Jesus is the exclusive normative reference point for the moral life.[3] This view obviously presupposes a specific moral epistemology that rejects the appeal to a creation order. Our fallenness has limited, perhaps even obliterated, our cognitive access to any divine ordinances that might have been discernible in the original creation. Our only option is to create communities that follow the Way of Jesus as set forth in the Sermon on the Mount and as displayed in his own radical willingness to take up the cross. The available revealed guidance for living the good life is to be found in our moral exemplar, Jesus of Nazareth. In becoming his disciples, by immersing ourselves in the practices of Christian community, we can cultivate the virtues he displayed in his earthly ministry.

This perspective is often reinforced these days by an appropriation of the stern "Nein!" that Karl Barth pronounced against natural theology in his debate with Emil Brunner during the 1930s.[4] Barth was offering a theological critique of the "culture religion" that prepared the way for the widespread German acceptance of Hitler's ideology. In providing that critique, Hauerwas has insisted, Barth was able to see that the theologians in Germany "who had spent their careers translating the faith in terms that could be understood by modern people" had thereby rendered themselves "unable to say no" to the Nazi threat.[5]

Not all of us in the Reformed tradition are willing to join Barth in pronouncing a straightforward "Nein!" to the sort of "translation" project that Hauerwas has in mind. Not that we question that Barth was speaking out against a theological system that was seriously — even horribly — defective. But for all of that, we would want to argue, the theological approach that Barth was rightly condemning was, to borrow an apt phrasing from H. Richard Niebuhr, "evil as perversion, and not as badness of being."[6]

On such a view, what Barth was rightly doing was speaking a clear word to a specific historical situation in which an identifiable culture, reinforced by a theology that supported that culture, had generated evil practices. He correctly saw that a certain "translation" project had gone terribly awry.

3. Stanley Hauerwas and William Willimon, *Resident Aliens: Life in the Christian Colony* (Nashville: Abingdon, 1989), 23.

4. Cf. Emil Brunner and Karl Barth, *Natural Theology,* trans. Peter Fraenkel (London: Centenary Press, 1946).

5. Hauerwas and Willimon, *Resident Aliens,* 25.

6. H. Richard Niebuhr, *Christ and Culture* (San Francisco: Harper and Row, 1951), 194.

Where Barth and his present-day fellow "Nein!"-sayers go wrong, however, is in taking that specific cultural situation to be a paradigm that reveals, precisely because of the clarity of the crisis that characterized it, the inevitable defects of any theological approach that attempts "a generic moral project."

When Barth and Brunner debated the question of natural theology in the 1930s, each accused the other of betraying the basic aims of Reformation thought. This was to be expected in an argument between two Reformed theologians, each of whom was calling for a return to something that had been betrayed in recent history. While Barth insisted that the return required a firm rejection of natural theology as such, Brunner issued a more modest call for "our generation to find the way back to a true *theologia naturalis*,"[7] one that avoids the pitfalls of what Brunner set forth as the Roman Catholic version.

Again, it is understandable that two Reformed theologians would go out of their way to argue that their respective views are consistent with those of Calvin and his fellow Reformers. And it is also understandable that they could find support in Calvin's writings for their differing viewpoints, since Calvin seems to nod in each's direction at various points in the *Institutes*. While Barth acknowledges the presence of favorable comments by Calvin about the possibility of a "natural knowledge" of things divine, he dismisses their importance. Calvin, Barth insists, was misled by Augustine, failing to see "the extent to which . . . [Augustine] has to be regarded as a Roman Catholic theologian."[8] But we should not allow "that little corner which has been left uncovered in Calvin's treatment" to lure us into an endorsement of natural theology.[9] Instead, we must recognize that "[w]hat Calvin wrote in those first chapters of the *Institutes* has to be written again and this time in such a way that no [present-day natural law theologians] can find in it material for their fatal ends."[10]

Brunner obviously sees things differently. And the kind of reading of Calvin that he offers is presented in the form of an elaborate historical scenario by Grabill in his book-length study of Reformed natural theology. "While Calvin neither constructs nor sanctions a robust natural theology," Grabill argues, "he certainly does not deny the formal possibility of developing subsidiary doctrines of natural theology and natural law on the ba-

7. Emil Brunner, "Nature and Grace: A Contribution to the Discussion with Karl Barth," in *Natural Theology*, 59.

8. Karl Barth, "NO!: Answer to Emil Brunner," in *Natural Theology*, 101.

9. Barth, "NO!" 103.

10. Barth, "NO!" 104.

sis of God's reliable but obfuscated natural revelation within creation, design of the human body, and conscience." This direction in Calvin's thought was taken up by other Reformed theologians — rather immediately, in fact, by Calvin's contemporary Peter Martyr Vermigli, who "formulated a more sophisticated doctrine of natural law on the basis of a modified Thomist understanding of the natural knowledge of God."[11] This theological project was then expanded and solidified by subsequent generations of Reformed thinkers, such as Johannes Althusius and Francis Turretin, with the result that an appreciation for some sort of "natural knowledge" of God found a place in much Reformed theology.

Until, of course, Barth came along. On the Brunner-Grabill telling of the story, then, Barth is the primary villain. And they insist that anyone claiming a Reformed identity has no option but to reject Barth's negative verdict in favor of the sort of robust natural theology/natural law thinking that they advocate.

There is a problem, though, in presenting this as an unavoidable choice. The fact is that there are theologians who claim a strong allegiance to the Reformed tradition who, while refusing to utter the Barthian "Nein!" against "natural knowledge," are nonetheless reluctant to endorse the kind of robust advocacy of "natural knowledge" that was developed by Reformed theologians who came after Calvin. This is true particularly of those of us who have drawn heavily on the Dutch "neo-Calvinist" thinking represented in the theological writings of Abraham Kuyper, Herman Bavinck, and G. C. Berkouwer.

Grabill refuses, however, to allow this perspective to stand as a clear alternative to a robust natural theology perspective, on the one hand, and the Barthian rejection of that kind of theology, on the other. Instead he construes this apparent alternative to be in effect a less stern version of the Barthian "Nein!" Since those of us who adhere to this viewpoint would not interpret our aims in that manner, it will be helpful to look carefully at Grabill's reasons for placing neo-Calvinists in the Barthian camp.

An Alternative Option?

Grabill sets the stage for his characterization of the Dutch neo-Calvinist approach to natural law thinking with this brief summary statement: the

---

11. Grabill, *Rediscovering*, 96-97.

kind of critique of a robust natural theology set forth in this school of thought can be found in the writings of "Herman Dooyeweerd and G. C. Berkouwer, a devotee of Barthianism for much of his long career at the Free University of Amsterdam, and is reiterated at points in Henry Stob's and Richard Mouw's treatment of natural law."[12] The suggestion of a significant Barthian influence is repeated a little further on when Grabill observes, with reference to Stob's perspective, that "it is possible to detect the influence of a Barthian-style actualism in his mature criticism of natural-law ethics, most likely filtered through the anti-scholastic and Christo-centric theology of G. C. Berkouwer that was popular in Christian Reformed circles during the 1960s and 1970s."[13] And from Grabill's further observation that Stob's views "had a significant influence on such philosophers and ethicists in the Dutch Reformed tradition as Richard Mouw, Lewis Smedes, and Nicholas Wolterstorff," one might be led to the conclusion that the perspective at work here is basically a Barthian one.

It is not necessary to go into great biographical (or autobiographical!) detail to cast doubt on the implication of serious Barthian influence. Suffice it to say that while Berkouwer may have been a Barth "devotee" on some issues, he was quite critical of Barth on the subject at hand, especially in Barth's handling of the biblical material regarding general revelation. Of Barth's treatment of the key Pauline passages in Romans 1 and 2, for example, Berkouwer notes that Barth's "exegesis is more the result of an *a priori* view of revelation than of an unprejudiced reading of the text itself."[14] Furthermore, Barth's account of unbelief, says Berkouwer, "is in contradiction with the permanent confrontation of man with God's revelation," and Barth's "characterization of the universal element of all religions as unbelief is a distortion."[15] Here is Berkouwer on Barth's treatment of John 1: "It is remarkable that Barth does say that John mentions a cosmological function of the Logos, but, nevertheless, neglects this in favor of the soteriological aspect."[16] Significantly, when Berkouwer states his own positive views, he points to a sense of the divine in human beings that "is preserved by God in the human heart" in a manner that "does not relieve the darkness, but it does help explain how it is that religions still arise in a

---

12. Grabill, *Rediscovering,* 39.
13. Grabill, *Rediscovering,* 43.
14. G. C. Berkouwer, *General Revelation* (Grand Rapids: Eerdmans, 2001), 154.
15. Berkouwer, *General Revelation,* 164.
16. Berkouwer, *General Revelation,* 242.

fallen world and how it is possible that these false religions bear a marked semblance of order."[17]

The fact is that Berkouwer and Stob, and others significantly influenced by them, were drawing primarily on a fairly well defined pre-Barthian strand of thinking about these matters. While the most immediate theological influence was the "neo-Calvinism" of Abraham Kuyper and Herman Bavinck, Berkouwer and Stob also appealed directly to Reformation-era themes that have not figured prominently in the Barth-Brunner kind of debate. And in doing so, I want to insist here, they were representing a perspective that counts as a distinct alternative to both a robust natural theology and a firm rejection of such a theology.

Extracognitive Motifs

A central matter of contention between Barth and Brunner was the merits of Calvin's notion of the twofold knowledge — the *duplex cognitio* — of God. While this focus on the possibility of at least two ways of "knowing" about God is certainly important, it is not the only subject that deserves attention in reflecting on the possibilities of some sort of moral and spiritual awareness that Christian believers share with their fellow human beings.

In his work in theological ethics, Max Stackhouse has regularly pointed to the need for contemporary theology to keep alive the awareness of the fact "that human life has, at its root, a very profound *logos,* rooted in *theos,*" that enables people with very different worldviews "in some measure [to] talk across boundaries and more or less discern what is valid and not valid in what others say."[18] Stackhouse also sees this as a catholic conviction of sorts, one that is "embraced," he observes, "by Augustine, Thomas, Luther, Calvin, Wesley and Edwards — and, for that matter, by Locke, Kant, Weber, Troeltsch, Whitehead and the Niebuhrs." Like Grabill, Stackhouse also sees the need for a contemporary "rediscovery" of a theological basis for moral commonalities: we must, Stackhouse says, "continually rediscover, extend and thereby refine our understanding of this capacity so that it may help sort through the religious stories, principles and actions that people use to see which are most adequate to God and for holy living."

17. Berkouwer, *General Revelation*, 169.

18. Max L. Stackhouse, "Liberalism Dispatched vs. Liberalism Engaged," *Christian Century* 112, no. 29 (October 18, 1995): 963.

Significantly, though, when Stackhouse offers examples of the theological themes that we do well to "rediscover" in our contemporary theological quest for commonalities, he does not specifically include natural law in his list of resources that we can look to, even though they are "all distorted but not erased by sin." He offers this list of examples: "'general revelation,' *justitia originalis,* the gift of reason in the *imago dei.*"[19]

I emphasize that Stackhouse is offering merely a *sampling* of resources here. His list is not meant to be taken as canonical. Not only does he not mention natural law, neither does he include in his list common grace — a favorite of many of us in the Reformed tradition and one that he himself employs elsewhere in his writings. But his sampling of the options does point to the fact that a Reformed treatment of human commonalities has a fairly broad repertoire of resources to choose from.

And not all these resources have to do with *cognitio.* The almost exclusive focus of Barth and Brunner on the possibility of a natural *knowledge* is, from the perspective of some strands of Reformed thought, somewhat myopic. This is certainly the case for the Dutch neo-Calvinists. Kuyper and Bavinck addressed moral and spiritual continuities between believer and unbeliever by appealing to the notions of common grace, while Berkouwer departed from Barth by expressing a positive appreciation for the notions of general revelation and the *semen religionis.* Unlike natural theology, these resources can be thought of as extracognitive, since they do not attribute to the believer any sort of clear cognitive access to correct information about God's nature or about God's will for moral behavior.

Take the notion of common grace. One of the ways in which Reformed thinkers have seen it as functioning is in the promotion of positive moral achievements on the part of unredeemed persons. As Kuyper put it, common grace "is operative wherever civic virtue, a sense of domesticity, natural love, the practice of human virtue, the improvement of the public conscience, integrity, mutual loyalty among people, and a feeling for piety leaven life."[20] While Kuyper is certainly attributing quite a bit of God-pleasing behavior here to the unregenerate person, he does not see this behavior as necessarily flowing from some kind of cognitive access to God's will for human beings. Max Stackhouse captures an important neo-

---

19. Stackhouse, "Liberalism Dispatched," 963.

20. Abraham Kuyper, "Common Grace," in *Abraham Kuyper: A Centennial Reader,* ed. James D. Bratt (Grand Rapids: Eerdmans, 1998), 181.

Calvinist emphasis in this regard when he refers to the way the gospel "promises fulfillment of that [which is] *almost known* by common grace."[21]

Because they wanted to avoid the more optimistic views of fallen human nature set forth by Catholics and others, the neo-Calvinists have been reluctant to concede too much by way of a "natural knowledge" to the unregenerate consciousness. In this regard it is important to distinguish clearly between the Kuyperian understanding of common grace and the notion of "prevenient grace" that is popular in other traditions. The neo-Calvinists see the appeal to prevenient grace as a way of downplaying the extent of human depravity by positing a kind of automatic universal upgrade of those dimensions of human nature that have been corrupted by sin. To put it much too simply, the goal of prevenient grace *is* the upgrade; it is to raise the deeply wounded human capacities to a level where some measure of freedom to choose or reject obedience to God is made possible. Common grace, on the other hand, is typically set forth by the neo-Calvinists as a divine strategy for bringing the cultural designs of God to completion. Common grace operates mysteriously in the life of, say, a Chinese government official or an unbelieving artist to harness his or her created talents to prepare the creation for the full coming of the kingdom. In this sense, the operations of common grace — unlike those of prevenient grace — always have a goal-directed ad hoc character.

The appeal to Calvin's notion of the *semen religionis* is similarly noncognitive. One can have a vague awareness of — to use Carol Zaleski's apt phrasing — being "hunted down by the God who instills transcendent longing"[22] without necessarily knowing that it is in fact the deity who is doing the pursuing. The *sensus divinitatis* need not be a "sense" that is capable of cognitive articulation.

What looms large for the neo-Calvinists, however, is the confessional address to the question of a "natural" awareness of the divine. Because they stand in a tradition that places a strong emphasis on fidelity to the Reformation-era confessions, they take the relevant confessional passages to have a direct bearing on their theological formulations on a given sub-

21. Max L. Stackhouse, "Covenantal Justice in a Global Era," Institute for Reformed Theology Web site, at http://reformedtheology.org/SiteFiles/PublicLectures/StackhousePL.html.

22. Carol Zaleski, "Case for the Defense," *Christian Century*, June 26, 2007, at http://www.christiancentury.org/article_print.lasso?id=3462.

ject. In this case much attention has been given to article 2 of the Belgic Confession, which has the heading "By What Means God Is Made Known unto Us":

> We know him by two means; first, by the creation, preservation and government of the universe; which is before our eyes as a most elegant book, wherein all creatures, great and small, are as so many characters leading us to contemplate the invisible things of God, namely his power and divinity, as the apostle Paul says, Rom. 1:20. All which things are sufficient to convince men, and leave them without excuse. Secondly, he makes himself more clearly fully known to us by his holy and divine Word, that is to say, as far as is necessary for us to know in this life, to his glory and our salvation.[23]

The felt obligation to square any assessment of a continuing consciousness of the divine presence on the part of sinful humanity with this confessional statement has made it difficult for neo-Calvinists to endorse the Barthian "Nein." But neither have they seen this article as requiring the acceptance of a natural theology as such. For one thing, the article does not require ascribing cognitive access to the divine: the manner in which the "characters" in creation's "book" are to be thought of as "leading us to contemplate the invisible things of God" need not be taken as providing us with knowable information about God. For another, the article simply stipulates that, on the basis of what is made available by means of nature's "book," the unregenerate consciousness is "without excuse" in its willful disobedience.

The "Voluntarist" Factor

Grabill observes that the fondness of some neo-Calvinists for the doctrine of common grace allows for, at best, a "hesitant juxtaposition" of common grace with natural law.[24] In his brief attempt to explain this hesitancy he rightly points to the neo-Calvinist attraction to a "voluntaristic" insistence on God's unrestricted sovereign will. This means, he says, the legislation

23. Belgic Confession, article 2, in Philip Schaff, ed., *The Creeds of Christendom, with a History and Critical Notes*, vol. 3 (Grand Rapids: Baker, 1996), 384.
24. Grabill, *Rediscovering*, 50.

that originates in that sovereign freedom calls for a human volitional response that in an important sense "mirrors" divine freedom.[25]

It is difficult to see how this will-to-will depiction of the most basic character of the God-human relationship can simply be expunged from Calvinism. One would expect that followers of John Calvin would always be nervous about any tendency to see God as somehow "bound" by, or "subject" to, a law that is coeternal with his own being. As Bavinck put it: "God does not stand outside of nature and is not excluded from it by a hedge of laws but is present in it and sustains it by the word of his power."[26]

And this being-present-to character of God's relationship to the creation in general has to be highlighted in a special way with reference to God's relationship to human beings. The notion of human lives, including rebellious human lives, being lived inescapably *coram deo* is a standard feature of Calvinist portrayals of the human condition — beginning, of course, with Calvin himself, who in the opening paragraphs of the *Institutes* emphasizes the need for us to know ourselves, not by thinking thoughts about God and his law, but by scrutinizing ourselves before the "face" of God.[27]

To be sure, human beings are subject to a cosmic legal system that is the expression of a sovereign divine will. But ultimately we are accountable, not to the law as such, but to the law's Author, who calls us into a covenantal relationship with himself, one to which we must freely respond. It is significant that the Canons of Dordrecht, often thought of as the harshest of the Calvinist confessional documents, nonetheless make much of the role of the human will in responding to God. "[T]his grace of regeneration does not treat men as senseless stocks and blocks," the authors of the canons insist, "nor take away their will and its properties, neither does violence thereto; but spiritually quickens, heals, corrects, and at the same time sweetly and powerfully bends it, that where carnal rebellion and resistance formerly prevailed a ready and sincere spiritual obedience begins to reign."[28]

Calvinism's critics have regularly raised the charge that the God of

25. Grabill, *Rediscovering*, 50-52. Grabill is referring here to my discussions in both *The God Who Commands: A Study in Divine Command Ethics* (Notre Dame, Ind.: University of Notre Dame Press, 1990) and *He Shines in All That's Fair* (Grand Rapids: Eerdmans, 2001).

26. Herman Bavinck, *Reformed Dogmatics*, vol. 1, *Prolegomena* (Grand Rapids: Baker, 2003), 370.

27. John Calvin, *Institutes of the Christian Religion*, ed. John T. McNeill, trans. Ford Lewis Battles (Philadelphia: Westminster, 1960), 1.1.2, p. 37.

28. Canons of the Synod of Dort, Third and Fourth Heads of Doctrine, article 16, in Schaff, *Creeds*, 3:591.

Calvinism operates in a fundamentally ad hoc fashion, issuing arbitrary and disconnected commands in the manner of a despot. And the fact is that many Calvinists have operated with an understanding of their relationship with God that closely conforms to this picture. Indeed, for many Calvinists this extreme moral voluntarism is bounded by an even more poignant soteriological voluntarism. There is a strong strand of Calvinist piety that views God as arbitrary not only in his moral negotiations but also in the manner in which he distributes his redemptive benefits as such. Thus the phenomenon of pious Calvinists who fret about their elect status as individuals who are at the mercy of a deity who dispenses his saving grace in a purely arbitrary manner.

What is missing in such a perspective, of course, is precisely a sense of lawfulness. While the Calvinists who endorse this picture of things may actually make frequent use of the *word* "law," for them this divine law actually functions as a series of arbitrary, disconnected, fiat-type commands, with no obvious unifying pattern of rational coherence.

It is precisely at this point that neo-Calvinist thinkers have insisted that it is important to emphasize the lawful ordering of creation. While they have not simply rejected the voluntaristic component of traditional Calvinist thought, they have been wary of giving it too much play. Thus their refusal simply to take sides in what G. C. Berkouwer describes as the "bitter conflict between Roman Catholic thinking and voluntarism."[29]

A Lawful Ordering

It is precisely in their understanding of divine law that neo-Calvinists have intentionally distanced themselves from a thoroughgoing Calvinist voluntarism. Because God regularly speaks and acts lawfully, believers do not need to stand in primitive fear before a divine despot whose ways are totally unfathomable to human beings. The harsher tones of the divine mystery have been softened by God's own publicly announced commitment to juridical fidelity. The God of the Bible — so insists the neo-Calvinist — has committed himself to acting toward his creation in ways that are reasonable and reliable. He is a faithful God who redeems his people so that they may come to understand and obey his ordinances. Thus divine sovereignty is administered in accordance with lawful patterns. This emphasis

29. Berkouwer, *General Revelation*, 196.

looms so large in neo-Calvinism that the philosophical movement associated with Herman Dooyeweerd's thought labeled itself *de wijsbegeerte der wetsidee* — the philosophy of the law-idea.[30]

In our shared human nature we have been designed by the Creator to respond in obedience to this lawful ordering of reality. But in our sinful rebellion our response has become one of disobedience. The redemptive mission of Christ was required to make it possible for depraved sinners to be redirected toward paths of obedience. The moral life that Christ came to inaugurate, then, is not, on this view, something brand-new. Rather it is the reclaiming and restoring of that which had been seriously marred by original sin. Kuyper makes the point forcefully in a much-quoted passage in his Stone Lectures:

> Can we imagine that at one time God willed to rule things in a certain moral order, but that now, in Christ, He wills to rule it otherwise? As though He were not the Eternal, the Unchangeable, Who, from the very hour of creation, even unto all eternity, had willed, wills, and shall will and maintain, one and the same firm moral world-order! Verily Christ has swept away the dust with which man's sinful limitations had covered up this world-order, and has made it glitter again in its original brilliancy. . . . [T]he world-order remains just what it was from the beginning. It lays full claim, not only to the believer (as though less were required from the unbeliever), but to every human being and to all human relationships.[31]

While this lawful ordering of the creation "lays full claim" on believer and unbeliever alike, this does not mean that the unregenerate consciousness has a clear cognitive access to this ordering. The most that can be said is that unbelievers are "without excuse" with regard to the divine expectations, because they are in the presence of that which they refuse to acknowledge. As Gordon Spykman summarized the neo-Calvinist perspective on this matter, "the creation order establishes an ontic commonality and solidarity among all peoples, even in the midst of the radical noetic polarities among differing faith communities."[32]

30. Cf. Herman Dooyeweerd, *A New Critique of Theoretical Thought,* vol. 1, trans. David H. Freeman and William S. Young (Philadelphia: Presbyterian and Reformed, 1953), 93f.

31. Abraham Kuyper, *Lectures on Calvinism* (Grand Rapids: Eerdmans, 1931), 71-72.

32. Gordon J. Spykman, *Reformational Theology: A New Paradigm for Doing Dogmatics* (Grand Rapids: Eerdmans, 1992), 180.

This emphasis on a "commonality and solidarity among all peoples" that is "ontic" but not "noetic" should make it clear that the neo-Calvinist position is indeed a distinct alternative both to the natural law tradition and to the Barthian rejection of natural law. Human beings are seen as inescapably confronted with God's ordering of the creation in which they carry on their lives. This confrontation includes an awareness of this creation order, albeit one that falls short of cognitive access — thus the neo-Calvinists' very un-Barthian appeal to the notions of general revelation, common grace, and the *semen religionis*. In this scheme of things, a lawful moral ordering of reality is not only acknowledged — it is a central theme. In that sense, the disagreement with the natural law tradition is not over the "ontic" but about the "noetic."

Covenant and Moral Reality

I have been treating the neo-Calvinist insistence on a lawfully ordered creation as, among other things, a strategy for softening the harsh tones of what has often amounted to a thoroughgoing voluntarism in the Calvinist tradition. But I must also confess to some dissatisfaction with the way the idea of God as Legislator has sometimes functioned in neo-Calvinist thought. The worrisome tendency shows up particularly in the way Dooyeweerd and his followers featured "the conception of the lex as the boundary between God and the creation."[33] As Professor Henk Geertsema of the Vrije Universiteit, himself a proponent of Dooyeweerd's overall perspective, once observed at a neo-Calvinist gathering,[34] this emphasis on law as *the* "boundary" between Creator and creature can give the impression that our individual relationships with God are always in some sense "mediated" by laws — a tendency that, Geertsema also observed, has been on display in frequent criticisms of various forms of pietism by *wetsidee* thinkers.

What Geertsema was insisting that Calvinism cannot relinquish is the "I-Thou-ness" of the individual's relationship to God — the very aspect of Reformation thought that Alasdair McIntyre complained about when he

33. Dooyeweerd, *New Critique,* 99 n. 1.

34. Geertsema's observation was made during discussion time at a symposium commemorating the 100th anninversary of the birth of Herman Dooyeweerd, sponsored by the Vereniging voor Reformatorische Wijsbegeerte, held in Hoeven, the Netherlands, August 1994.

We become r oled after

criticized Calvin and Luther for having produced in their theologies the ancestor of the postmodern "emotivist self," the de-roled individual, stripped of all social characteristics, who stands alone before God.[35]

Needless to say, there are dangers in such a conception — dangers that are magnified in the thoroughgoing Calvinist voluntarism described above. It is necessary, then, to insist on a voluntarist *component* — a "moment" in our relationship with God — as opposed to voluntarism as an all-encompassing characteristic of the God-human relation. Kuyper regularly pointed to this component, as in his comment that "God's sovereign election from all eternity binds the inward soul directly to God Himself," so that "the ray of divine light enters straightway into the depths of our heart." And it is only when this happens, he adds, that "religion, in its most absolute sense, gains its ideal realization."[36] Kuyper is acknowledging in these remarks that, while it is important to acknowledge the crucial role of law in God's relationship to the creation, we may not wholly subsume our relationship with God under the umbrella of lawfulness.

This is the point at which neo-Calvinism very much needs a strong reliance on the idea of *covenant*. In Reformed theology the covenant motif has also, along with the stress on lawfulness, made an important contribution to the kind of "softening" of Calvinist soteriology that is necessary if a thoroughgoing voluntarism is to be avoided. It is surprising, then, that the covenant idea has not been more prominent in neo-Calvinist ethical and social theory. In this regard, Max Stackhouse is a welcome exception. While endorsing many of the key concepts of neo-Calvinism in his approach to public theology, he has given significant attention to the covenantal motif, not only as it applies to specific moral relationships, such as marriage and family life, but also as it relates to the fundamental character of moral reality as such.

Stackhouse observes, for example, that there is a school of thought in the Reformed tradition that posits the existence of covenant between God and human beings — typically referred to as the "covenant of works"[37] — that operated in the pre-Fall Garden. On this view, says Stackhouse, a covenant is not just a handy device for structuring a salvific arrangement;

35. Alasdair McIntyre, *A Short History of Ethics: A History of Moral Philosophy from the Homeric Age to the Twentieth Century* (New York: Macmillan, 1966), 121-24; see also his *After Virtue: A Study in Moral Theory,* 2nd ed. (Notre Dame, Ind.: University of Notre Dame Press, 1984), 52-53.

36. Kuyper, *Lectures on Calvinism,* 49.

37. See Louis Berkhof, *Systematic Theology* (Grand Rapids: Eerdmans, 1941), 211-14.

rather, covenant is "given by God to Adam in the very fabric of creation," so that "the primal relationship of God to humanity is covenantal."[38] This insight can motivate us to be on the lookout for "the presence of covenant-like possibilities in many, perhaps all, cultures," and this in turn "suggests that in the very structure of human relationships we find traces of what God graciously revealed to humanity in the fabric of creation."[39]

The idea of covenant helps us to be sensitive to the nonnegotiable voluntarist component in the Calvinist view of selfhood. *Trust* is a key feature in a covenant. Covenantal trust is more open-ended than the sort of trust that characterizes contractual arrangements. In a contract the trust is more limited; it is bracketed by clearly defined expectations. In a covenantal relationship the promise is not so much to be faithful to a set of conditions; it is a commitment to be faithful *no matter what.*

 Human beings, as volitional creatures, do have a special relationship to law. Unlike animals and plants, which are also subject to God's lawful ordering of the creation, human beings have the choice of obeying or disobeying the divine ordinances. To understand this is to discern the nature and reality of our sinfulness, as a willful rebellion against the divine Lawgiver. It is also to grasp the basic pattern of God's gracious provision of a remedy for our fallenness — Jesus as the incarnate Son of God fulfilled the demands of the law on our behalf and made the payment that was necessary to purchase our redemption. By accepting this substitutionary work on our behalf, we enter into a renewed covenant with our Creator.

Since this covenant is initiated by the triune God, it is important also to see the role of law in its Trinitarian context. The First Person is indeed a Lawgiver, but this does not mean that we experience him in that way in all aspects of our relationship with him. In the Old Testament God is portrayed in numerous ways that seem to supplement, rather than to be subordinate to, his legislator status. While a human parent makes the rules that "govern" the life of a child, a child also can experience parent as caregiver, nurturer, teacher, guide, and even playmate. Similarly the God who is the legislator is also portrayed by the biblical writers as a father who showers tender mercies upon his children, and as a mother who gives birth to us and protects us by drawing us close to herself in times of danger. In both the human and the divine cases, the juridical framework may never be

38. Max L. Stackhouse, *Covenant and Communities: Faith, Family, and Economic Life* (Louisville: Westminster John Knox, 1997), 150.

39. Stackhouse, *Covenant and Communities,* 144.

completely absent, but there are times — importantly so — when law stays in the background and more intimate, face-to-face, dimensions of the relationship come to the fore.

This intimacy is intensified in our relationship to Christ, who as the incarnate Son descended to our station "under" the law, experiencing the pain, abuse, and temptation that are part and parcel of our fallen brokenness (Heb. 2:10-18). In Jesus we experience God, not so much as Lawgiver, but as one who became one of us in order to qualify as a fellow Law-obeyer.

And the Holy Spirit functions in our lives not so much as a legislator but as a guide and enabler to obedience. The Spirit's place in reference to the law is not above the human self, as a Lawgiver, but alongside those who have received the law, as their divine Comforter.

Continuing the Exploration

Early in this discussion I pointed to Max Stackhouse's call for contemporary theological ethics to explore in new ways what makes it possible for human beings with very different worldviews and living in many different cultural locations "in some measure [to] talk across boundaries and more or less discern what is valid and not valid in what others say" — an exploration, Stackhouse insists, that must be "catholic" in its scope.

My intention here has not been to inhibit this recognition of the need for the much-needed catholicity in any way. While the contemporary opposition to the Christian message and its moral resources may not be expressed in as dramatic form as it was, for example, in the Nazi era, the opposition still poses significant threats, not only to the cause of the gospel in particular, but also to the larger common good. Christian thinkers would do well to commit to a catholic engagement of the issues, a joint exploration of what can best promote in our difficult times what Klaas Schilder referred to as a human "*sunousia*, a being-together,"[40] in fulfillment of the ancient mandate given to God's people in the midst of a moral and spiritual environment not unlike what many of us struggle against today: "But seek the welfare of the city where I have sent you into exile, and pray to the LORD on its behalf, for in its welfare you will find your welfare" (Jer. 29:7).

40. Klaas Schilder, *Christ and Culture*, trans. G. van Rongen and W. Helder (Winnipeg, Manitoba: Premier Printing, 1977), 55.

My main concern here has been to see to it that we do not unnecessarily limit our options in thinking about the possibilities of better understanding our human *sunousia*. We need to draw on all the theological resources available to us.

The natural law tradition certainly deserves a more adequate consideration than I have given it here. Whatever new strengths we might discover in that tradition, though, we will surely need also to draw upon a broader ethic, one undergirded — in Max Stackhouse's apt formulation — by the "fidelity, trust, forgiveness, mutual edification, and acceptance" that are necessary for the kind of "graciousness of living [that] takes us out of ourselves and makes alive in us a consciousness of the mystery of another realm of being, which we come to know in love."[41]

---

41. Stackhouse, *Covenant and Communities*, 160.

Educational Choice and Pillarization:
Some Lessons for Americans from the
Dutch Experiment in "Affirmative Impartiality"

Our present debates about educational choice in the United States are characterized by a variety of arguments for and against the encouragement of educational pluralism. Some of the considerations presented on both sides are superficial ones, as when a voucher plan is defended by broadsides against a public educational system that is bent on brainwashing children into secular or "occult" thoughts and practices, or when vouchers are opposed on the grounds that they will encourage "outdated" religious teachings. At their best, however, the discussions are healthy ones that assess the challenges of contemporary pluralism, with one side insisting that we ought to promote a plurality of educational philosophies and programs, and the other worrying about the fragmenting impact of such a plan.

My purpose here is to explore some of the underlying issues relating to educational choice. Let me make it clear at the outset that my own sympathies are with those who call for equitable funding for a variety of educational programs. But I must also confess that, while I think a good case can be made for such an approach on the level of principle, I have some serious qualms about the feasibility of implementing a program of equitable funding in our present North American context.

In what follows I will explain my misgivings. I will begin by briefly discussing the "school settlement" that was established by law in the Netherlands in 1917, and the way in which it has influenced some patterns of thinking — including my own — about educational choice. Some defend-

This essay previously appeared in *School Choice*, ed. Alan Wolfe (Princeton: Princeton University Press, 2003). It is printed here with permission.

ers of a voucher system for North America have rightly pointed to the Dutch program as one where government-sanctioned educational choice has met with much success. I am convinced, though, that it is important to pay attention to the cultural circumstances that gave rise to the Dutch settlement; I will do this, comparing those conditions to the context of our own present-day North American debates. Finally, I will assess the recommendation, made by several commentators on educational choice policies, that the Dutch system can provide an instructive reference point for a voucher program in the United States — and in doing so, I will spell out some of my qualms about the applicability of the Dutch experiment to our own North American context.

The Dutch "Peace Treaty"

The 1917 Dutch agreement — which provided equitable funding for a variety of religious and nonreligious school systems — was engineered by several Calvinist thinkers in the Netherlands, with Abraham Kuyper leading the way. Kuyper (1837-1920) was an important figure in Dutch life during the last half of the nineteenth century and the opening decades of the twentieth — he founded two newspapers as well as the *Vrije Universiteit* (Free University) of Amsterdam. Also a prominent church leader, he headed a group that broke away from the state church in the 1880s to form the country's second-largest Dutch Reformed denomination. And he founded the Anti-Revolutionary Party, which he led as a member of the Dutch parliament, and eventually — for a few years just after the turn of the century — as prime minister of the Netherlands.

Kuyper has long had an influence among Dutch Calvinists in North America, especially in the Christian school system and higher educational institutions (the best known being Calvin College in Grand Rapids, Michigan) associated with the Christian Reformed denomination. In recent years, however, interest in his thought has spread in North America, especially with regard to his social-political thought. John Bolt's study of Kuyper's thought makes a special point of exploring the relevance of his ideas to the North American context — Bolt even chose as his subtitle "Abraham Kuyper's American Public Theology."[1] Nor has this interest

1. John Bolt, *A Free Church, a Holy Nation: Abraham Kuyper's American Public Theology* (Grand Rapids: Eerdmans, 2001).

been restricted to people who share Kuyper's Dutch Calvinist convictions. In his 1979 presidential address to the Canadian Political Science Association, Kenneth McRae proposed that his colleagues think about reshaping the typical curriculum in political studies so that attention could be given thinkers who have been pretty much ignored thus far in the mainstream of North American discussions. Have we arrived at an appropriate time, he asked, when we might consider giving preference to "Althusius over Bodin, Montesquieu over Rousseau, von Gierke over Hegel, Acton over Herbert Spencer, Abraham Kuyper over T. H. Green, Karl Renner and Otto Bauer over Marx and Engels?"[2]

The 1917 educational policy that Kuyper was instrumental in forging is commonly referred to as a "peace treaty," and rightly so, since it was accepted only after a century of much controversy in Dutch society over the government's responsibility toward schools that had been established by religious groups. The controversies can be traced back to 1807, when the Dutch government effected a significant shift in the country's educational arrangement, by assuming control over the system of elementary education.[3] Prior to that the school system had been officially administered by the national Reformed Church. While there was little immediate change in the substance of religious education as a result of the new regulations of 1807 — the practices of daily worship and regular catechetical instruction were continued in the schools — gradually the religious content moved in a more "generic" direction. These developments were especially troublesome to the dissident Reformed groups that emerged in the 1830s. Unhappy with the influence of Enlightenment thinking in both the state churches and the schools, they distanced themselves from both entities. The combined opposition of both the state and the national church made their efforts difficult, however. Stringent conditions were imposed for the establishment of alternative schools, and even when permission was granted, the high costs had to be borne by the parents.

When a new Dutch constitution came into effect in 1848, the rights of alternative school systems were guaranteed — although the procedures for

2. Kenneth D. McRae, "The Plural Society and the Western Political Tradition," *Canadian Journal of Political Science* 12 (December 1979): 682.

3. For my brief sketch here of nineteenth-century developments I am drawing on more detailed discussions in Bolt, *Free Church*, 332-39, and John Sturm and Siebren Miedema, "Kuyper's Educational Legacy: Schooling for a Pluralistic Society," in *Kuyper Reconsidered: Aspects of His Life and Work*, ed. Cornelis van der Kooi and Jan de Bruijn, VU Studies on Protestant History 3 (Amsterdam: VU Uitgeverij, 1999), 239-43.

doing so were still difficult and no financial support was offered to these schools. The public debate heated up considerably in 1857, when a new educational law stipulated that the public schools were to teach "Christian and civic virtues." As Bolt observes, however, it soon became clear that "the former was understood in terms of the latter," so that "'Christian' came to mean nothing more than what is socially and civically important, [and] the schools became effectively de-Christianized."[4] As Kuyper emerged as a public leader, he took up the cause of the alternative schools, arguing for equitable financial support for all schools, religious and nonreligious. The 1917 agreement granted full government funding for all schools, with the exact subsidies based on student numbers.

The social arrangement that provided the context for the school agreement is known as "pillarization" *(verzuiling).* The Dutch sociologist J. P. Kruijt provides this fairly concise explanation of the use of the pillarization metaphor:

> A pillar or column is a thing apart, resting on its own base (in our case a particular religious or non-religious faith) separated from other pillars, which are units similar to the first: they are standing upright, perpendicular sets of persons and groups separated from other sets. Perpendicular means that each pillar is cutting vertically the horizontal socio-economic strata that we call social classes. For a pillar is not a social class; it contains persons out of every social class or stratification. . . . Further, a pillar is solid; the ideological pillars of the Dutch nation are indeed strong super-organizations . . . [and] all the pillars together generally serve as a support to something resting on top; in our case that something is the whole Dutch nation.[5]

Each Dutch pillar, then, is encouraged to support its own pattern of primary and secondary education. Education, however, is viewed in the Dutch scheme as only one among many pillarized activities. It is a part of a larger set of pillarized activity — held together by a fairly comprehensive understanding of what life is all about — that includes such things as labor unions, farming organizations, radio stations, and political parties.

4. Bolt, *Free Church,* 336.
5. J. P. Kruijt, "The Netherlands: The Influence of Denominationalism on Social Life and Organizational Patterns," in *Consociational Democracy: Political Accommodation in Segmented Societies,* ed. Kenneth McRae (Toronto: McClelland and Stewart, 1974), 130.

The Kuyperian Rationale

Kuyper had his own unique version of Calvinist thought that provided a rationale for this overall pillarization scheme. To be sure, other pillar groups also provided their unique philosophical underpinnings for pillarization. But Kuyper's perspective not only served to convince the Calvinist rank and file of the merits of pillarization; it also provided a benchmark for other groups to articulate detailed alternative rationales.

One of Kuyper's most original themes was his idea of "sphere sovereignty."[6] God, he insisted, built into the creation a variety of cultural spheres, such as the family, economics, politics, art, and intellectual inquiry. Each of these spheres has its own proper "business" and needs its own unique pattern of authority. When we confuse spheres, by violating the proper boundaries of church and state, or when we reduce the academic life to a business enterprise, we transgress the patterns that God has set for created existence.

Kuyper's perspective on social issues has much in common with the views being put forth today by thinkers who are concerned with the proper shape of "the good society." A number of North American social critics (Peter Berger, Robert Bellah, Mary Ann Glendon) have emphasized in recent years the important role that "mediating structures" play in providing a buffer zone between the individual and the state. Families, churches, and service organizations protect us from the all-encompassing tendencies of the state on the one hand and an isolated individualism on the other.

Like these contemporary thinkers, Kuyper was eager to curb the power of the state. The various cultural spheres, he insisted, do not exist by governmental permission. They are established by God, and no human authority has the right to violate the Creator's intentions. Nor are the created "spheres," as he saw things, completely disconnected. They are a part of a larger created reality whose unity we can fully grasp only by developing a comprehensive "biblical world-and-life view" (one of his favorite phrases). And Christians are obligated, he argued, not only to ask the state to allow them to work out the implications of their own comprehensive vision of life; they must also demand that the state grant the same rights to other

6. For the best presentation by Kuyper in English of his idea of "sphere sovereignty," see his 1898 Stone Lectures, published as *Lectures on Calvinism* (Grand Rapids: Eerdmans, 1931); also his "Sphere Sovereignty," in *Abraham Kuyper: A Centennial Reader,* ed. James D. Bratt (Grand Rapids: Eerdmans, 1998), 461-90.

worldview groups, even if Christians disagree seriously with the content of those alternative perspectives on life.

A key virtue of the Dutch educational settlement from the Kuyperian perspective, then, is its recognition that any educational program is inevitably guided by a "world-and-life view." The so-called public school system is not really "neutral" with regard to the basic issues addressed by religious and philosophical creeds. Such neutrality was viewed by Kuyper and his followers as impossible. In the Dutch case the public schools were shaped by the ideals of the Enlightenment. In a pluralistic society, Kuyper argued, people who genuinely embrace these ideals should be permitted, even encouraged, to educate their children in conformity to this philosophy of life. But parents with other worldviews should also be granted the right to give educational shape to their convictions. And the government should maintain a position of impartiality toward these various worldview "pillars."

American Kuyperianism

Again, this perspective on educational pluralism has had some currency in the United States and Canada. One of the most carefully formulated statements of this view was set forth by Nicholas Wolterstorff in a pamphlet that he published in the mid-1960s, *Religion and the Schools*. Wolterstorff argues that the government's primary educational aim is to see to it that all citizens are educated. There is no reason, he argues, why this aim cannot be met by the encouragement of a plurality of school systems based on a variety of pedagogical and philosophical perspectives. Wolterstorff calls for a governmental posture where schools are supported in a way that respects their religious or nonreligious perspectives. The fact that this means that the government will provide aid to specifically religious programs of education ought not to bother us, argues Wolterstorff; the main concern must be that the government not have *as its purpose* the favoring of a particular religious or philosophical perspective. Governments cannot be neutral in these matters. Neither can they avoid doing things that will in fact promote the cause of one or another religious or nonreligious perspective. Wolterstorff advocates a governmental posture of "affirmative impartiality," where nothing that a state "says or does manifests a lack of impartiality on its part" with respect to the "religion or irreligion" of various groups. "[F]or the state to be affirmatively impartial," explains Wolterstorff, "it is not necessary that it not say or do anything contrary to the tenets of any religion or irreligion." He observes that municipalities that require peddlers to be licensed in fact violate the convictions of Jehovah's Witnesses who stand on street corners selling copies of *The Watchtower*. This need not be construed as a violation of governmental impartiality: "in our society there can be no such thing as a state all of whose policies and practices are in accord with the conscientious convictions of all its citizens." But what *is* required, he insists, is that the government "not have *as its purpose* to lend support to any religion or irreligion; and, in addition, what is demanded is that whenever one of its legitimate purposes can be achieved without violating the tenets of some religion or irreligion, it be so achieved."[7]

While Wolterstorff made his case long before the voucher question became a matter of broad public interest, the applicability of his Kuyperian perspective on educational freedom to this contemporary discussion is obvious. And more recently the application has been made explicit by a number of writers. Stanley Carlson-Thies, for example, states the case for the applicability of the Dutch arrangement to our context in very direct terms. In North America these days, he argues, we are facing "the same issues" that led to the Dutch plan. And for our own situation, "[v]ouchers represent the American way to make public education plural by funding every variety of school, secular or religious."[8]

What is intriguing about the case Carlson-Thies makes for his recommendation, however, is that he also makes much of the *differences* between our present North American context and that of nineteenth-century Holland. For one thing, while the nineteenth-century Dutch dissidents generally agreed that the government should subsidize their alternative educational projects,

> [not] all those who reject the public schools as unsuitable on religious grounds favor pluralizing public education through vouchers. Many are proponents instead of home schooling, sometimes for financial reasons but often because they interpret the biblical injunction that raising children is the responsibility of parents to mean that parents should not

7. Nicholas Wolterstorff, *Religion and the Schools*, Reformed Journal Monograph (Grand Rapids: Eerdmans, 1965, 1966), 22-23.

8. Stanley W. Carlson-Thies, "The Meaning of Dutch Segmentation for Modern America," in *Sharing the Reformed Tradition: The Dutch–North American Exchange, 1846-1996*, ed. George Harinck and Hans Krabbendam, VU Studies on Protestant History 2 (Amsterdam: VU Uitgeverij, 1996), 164-65.

send their children out to school. Home schoolers do not agitate for pluralized public schools but rather to be left alone by the government. Similarly, a growing number of supporters of non-public schools reject vouchers on the grounds that "government shekels" always bring "government shackles." Their goal is the "separation of school and state." Yet others are home-school or use private schools only until they can win the public schools back for God.[9]

Carlson-Thies admits that this kind of plurality of motives within the forces that are critical of public education means that it is not

clear what the broader social consequences might be if vouchers were widely adopted. In the Netherlands, the *schoolstrijd* [school struggle] catalyzed the formation of subcultures, and the adoption of equal funding for all schools established the precedent for pluralizing other state services. In America, concern about the public rights of believers is only one of the causes of the school wars, and defenders of the right of religious people to carry out their belief into the public square are divided between pluralists and theocrats.[10]

These are important observations — ones that, as I see things, raise some significant questions about the case for vouchers that Carlson-Thies means to be making. To weigh these considerations in more detail, it will be helpful to look a little more closely at some of the conditions that have given rise to the present debate over school choice in North America.

Suspicion of Public Education

When Wolterstorff made his case for affirmative impartiality in the mid-1960s, he was doing so as a supporter of a Christian school movement that was very much on the margins of North American life. The folks then advocating a uniquely "Christian" pattern of elementary and secondary education were in a rather small minority. The most visible were the Roman Catholics; other school systems were maintained by the Missouri Synod Lutherans, the Christian Reformed, some Mennonites, and Episcopalians;

9. Carlson-Thies, "Meaning," 165.
10. Carlson-Thies, "Meaning," 167.

some Jewish groups also sponsored their own religiously based schools. And in that setting "homeschooling" was pretty much the sort of thing that the Amish and some countercultural commune types tried to get away with.

Most fundamentalist and evangelical Christians at that stage were strong supporters of the public school system. Indeed, in many ways their commitment to the public schools was stronger than their commitment to the culture at large. Fundamentalist and evangelical Christians had long lived with a deep ambivalence toward the dominant patterns of American culture. As heirs of the Puritans, they nurtured the hope that the United States would someday return to its "Christian nation" status. But at the same time, they were quite aware of trends that made this return an unlikely prospect. This ambivalence also characterized their relationship to public education. But both of the pulls — optimism and pessimism — seemed to dictate a "hang in there" posture regarding public education. If there was hope for a "Christian America," the public school system would be an important instrument of moral reform. But if the negative trends continued, it was still important to offer support to the public schools system: even if they were critical of some of the practices and teachings in those schools, many Christian parents were still convinced that their children could be a good "Christian testimony" within that system for values that the believing community held dear.

In the early 1970s, however, things began to change significantly, and disillusionment with public education began to take hold. New Christian schools began to sprout up, many of them under the sponsorship of local Pentecostal and "Bible church"–type congregations. Many observers simply attribute this growth to racial issues, as busing and other programs for integrating the public schools became controversial topics. And racism was undoubtedly a factor. But it was not the whole story, and to attempt to make it so is to ignore some important topics that have a bearing on the present-day debates over school choice.[11]

Many Christian parents in the 1970s experienced a new sense of cultural alienation as secularism — the "secular humanism" that had long been a worrisome presence to many people of faith — began to display a new stridency in the form of the "sexual revolution." As pornography, ho-

11. The complex motivations for increased support for religiously based schools are nicely charted by David Sikkink in his essay "The Social Sources of Alienation from Public Schools," *Social Forces* 78, no. 1 (1999): 51-86.

mosexual rights, abortion on demand, the pill, rising divorce rates, sex education in the schools, and the like became increasingly prominent on the cultural agenda, many concerned parents feared that their defenses against secularism had been seriously damaged. Previously they had taken it for granted that a strong family life could inoculate their children against whatever secularism might be at work in public education. Now they began to suspect that public education had itself become a chief propagator of values that were antithetical to many of their most cherished convictions.

"Worldviews" and the American Context

While conservative Protestants are not the only ones who have established alternative schools during the past decades, they are among the most vocal advocates of educational choice these days. It isn't clear, however, that their pleas for government support for their school programs are typically based on a nuanced philosophy of pluralism. Nor is it clear that the Kuyperian perspective set forth by Wolterstorff and Carlson-Thies — which calls for a government posture of impartiality to all schools, whether Christian, Muslim, Scientologist, or atheist — applies well to the kinds of plurality of educational experiments that prevail in contemporary North America.

One obvious difference between our situation and that of nineteenth-century Holland is the nature of the entities the government is asked to be impartial toward. As already noted, the key term in the Dutch arrangement is "pillarization." The "pillars" in the Netherlands have been relatively stable, long-standing patterns of life and thought. Kuyper's favorite term to describe this sort of pattern was "worldview."[12] He saw his brand of Calvinism as the most coherent of competing worldviews, but he also attributed a coherence to the other "pillar" worldviews, the most prominent ones in the Dutch scheme being Roman Catholicism, Lutheranism, socialism, and secularism.

Governmental impartiality in North America, on the other hand, would have to make decisions regarding a very different range of perspec-

12. For a good summary of Kuyper's use of this concept, see Peter S. Heslam, *Creating a Christian Worldview: Abraham Kuyper's Lectures on Calvinism* (Grand Rapids: Eerdmans, 1998), 88-96; for more extensive discussions of the Kuyperian notion of worldview, see the essays in Paul A. Marshall, Sander Griffioen, and Richard J. Mouw, eds., *Stained Glass: Worldviews and Social Science* (Lanham, Md.: University Press of America, 1989).

tives. And the truth is that very few of them deserve to be thought of as "pillars" — or even as very coherent "worldviews." Indeed, if anything, we seem to be experiencing considerable worldview fragmentation in American culture. This phenomenon was nicely illustrated for me by a leader of an evangelical ministry on university campuses, who reported that his organization is struggling with difficult questions about how to present the claims of the Christian faith to present-day students. In the not-so-distant past, he observed, evangelicals would employ an apologetic approach that placed a strong emphasis on the coherence of a Christian view of reality. The biblical perspective was shown to tie things together, to answer more questions adequately than other worldviews. Such an approach challenged students to make a clear choice between Christianity and, say, a naturalistic or an Eastern religious perspective. But today's students, he observed, don't seem to put much stock in coherence and consistency. They participate in an evangelical Bible study on Wednesday night and then engage in a New Age meditation group on Thursday night, while spending their daily jogging time listening to a taped reading of *The Celestine Prophecy,* with a stop for an infusion of nutrition at the local Holistic Herbal Healing Center — and have no sense that there is anything inappropriate about moving in and out of these very different perspectives on reality.

The fragmentation phenomenon was raised for me in a poignant manner a few years ago by a brief comment from a person who called in to a radio talk show. I was a guest on this particular program, and I was paired with another theologian in a discussion about the continuing fascination in our culture with the person of Jesus of Nazareth, as evidenced in frequent cover stories in weekly newsmagazines, TV specials, and the like. My fellow guest was a very liberal Protestant who expressed some strong skepticism about the reliability of the New Testament accounts of the resurrection of Jesus. I strongly disagreed with his assessment, and made it clear that I believe that what occurred on Easter morning was a literal bodily resurrection. When we opened the discussion to questions from our listening audience, one of our callers was a teenager who identified herself as Heather from Glendale. Heather expressed herself in typical "Valley Girl" tones: "I'm not what you would call, like, a Christian," she began. "Actually, right now I am sort of into — you know — like, witchcraft and stuff? But I want to say that I agree with the guy from Fuller Seminary. I'm just shocked that someone would, like, say that Jesus wasn't really raised from the dead!"

I was taken aback by Heather's way of offering support for my position.

Her comment still strikes me as rather bizarre — combining a fascination with "witchcraft and stuff" with a belief in the literal resurrection of Jesus. And the more I have thought about what Heather said, the more I worry about her and what she represents in our contemporary culture. I am concerned about the way she seems to be piecing together a set of convictions to guide her life. While I did not have the opportunity to quiz her about how she makes room in her psyche for an endorsement of both witchcraft and the Gospels' resurrection narratives, I doubt that Heather subscribes to both views of reality, Wicca and Christianity, in their robust versions. She is placing fragments of worldviews side by side without thinking about their relationship. And it is precisely the fact that these disconnected cognitive bits coexist in her consciousness that causes my concern.

My worries are reinforced by the realization that certain intellectual leaders actually celebrate this kind of disconnected selfhood. Take the case of Kenneth Gergen, a psychologist who has written a much-discussed study of contemporary selfhood, his 1991 book, *The Saturated Self: Dilemmas of Identity in Contemporary Life.* There Gergen argues that traditional conceptions of how to understand personhood — that we do or do not have souls or unconscious minds, that people have "intrinsic worth" or "inherent rationality" — have been exposed by "the postmodern turn" as inappropriate: "These are, after all, ways of talking, not reflections of the actual nature of persons. In contrast to the narrow range of options and the oppressive restraints favored by totalizing systems of understanding, postmodernism opens the way to the full expression of all discourses, to a free play of discourses."[13] From this way of viewing things, we help people best, says Gergen, by inviting them into an "endless wandering in the maze of meaning," in which they regularly experience "the breaking down of oppositions."[14] To be sure, Gergen wants individuals to find some way of blending, through both internal and external dialogues, various "richly elaborated discourses into new forms of serious games that can take us beyond text and into life."[15] But it is not clear exactly what standards are to guide this process in a world in which all comparative judgments are arbitrary, indeed "imperialistic." Why should my Dodger-fan self have any less status in my life than the self that senses a need to serve the poor? Why

13. Kenneth J. Gergen, *The Saturated Self: Dilemmas of Identity in Contemporary Life* (New York: Basic Books, 1991), 247.
14. Gergen, *The Saturated Self,* 256.
15. Gergen, *The Saturated Self,* 259.

should I prefer any instinct or preference over any other one? In such a world, what is the difference between a healthy and an unhealthy self? What would keep each of us from proclaiming, like the young demoniac whom Jesus encountered, "My name is Legion; for we are many" (Mark 5:9)?

Something like this same pattern — although in a more subdued form — prevails in the larger religious culture. Several commentators have pointed to a widespread cafeteria approach to religious belief these days. Of course, this metaphor takes on added significance in the light of the ways in which literal cafeterias have changed in recent years. For example, providers of campus food services have transformed college cafeterias, which were once places where people sat and "dined" together, into spaces containing a variety of "grazing stations." A student will first go to a salad bar, then to a sandwich preparation area, then to a dessert stand, and finally grab a cone from the frozen yogurt machine on the way out. Quite likely she will not actually sit and "dine" with a specific group of people during this time; instead she will touch down at a variety of points to eat various portions of her meal. Nor is this a substantial shift from the habits she learned at home, where the family meal — as a regularly scheduled communal experience — was at best a rare occurrence.

Religious grazing, then, where people sample bits and pieces of a plurality of religious offerings, putting together their own personal combinations, is a part of a larger grazing culture. In the realm of educational choice, for example, it is not at all uncommon to find parents who are members of an evangelically oriented Presbyterian church and who also attend Catholic charismatic prayer meetings on Wednesday evenings, while sending the occasional contribution to a Southern Baptist TV evangelist — and who, having sent their children for three years to a Lutheran school, now have enrolled them in a Christian school sponsored by a local Pentecostal congregation.

What "pillar" does this family's religious perspective represent?

And even where we *can* identify long-standing "pillars" in American life — for example, Judaism, Roman Catholicism, Lutheranism, Islam — we still must take into account the greatly increased mobility *between* these pillars, in contrast to the Netherlands of Kuyper's day. People change religions frequently in our culture, so that even the relatively stable worldview-pillars that do exist on the American scene are not populated by correspondingly stable constituencies. Furthermore, the very fact of this mobility suggests that in our context a plurality of schools encourages a competitive educational market environment. And this is only likely to increase when the competition focuses on vouchers available to parents whose own sense of religious identity is not well defined.

Anyone, then, who wants to apply the lessons of the Dutch educational settlement to the North American context must seriously wrestle with this important question: Where are the "pillars" to be found in our culture?

New Social Conditions

Another key item in the Dutch equation must also be looked at carefully from the perspective of North American culture. It was *families* in the Dutch context who were expected to make their educational choices in the light of their worldview commitments. More specifically, it was assumed that the decisions would be made by *parents*.

This motif is also featured prominently in many American formulations, where a strong emphasis is placed on "parental choice." But how are we to think about parental decisions amidst the shifting patterns of parenting in contemporary life?

Kuyper and his contemporaries spoke much about the fundamental right and obligation of parents to determine the basic patterns of the education of their children. This same formulation characterizes the cases made by Wolterstorff and Carlson-Thies. Wolterstorff, for example, praises the Supreme Court ruling in the case of Pierce versus the Society of Sisters, where the court struck down a 1920s law requiring all children to attend public schools. "The child is not the mere creature of the State," the justices wrote; "those who nurture him and direct his destiny have the right, coupled with the high duty, to recognize and prepare him for additional obligations."[16]

The problem with this way of putting things, of course, is that the patterns of American family life have changed significantly in recent decades: many children now live in single-parent or blended families, and increasing numbers are even moving back and forth between two or more family units. The question of what "parental choice" means in situations where *competing* parental choices are a fact of life for many children cannot be ignored.

16. Quoted by Wolterstorff, *Religion and the Schools,* 34.

Societal Health

In the case that he set forth in the 1960s, Wolterstorff made a point of insisting that affirmative impartiality must always be carried on within a framework where "the good order and health of society must be preserved."[17] This concern must certainly figure prominently in our present debates. Will a voucher plan, or some other strategy for encouraging school choice, promote a healthy pluralism or will it further fragment our culture in unhealthy ways?

The question of the relationship between educational choice and societal health is also being raised in the Netherlands these days.[18] The Dutch pillars have been visibly crumbling in recent decades, and while the educational patterns established on the basis of pillarization thinking do still remain intact, many people, including many Christian supporters of Dutch religious schools, wonder these days whether the effects of educational impartiality continue to be primarily beneficial for either religious groups or the larger culture. And as Dutch life continues to become more religiously and ethnically diverse, the Dutch educational arrangement must now distribute benefits over an increasing number of worldview units. At what point, many critics are asking, does the expansion of pillarization *(verzuiling)* actually become a force for de-pillarization *(ontzuiling)?*

Obviously, many of the issues being raised in these Dutch discussions parallel those that dominate our own North American discussions of pluralism. But it is significant that in the Dutch case the arguments are informed by many decades of actual experience with a system that is only in the advocacy stage in North America.

One issue that is never far from the surface, whenever and wherever these issues are discussed, is the question of religion's role in the promotion of civic virtues. Here is one report about the way in which the concern is presently being articulated in the Netherlands:

> Nowadays, it is broadly accepted that all young people need to learn to cope with and fully accept ideological diversity in today's open and multicultural society. In the light of the pervasive secularization and plurality of modern Dutch culture questions are being raised as to the

17. Wolterstorff, *Religion and the Schools,* 12.
18. See the summary of these present-day discussions in Sturm and Miedema, "Kuyper's Educational Legacy," 243-46.

advisability of so many still being sent to schools professing only one particular conception of "the good," even if all the teachers in any given school are required by law to introduce all their students to different ideas and cultures. All citizens should respect and value — or learn to respect and value — multiformity, and no student ought to be confined to the self-imposed ghetto of a denominational school, say the advocates of a uniform public multicultural school system.[19]

This is an important concern, and no defender of educational freedom can ignore the fact that religion has indeed often promoted a "ghetto" mentality in which the civic virtues of tolerance and respect for diversity have been ignored, and even on occasion aggressively undermined. This is not the place to explore the complexities of the relationship of religious conviction to what Wolterstorff describes as "the good order and health of society." But I do want at least to offer a brief personal testimony on the subject.

Part of my own elementary education took place in a small Dutch Calvinist school in Paterson, New Jersey. Most of the students in that school came by bus, and we all brought our lunches. During our noon hour, the boys would play baseball in a nearby field, at a time when groups of students would be returning to the local public school from their lunchtimes at home. These encounters were often not very peaceable. On one particular day, some taunting words between my friends and a group of African American public schoolers turned into a rock-throwing fight. A stone thrown by one of the blacks grazed my head, and I was enraged. I yelled out the "N" word in his direction, and ran back to the school.

Unbeknownst to me, the young stone-thrower followed me and marched into the principal's office to report my verbal insult. Soon the principal and I were facing each other, alone in his office. Mr. Dykstra told me how disappointed he was with me. Through my tears, I protested: "But he threw a *stone* at me! He *hit* me with it!"

Mr. Dykstra's response was kind but firm. "Yes, he should not have done that. I'm sorry it happened to you. But, Richard, you have done something much worse. He tried to harm your body. You responded by trying to harm his soul. God is much more saddened by what you did to that young man than by what he did to you."

A common punishment in that school was to "write lines" — the

19. Sturm and Miedema, "Kuyper's Educational Legacy," 245.

punishee was made to write a sentence such as "I will not chew gum in class" a prescribed number of times. My punishment for saying the "N" word set a school record. I had to copy the Ten Commandments one hundred times, and then take the result to the principal after the sheets were signed by my parents.

Mr. Dykstra's way of handling this case had a lasting impression on me. I came to see the theological wisdom of what he made me do. What I had done was not only an insult to the young stone-thrower, it was an offense against the God who had created both of us. My angry retort was an act of bearing false witness against my neighbor. I had violated God's law.

This experience, in an all-white, predominantly Dutch-ethnic, Christian school, shaped my convictions about race relations in a way that was unmatched by any other lesson on the subject I was later to learn in the broader environs of multiculturalism. There is no question in my mind that religion can be a positive force in promoting civic virtues. Indeed, I believe that it has a crucial role to play in that endeavor.

"Thick" and "Thin"

Again, this is a complex topic that I have only touched upon with this example. But the larger picture has been nicely sketched out by Professor Bryan Hehir, of Harvard Divinity School. Father Hehir, who has been a key adviser to the United States Roman Catholic bishops on matters of public policy, acknowledges that he has been deeply influenced by the natural law tradition, which has led him to work as an ethicist with the assumption "that when speaking to the state, the church must use a language the state can comprehend." While he still basically adheres to this position, he has come to see the limits of such an approach: "in surveying the principally social policy debates of the 1990s," he writes, "I am also struck by the limits of the ethical, that is to say the failure of the purely moral argument to address the underlying dimensions of our public policy disputes and decisions." It is important for us to attend especially to "the premoral convictions that must be addressed to confront the societal questions we face today." And on these matters, he says, "the comparative advantage is with communities that are convinced of the kind of theological truths the Christian community takes for granted. These are embedded convictions — capable of being articulated, so not unintelligible for public discourse." What this means in practice, Hehir suggests, is that we are severely limited in our use of theological language "when we finally address the state on law and policy . . . but prior to stating the policy issue we can and should expansively engage the wider civil community in the deeper questions that undergird policy choices, and that may take theological argument to surface, because they are about our basic relationships as a society and a human community."[20]

Hehir's suggestion here that it can be helpful to introduce theological language into our public discussions is an important one. He is right, of course, also to insist that this sort of "thick" language becomes less appropriate at that point where we begin directly to "address the state on law and policy" — here a "thinner" language becomes necessary.[21] But proposing formulas for the official policies that will guide our collective lives is not the only proper mode of public discourse. There are also many opportunities in public life for us to testify to each other about how our policy proposals connect to our deepest convictions about the human condition. Nor ought we even to pretend that those connections do not matter much, since for many of us — perhaps for all of us — it is precisely *in* the awareness of the particularities of our deepest convictions that we know the proper limits of our public discourse. We should never promote a ban, then, on all thick expressions in our public conversations, for the public square ought to provide us with a forum where — at least on important occasions — we talk to each other about the sources of the hope that lies within us. There are, to be sure, also moments when thin discourse becomes the important mode of conversation — especially when we come to those points when we must hammer out those consensus formulations that will allow all of us, people of faith as well as those with no faith at all, to live out our deepest commitments together with integrity.

I am convinced that faith-based schools can serve as important workshops for training in this kind of citizenship in a pluralistic society. Ronald Thiemann put it well when he observed that various sorts of particularistic Christian communities can function as "schools of public virtue," where people of faith work at forming "the kind of character [that is] necessary

20. J. Bryan Hehir, "Personal Faith, the Public Church, and the Role of Theology," *Harvard Divinity Bulletin* 26, no. 1 (1996): 5.

21. My use of "thick" and "thin" here follows the pattern employed by many commentators in recent years. The imagery was made popular by Clifford Geertz, who in turn borrowed the terms from Gilbert Ryle. Cf. Clifford Geertz, "Thick Description: Toward an Interpretive Theory of Culture," in his *The Interpretation of Cultures* (New York: Basic Books, 1973), 3-30.

for public life."[22] All we need to add, to link his claim to our present discussion, is the insistence that actual faith-based schools be numbered among these "schools of public virtue." My own lesson about racism serves as a case in point. It is in the very thickness of the kind of theological language that can be freely employed in religious school settings that we are encouraged to reflect on the deeply human questions that are so crucial to the thinner discussions that take place in the public square. To be sure, religion at its worst, and even when it is functioning in a mediocre fashion, does not contribute in a healthy manner to this larger discussion. But in assessing the overall merits of religiously oriented school systems, we ought not simply to ignore what might happen when religion is in fact functioning at its best.

I hasten to add the acknowledgment that there are Christian thinkers who get nervous when someone even hints that religion might be good for the larger pluralistic culture. Debates within the theological community can get pretty heated these days about the dangers of sacrificing the thick texture of Christian discourse for the alleged benefits of a thin ethical contribution to the larger public arena. And these worries are legitimate when they stem from a concern that we not assess the merits of religion exclusively with reference to the utilitarian benefits it can bring to the larger society. People of faith will serve the larger culture best by nurturing convictions that sometimes go against the cultural grain. But that does not rule out the real possibility that religious training can also lay the groundwork for healthy citizenship.

The Virtues of Sacrifice

My own musings on the issues of educational choice, then, are shaped by the strong belief that religiously oriented schools can make an important positive contribution to the health of society. But while I do believe, given my Kuyperian convictions, that affirmative impartiality is a healthy posture for government to take toward educational pluralism, I am also convinced that the actual policies for implementing the concerns associated with that posture — including the financial support systems that might be appropriate — must be decided on the basis of prudential considerations.

22. Ronald Thiemann, *Constructing Public Theology: The Church in a Pluralistic Culture* (Louisville: Westminster John Knox, 1991), 43.

One such consideration is the need for educating people for the common good — a task that, as I have just been arguing, *can* be accomplished by faith-based schools but is not likely to happen without stronger worldview-pillars than presently populate the American scene. Another crucial consideration is the need to attend in special ways to what will promote the well-being of the disadvantaged. This need is not adequately provided for in most of the schemes being proposed these days — a fact that leaves me with nagging doubts about the prudence of moving ahead with a program of government support that relies too heavily on the Dutch model.

Not that I am pessimistic about finding productive new strategies for implementing some sort of affirmative impartiality program. I see much wisdom in the idea, for example, that instead of a voucher plan we should legislate in favor of tax credits for parents who send their children to nonpublic schools. But we must work harder than we have thus far to ensure that such a move would in fact be good for, say, the urban poor. In a helpful discussion in the *New Republic*, Sarah Wildman has argued that tax credits are the one measure most likely to gain bipartisan support. But she also emphasizes that such a strategy would not guarantee the "one clear benefit" of a voucher plan: that of "enabling low-income kids to get out of failing public schools." As she rightly notes, "since the vast majority of people who get a tax credit are the ones rich enough to pay income taxes, it does virtually nothing for the very poor."[23]

But my own fear is that even a voucher system will not do much to make quality education more available to the poor. To achieve that goal, a stronger sense of justice must be at work in our culture. That is best achieved, at least for people with the kinds of religious convictions that I hold dear, when we take seriously our obligations to live sacrificially on behalf of, and for the sake of, those who are victims of injustice. And this in turn could be helped by encouraging a spirit of sacrifice in the hearts and lives of those who want to support alternatives to the dominant patterns of education in our contemporary context — including the sacrifice of promoting the cause of the poor and the marginalized while also learning to live with the fact that we ourselves are receiving less than we believe is appropriate from a government that is obliged to act with affirmative impartiality to all its citizens.

23. Sarah Wildman, "Who Says Conservatives Like Vouchers?" *New Republic*, February 26, 2001, 16.

There is good biblical support for such an approach. The ancient prophet spoke wisely to the faith community when suddenly they found themselves to be strangers in Babylon: "Seek the welfare of the city where I have sent you into exile, and pray the LORD on its behalf," he preached, "for in its welfare you will find your welfare" (Jer. 29:7).

Creational Politics:
Some Calvinist Amendments

The anthropologist James Peacock has offered an apt characterization of the ancient Hebrews' contribution to our understanding of "the idea of culture":

> The Book of Genesis addressed not only the important philosophical question "Why is there something rather than nothing at all?" (it was Yahweh who created matter, i.e., the heavens and the earth); Genesis also addressed the questions "Why is there life instead of simply nonlife?" (it was Yahweh that breathed in the breath of life) and "Why is there consciousness and not simply nonconscious activity?" (the distinction between human and animal existence in Yahweh's creation and the transition from Eden to the "real world"). Or to restate the final question, "Why is there culture and not simply nature?"[1]

Peacock's remarks would strike a sympathetic chord in many a Calvinist heart. Calvinists, more than any other group of Christians, have placed a strong emphasis on the cultural significance of the Genesis creation narrative. Henry Van Til states the case unambiguously in *The Calvinistic Concept of Culture:* culture, "that activity of man, the image-bearer of God, by which he fulfills the creation mandate to cultivate the earth, to have do-

1. James L. Peacock, *The Anthropological Lens: Harsh Light, Soft Focus* (New York: Cambridge University Press, 1986), 24.

This essay previously appeared in *Christian Scholars Review* 23, no. 2 (1993). It is printed here with permission.

minion over it and to subdue it," is no peripheral concern from a biblical perspective. "It is an expression of man's essential being as created in the image of God, and since man is essentially a religious being, it is expressive of his relationship to God, that is, of his religion."[2]

On the Calvinist reading of the opening pages of the Bible, as detailed by Van Til, the Creator's initial assignment to the first human pair is a "cultural mandate." The directive to "fill the earth" (Gen. 1:28) is not to be thought of primarily as a reproductive command. The "filling" of the earth is a *cultural* activity. God placed Adam and Eve in a "primary environment" — a garden containing animal and vegetative life — with the understanding that human beings would fashion a "secondary environment," a cultural one, out of those primal materials.[3] When our first parents fashioned tree branches into rudimentary tools, or when they invented a basic labeling system, or when they created schedules as a means of organizing their lives — in all this they were developing the cultural potential of the original creation, as a means of fulfilling their original mandate from God.

Nor has the centrality of cultural formation been in any way diminished by the entrance of sin into the creation. Under fallen conditions the question becomes one of cultural obedience versus cultural disobedience. Rebellious humanity distorts and perverts cultural activity. To be redeemed from sin, then, is to be restored to the patterns of obedient cultural formation for which we were created. This is why, as Van Til sees things, Calvinists must be very diligent in combating both the "pietistic withdrawal from the world and the Anabaptistic denial of the Christian's cultural calling."[4]

This is a perspective that I find to be attractive in its general contours. More specifically, I have found it helpful for developing a Christian perspective on political life. In my own teaching and writing on political topics, I have regularly drawn on the insights of this "cultural mandate" tradition, arguing that political culture in particular, like cultural formation in general, is in some important sense "grounded in creation."

But the more I have reflected on this perspective as it applies to the political dimension of human life, the more I have seen the need to amend it in significant ways. Some of my amendments are required for the sake of the internal coherence of the perspective itself. But others have to do with

2. Henry R. Van Til, *The Calvinistic Concept of Culture* (Grand Rapids: Baker, 1959), 7.
3. Van Til, *Calvinistic Concept of Culture*, 7.
4. Van Til, *Calvinistic Concept of Culture*, 22.

the ways in which defenders of this Calvinist cultural perspective have dealt with other Christian traditions in their formulations. For example, I have already provided one illustration of the way in which Calvinists have used the Anabaptists as a foil as they have explained and defended their position.

Some of my amendments, then, are necessitated by the requirements of ecumenical fairness. In my own political reflections, for example, I have learned much from the contributions that contemporary Anabaptist thinkers, especially John Howard Yoder, have made to Christian political thought. Not only have these Anabaptist formulations regularly failed to fit the common Calvinist stereotype; they have also helped me to understand better how the Calvinist cultural perspective can be enriched. I will attempt to elaborate on those patterns of enrichment in these reflections.

Politics and Dominion

The appeal to Genesis 1 as a rationale for Christian political involvement has taken visible shape in recent years in the movement known as Christian Reconstructionism. The Reconstructionist thinkers make much of the "dominion" theme of Genesis 1:28; one of their main publishing ventures bears the title Dominion Press.[5]

One recent critique of Reconstructionist thought has been offered by two fundamentalist-dispensationalist authors. These writers focus on, among other things, the political use of the "dominion" theme, insisting that the "have dominion" of the creation mandate does not apply to the way in which human beings are to treat each other, but only to an authority that human beings together are to exercise with regard to the nonhuman creation.[6]

We need not trouble ourselves here about whether these critics are being fair in their suggestion that Reconstructionist thinkers have confused the distinction between interhuman relations and human/nonhuman relations in their use of the "dominion" theme. Even if the Reconstruction-

---

5. For a good, albeit critical, introductory survey of this movement's program, see Richard John Neuhaus, "The Theonomist Temptation," *First Things: A Monthly Journal of Religion and Public Life* 3 (May 1990): 13-21. Neuhaus provides a short bibliography that lists several key Reconstructionist publications.

6. H. Wayne House and Thomas Ice, *Dominion Theology: Blessing or Curse? An Analysis of Christian Reconstructionism* (Portland, Oreg.: Multnomah, 1988), 141.

ists have been careful on this point, it is not difficult to find other Calvinist thinkers who have been less than clear in employing the theme. Take, for example, my own writings. Having observed, in one of my published discussions, that human beings are called by God in Genesis 1 to exercise dominion together in the good creation, I go on to comment that "[t]he ways of human government in a sinful world are perversions of the 'subduing' and 'dominion' which God intended as a part of the good creation."[7]

To be sure, one could take this sentence to be a somewhat imprecise vehicle for saying something that is quite plausible. But to be truthful, I do not think that was the meaning I intended. My underlying assumption in my various published treatments of "dominion" and politics[8] has been that the authority to exercise dominion, as granted by God in the creation mandate, is itself in a very direct sense the ground of the political authority that was bound to be necessitated by the existence of large numbers of human beings, even unfallen human beings. Thus, the dominion over plants and animals was logically extendable to an interhuman pattern of dominion relationships.

This now seems to me to be wrongheaded — and dangerously so. It is now generally accepted as a near truism among environmentally sensitive people that the "dominion" mandate has regularly been employed as a rationale for the manipulative exploitation of nonhuman nature. Even if we are convinced, as I am, that environmental domination is a perversion of the original dominion task, there can be no doubt that Genesis 1 has indeed sometimes been used in perverse ways. For this reason alone we should be cautious about encouraging anyone to think that "dominion" is an appropriate way of describing acceptable interhuman patterns. If there are no clear biblical grounds for taking risks in this area, it seems obvious to me that we ought to avoid doing so. And there is in fact no reason to take these risks with reference to interhuman relationships, since creational political authority is not directly grounded in the "dominion" command.

In what sense, then, *is* politics grounded in creation? It seems to me plausible to look for the answer in two other elements of the creation account. First, the political ordering of human life can be seen as included

7. Richard J. Mouw, *When the Kings Come Marching In: Isaiah and the New Jerusalem* (Grand Rapids: Eerdmans, 1983), 30.

8. See also the discussion of these matters in chapter 2 of my *Politics and the Biblical Drama* (Grand Rapids: Eerdmans, 1976).

within the command to "fill" the earth. We can understand the emergence of prelapsarian patterns of authority among human beings as one product of the larger task of cultural formation.

Second, political relationships can be viewed as emerging in the process of giving some degree of formal structuring to the patterns of human social interaction.

This latter point is where I failed to be clear enough in my own earlier reflections on the topic. I had come to see that the ideas of sociality and dominion were very important elements in the creation narrative. Fashioned by God to be "male and female" together (Gen. 1:27), we human beings are needful of "helpers" who are of our own kind (Gen. 2:18-23); thus we are inescapably communal by virtue of our created nature. And we are, in turn, given a communal task to perform — the exercise of "dominion" in the good earth in which God has placed us.

So far, so good. But I then went on to correlate these two biblical themes with two very basic questions of social-political philosophy: First, why ought human beings to be immersed in the patterns of social interaction? And second, how, if at all, do political relationships expedite proper human functions and goals? The matchup between these two philosophical questions and the two biblical themes seemed to me to be clear: the first question is answered by the Bible's insistence that we are created with deep communal longings and needs. And the second is answered by the "dominion" assignment: the political connotations of the term "dominion" suggested to me that God had from the very beginning invested the creation order with patterns of authority and power.

But the correlation I attempted here was too simple. The dominion assignment has, as we have already noted, nothing to do with the ways in which we human beings are to treat each other; and it has everything to do with our common task with regard to the nonhuman creation. The dominion theme, then, answers neither of the two questions of social-political philosophy. It does tell us about the overall obligations we should keep in mind — those having to do with the stewardship of nonhuman created reality — as we go about expediting our social and political interactions. But it tells us nothing about how those interactions themselves are *grounded* in created reality.

The two aforementioned questions of social-political philosophy, then, must both be answered — insofar as they are properly "answered" in biblical terms — with reference to the first biblical theme, the fact of our created sociality. The first question gets the rather direct answer that we gave above: we are social beings because God created us with deep communal longings and needs. The second question, on the other hand, is answered with somewhat less directness: politics enters the picture when it becomes necessary for us to give some structure to the "together" part of our exercising "dominion together"; as creatures who have been told by God to fill the earth with the patterns and products of cultural formation, we need not shrink from contributing a *political* culture to the world in which God has placed us.

Does all this have any real point or is it merely an exercise in terminological quibbling? I think there is a point and it is an important one. If "dominion" told us something about the nature of creational political authority as such, then it would not be too difficult to treat hierarchy and coercion as if they were a part of the very (created) nature of things. At the very least it would seem to provide a justification for a strong program of hierarchical-coercive politics as Christians attempt to fulfill their creational "dominion" obligations by engaging in political efforts to tame a world that is now pervaded by human sinfulness. But if we disallow any element of dominion to our understanding of God's original intentions for interhuman relations, then we are able to frame the question of present-day political obligation somewhat differently: How can we model, in the midst of a broken and distorted world, something of the original order of things — an order in which "dominion" had no proper place in the relationships that hold within the human community?

Calvinist Stereotypes of Anabaptism

When Calvinists offer their rationales for the proper patterns of "Christian politics" in a fallen world, they are very likely to frame the basic issue in the manner just suggested. The question has to do with the degree to which we can preserve something of God's original intentions for human social interaction in a situation that has come to be deeply scarred by human rebellion.

Anabaptists tend not to ask the question of "Christian politics" in creational terms. This apparent refusal to view our fallenness against the horizon of good creation order has convinced many Calvinists that the Anabaptists are operating with a very different fundamental theology of Christian discipleship. Henry Van Til expresses a traditional Calvinist consensus, then, when he refers to "the Anabaptist denial of the Christian's cultural calling." This general assessment has, in turn, taken on a special vehemence when Calvinists have characterized the Anabaptist community's relationship to political cultural in particular. Thus the polemical flourish with which the sixteenth-century framers of the Belgic Confession concluded their account of the God-ordained authority of civil magistrates: "Wherefore we detest the Anabaptists and other seditious people, and in general all those who reject the higher powers and magistrates and would subvert justice, introduce community of goods, and confound the decency and good order which God has established among men" (article 36).

Rhetorical asides of this sort have regularly served in Reformed writings as a substitute for a careful consideration of the actual teachings of the "radical Reformation." No one has answered the two Calvinist charges against Anabaptists — "anticulture" and "antipolitics" — more carefully and systematically than John Yoder. And his response seems to me to be quite convincing.

Do Anabaptists deny "our Christian cultural calling"? The Reformed assessment of Anabaptism's cultural posture presupposes, says Yoder, that there are no alternative ways of reading the call to cultural involvement: "The Reformed do not say that the Anabaptists misinterpret the cultural mandate but that they deny it. This only makes sense if that mandate's content is univocally that which the Anabaptist refuses to do."[9] Yoder insists that the Anabaptists are opposing, not the cultural mandate as such, but only the Calvinist's prescriptions about what it means to respond obediently to that mandate.

The differences between Anabaptists and Calvinists regarding political involvement in particular move along similar lines. If being politically involved means a desire to influence public policy in the light of biblical standards of righteousness, then there is no disagreement in principle between Calvinists and Anabaptists. Indeed, Yoder's *Politics of Jesus* is a full-scale argument for viewing the sort of communal witness that is central to the Anabaptist understanding of Christian discipleship as a legitimate mode of political involvement. From Yoder's perspective the real argument gets started at that point where the Reformed Christian insists that a willingness to give direct support to the civil ministry of "the sword" is a litmus test for genuine political involvement.

---

9. John H. Yoder, "Reformed versus Anabaptist Social Strategies: An Inadequate Typology," *TSF Bulletin*, May-June 1985, 2; see also my supportive response to Yoder's case in the same issue: "Abandoning the Typology: A Reformed Assist," 7-10. In some of my discussion in this present essay I am expanding upon points contained in that response.

The Political Relevance of Creational Patterns

There is no real disagreement here, then, over whether or not Christians are under a cultural mandate, or over whether or not Christians have political obligations as such. So where *do* the real differences lie?

One crucial area of difference has to do with the relevant biblical reference points for pursuing our cultural-political tasks. Calvinists show a strong interest in creational data, while Anabaptists are much more likely to look directly to the example and teachings of Jesus for normative guidance. Thus we might think in terms of tensions between "the politics of creation" and "the politics of Jesus."

Even here, though, we must be careful to avoid too stark a contrast. Calvinists certainly believe, for example, that the ministry of Jesus is relevant to Christian political discipleship. Anabaptists, on the other hand, need not reject the notion of an original creation order, nor is it necessary to their case that they deny that this original order had a political character. Yoder, for example, seems to operate with a clear distinction between prelapsarian and postlapsarian politics: "It is not as if there was a time when there was no government and then God made government through a new creative intervention; there has been hierarchy and authority and power since human society existed. Its exercise has involved domination, disrespect for human dignity, and real or potential violence ever since sin has existed."[10]

Calvinists believe, then, in a political Jesus; and Anabaptists have no reason to reject the idea of an original creation in which politics had a part. The main point of contention has to do with how these two political realities — the ministry of Jesus and the creation order — are to be ranked in the order of knowing. The question is where primarily we are to look for normative guidance.

Calvinists have regularly insisted, for example, that the incarnation did not introduce anything new by way of ethical content. Jesus came to restore a pattern of cultural obedience that had been with us from the beginning. This emphasis loomed large in Abraham Kuyper's thinking:

> Can we imagine that at one time God willed to rule things in a certain moral order, but that now, in Christ, He wills to rule it otherwise? As

10. John H. Yoder, *The Politics of Jesus: Vicit Agnus Noster* (Grand Rapids: Eerdmans, 1972), 203.

though He were not the Eternal, the Unchangeable, Who, from the very hour of creation, even unto all eternity, had willed, wills, and shall will and maintain, one and the same firm moral world-order! Verily Christ has swept away the dust with which man's sinful limitations had covered up this world-order, and has made it glitter again in its original brilliancy. . . . [T]he world-order remains just what it was from the beginning. It lays full claim, not only to the believer (as though less were required from the unbeliever), but to every human being and to all human relationships.[11]

The Anabaptists, on the other hand, do not share the Calvinists' confidence regarding our noetic access to this "moral world-order." They have preferred to focus directly on the ministry of Jesus as their normative reference point.

At first glance it is difficult to see why this preference for Jesus as a political model should be so offensive to Calvinist sensibilities. After all, if Jesus is the restorer of the original moral order, why should it make any difference whether we look for guidance to that moral order itself or to the restoration of it in the mission of the incarnate God? If one wants to build an eighteenth-century-style log cabin, it should not make much difference whether one looks at an original log cabin or an accurate restoration of one. Why doesn't the same thing hold for the creation-restoring work of Jesus?

The Calvinist answer, of course, is that we will inevitably misinterpret the ministry of Jesus if we do not view it against the background of what it is designed to restore. Jesus never intended that we would learn all that we need to know about Christian discipleship simply by looking to his example and teachings. We can make proper use of these incarnational data only by seeing them in the larger context of God's creating purposes. The politics of Jesus, then, presuppose an understanding of the politics of creation.

Understanding the Cultural Mandate

The Calvinist account makes much of an original creation in which human beings are called to engage in a rich variety of cultural formation, including

---

11. Abraham Kuyper, *Lectures on Calvinism* (Grand Rapids: Eerdmans, 1931), 71-72.

political formation. As we have seen, this theme is not, strictly speaking, an important matter to dwell upon in Reformed-Anabaptist arguments.

This is not to say that the kind of cultural theology developed by Calvinists is noncontroversial in the larger Christian community. But the controversial elements do not figure significantly into the debates between Calvinists and Anabaptists. Indeed, these two communities display a common commitment to a uniquely Christian mode of cultural formation. One can find in each group a strong emphasis on the need for specific manifestations of cultural obedience: Anabaptists have insisted, for example, that Christians ought to develop alternative technologies and problem-solving methodologies; and many Calvinists have been strong supporters of separate school systems and political parties. Unlike other conservative Christian movements, then, Anabaptists and Calvinists have insisted on the importance of cultural discipleship; but unlike many other culturally sensitive Christian groups, these two communities have both tended toward nonconformism in their patterns of cultural formation.

But again, the Anabaptists are less likely than the Calvinists to defend their commitment to cultural discipleship by appealing to an account of the original creation. More typically they will gain their inspiration from the Gospels rather than from Genesis.

Even though Anabaptists, then, need not dissent from the notion of an original cultural mandate, they do not want to make as much use of this theme as the Calvinists do. And the fact is that Calvinists build a lot more into the idea of a cultural mandate than would be suggested by the bare statement of this theme. This should not surprise us, since the bare statement of the fact of a cultural mandate supplies us with little by way of normative guidance for cultural involvement. Even if we take it as given that God's command to Adam and Eve to "fill the earth" meant that they should engage in cultural formation, this still leaves us with rather minimal information about the *kind* of cultural formation that God intended. Do large corporations fall within the scope of the original cultural mandate? Do pubs? Or gambling casinos? And what is mandated or permitted for cultural formation under sinful conditions? Prisons? Armies? Law firms that specialize in divorce settlements?

Calvinists tend to have answers to these kinds of questions. And they regularly offer their answers with the conviction that it is possible to discern the Creator's original intentions with regard to such topics. One device for fleshing out that conviction is the Kuyperian "sphere sovereignty" scheme, which posits a plurality of God-ordained spheres of cultural interaction (familial, ecclesial, educational, economic, political, etc.) whose creational integrity must be respected. Significantly, this scheme is regularly set forth as "the *biblical idea* of sphere sovereignty."[12] Calvinists seem to have an unusual facility for finding detailed cultural guidance in the biblical record.

I do not mean to disparage this way of construing the cultural mandate. My own world has more "spheres" and "ordinances" and "natural laws" in it than many of my non-Calvinist friends are willing to tolerate. But it does seem to me that we Kuyperian Calvinists have regularly erred in not being clearer about where the lines fall in our thinking between revelation and speculation *about* revelation. Much of what we have set forth in our talk about "sovereign spheres" and "creation ordinances" seems to me to be helpful speculation. These schemes are interpretive constructs that are at best "suggested" by, or serve as fitting supplements to, the biblical data. They make sense only after one has been captivated by the notion of cultural obedience; and even then they must be set forth with the awareness that there are other attractive ways of organizing the patterns of cultural discipleship.

Even if Anabaptists accepted the very same cultural-theological framework that Calvinists utilize in fleshing out their understanding of the cultural mandate, though, there would still be room for serious disagreement in applying that scheme to the challenges of actual discipleship. Differences can easily arise, for example, in assigning relative weight to this or that area of cultural formation. John Yoder rightly points out that Calvinists tend to treat the civil order as "the quintessence of the cultural mandate." He is also correct in suggesting that there might be other ways of arranging the variety of cultural activities in which the civil order does not occupy the favored position.[13]

The Knowability of the Original Order

It should be obvious by now that there need be no fundamental disagreement between Anabaptists and Calvinists on the importance of a cultural

12. See, for example, the various formulations of the "sphere sovereignty" notion as surveyed by Gordon J. Spykman, "Sphere-Sovereignty in Calvin and the Calvinist Tradition," in *Exploring the Heritage of John Calvin*, ed. David E. Holwerda (Grand Rapids: Baker, 1976), 163-208.

13. Yoder, "Reformed versus Anabaptist," 5.

formation that draws directly on the Scriptures for guidance. The disagreements arise on the question of which part of the Bible is meant to
serve the Christian community as the most important locus for that guidance. The Anabaptists are, as we have seen, wary of the Calvinist reliance
on the Genesis account in this regard. And much of this wariness relates to
an Anabaptist nervousness about the use to which creational themes are
put by the Reformed community.

But another matter of serious disagreement must be acknowledged. It
has to do with our ability to know enough about the original creation to
make effective use of it in our present-day programs of discipleship. This
disagreement about our noetic capacities has a special bearing on questions of what it means to be obedient political disciples under postlapsarian conditions.

It will be helpful here to sketch out some of the details of an Anabaptist way of stating the case. In doing so, I mean to be following the basic
patterns of Yoder's argument as he sets it forth in *The Politics of Jesus*.[14]

Whatever the original prelapsarian political patterns might have
looked like, the argument goes, the Fall has altered the situation in at least
two general ways. First, sinful rebellion changed the general "metaphysical" situation with reference to the ways in which authority gets exercised.
The good "powers" that were meant in some sense to order our political
activity in healthy ways have become *fallen* powers.

Reformed Christians tend to portray the situation as one in which human wills are responding to a creation that is governed by divine ordinances. The basic political problem, then, is that fallen human wills are
failing to respond properly to divine ordinances. To correct the situation,
all we need to do is substitute obedient human wills for disobedient ones.
Thus the Calvinist celebration of "godly magistrates."

But this is too simple, the Anabaptist is insisting. It fails to account for
a more-than-human layer of perversity that is now present in the cosmos:
the perversity of the principalities and powers. Under sinful conditions,
human political action is itself a response to a perverse political environ-

14. For an analysis of how the case I am developing here applies specifically to issues in
political science, see my "Alternative Approaches to Political Science: Toward a More Comprehensive Perspective," in *The Reality of Christian-Learning: Strategies for Faith-Discipline
Integration*, ed. Harold Heie and David L. Wolfe (Grand Rapids: Christian University Press,
1987), 38-52; the essay, in the same volume, to which I am responding in that discussion is
James Skillen, "Can There Be a Christian Approach to Political Science?" 17-37.

ment. Whether there are divine ordinances, then, is beside the point, since our access to them is blocked by the rebellious spiritual powers.

Second, there is, of course, the perversity that does reside in human-kind itself. We are indeed sinners, prone to rebellion against God's rule. We have, then, a double problem in gaining access to original creation ordinances. Our ability to discern such normative patterns is blocked by the more-than-human distortedness of the fallen powers; and it is blocked by our own human perversity.

Indeed, the Anabaptist argues, Calvinism often underestimates the radical effects of sin on our political consciousness. To be sure, Reformed Christianity insists that our political perversity is so deeply embedded that only a redemptive solution will alter the situation. But on the Anabaptist account, the work of Jesus institutes and models a political alternative that stands in stark contrast to the kind of politics that is taken as "normal" in a sinful world. And the fact that Calvinism's political alternative is less radical than that envisioned by Anabaptists means that Reformed Christianity, for all its talk about "total depravity," really does not take the depths of sinful politics seriously enough.

Our political problems are so desperate that nothing less than "the politics of Jesus" will do. The kingdom of Christ restructures the patterns of our communal life so that group organization and decision making come to be modeled on the pattern of mutual servanthood. This is not a pattern that we can hope to implement on any large scale in the contemporary world. It is possible only where human beings have covenanted together to live in conformity to the demands of radical discipleship. Thus the Christian community is called to live in anticipation of a new order that is yet to come in its fullness.

When we live out these patterns of discipleship, are we also reestablishing the politics of the original creation? Anabaptists typically do not worry about the answer to this question. Whether the gospel restores a long-lost order is a topic of useless speculation. We must be content to submit to the rule of Jesus by focusing on the clear teachings of the gospel, so that we can live out an alternative political style in a politically broken world.

Amending Calvinism

How should Calvinist creational theology be amended in the light of these considerations? There is much to say on this subject — too much, indeed, to treat adequately in this chapter. But many of the issues cluster around the need for Reformed Christians to pay much closer attention to the politics of Jesus — and in a way that does not treat the New Testament's witness to the life and ministry of Jesus as little more than a "republishing" of the politics of creation.

This does not mean that Calvinists have to abandon altogether their insistence on the relevance of creational norms for Christian discipleship. We do not arrive at a proper understanding of the proper patterns of Christian political involvement by a naive reading of the Gospel accounts. We need an interpretive framework for sorting out what in those accounts is relevant to our contemporary witness.

That we must have some criteria of relevance in our attempts to understand the politics of Jesus is a point that Yoder himself emphasizes. He does so in two ways. First, he insists that the biblical call to "be like Jesus" is not an unqualified one; there is no general expectation that Christians will be celibates or carpenters or exemplars of "barefoot itinerancy." Yoder finds the proper contours of the *imitatio Christi* in the taking on of those sufferings of Christ that are displayed in "his social nonconformity."[15]

Yoder is underscoring here the importance of looking at the data of Jesus' life and ministry in the light of other biblical materials — his own views on the *imitatio Christi* draw specifically on Pauline teachings. But he also allows that the biblical materials themselves are not adequate for the complexities of contemporary decision making. We cannot hope to gain "a specific biblical ethical content for modern questions"; we must also make use of "broader generalizations, a longer hermeneutic path, and insights from other sources."[16]

I see my own Calvinist reliance on creational themes to be an extension of these themes. This extension may make Professor Yoder and other Anabaptists nervous; but it is important at least to make it clear that the Calvinist importing of creational data is not completely unlike the kinds of moves that Yoder himself makes. A proper devotion to the politics of Jesus requires the use of criteria that enable us to discern what elements of the Gospel materials are especially relevant to contemporary discipleship. It seems to me to be perfectly legitimate to employ in this regard a background understanding — shaped by the study of, and reflection upon, Old Testament materials — of God's overall intentions in calling people to cul-

15. Yoder, *The Politics of Jesus*, 96-97.
16. Yoder, *The Politics of Jesus*, 192.

tural obedience in general and political obedience in particular. Furthermore, as we attempt to formulate those "broader generalizations . . . and insights from other sources" that Yoder insists are necessary components of our operating ethical content, I find it helpful to think of this process as relying upon some sort of — admittedly imperfect — grasp of the original "world order" to which Kuyper referred.

In saying this, however, I do not mean to revert to the notion that Jesus is simply the restorer of the moral order of the primal creation — any more than I want to suggest that Jesus merely exemplifies the righteousness required by the Old Testament law. It is certainly plausible to posit some significant continuities between God's purposes in Eden and Sinai and God's purposes in Jesus' ministry. But the differences are, in the final analysis, very striking — just as the earliest hints of dawn are very different from the full brightness of noonday.

My formulations here obviously still betray my strong Calvinist loyalties. We Reformed Christians are much fonder of continuities and fulfillments than we are of disruptions and novelties. But for all that, I am also convinced that the newness of Jesus' witness needs to be stressed more energetically in Calvinist ethics. While Jesus is indeed the fulfillment of the potentials and yearnings of the older patterns of righteousness, he also radically changes those previous understandings of God's will for human beings.

There is something intriguing about the Scotist notion that the incarnation would have had to occur even if sin had never invaded the creation. The cultural-moral content of the universe has surely been qualitatively transformed by the actual appearance in human flesh of the Righteous One, Emmanuel, who "In olden time didst give the Law / In cloud and majesty and awe." Given the arrival of Jesus in our midst, we can never again be content simply to guide our lives with reference to creational ordinances or revealed laws.

All this applies to political discipleship as well. Whatever normative status we might still attribute to the data of the political deliverances that were received in the ancient wilderness, and the even more ancient Garden, they are far outweighed by the political ministry of the incarnate Servant Ruler. Let me put my point here as clearly as I can: if there is a seeming tension between the older political advice and the kind of political guidance we receive from Jesus — if, for example, the older way seems to encourage us to use the sword in a manner that the Gospels seem to forbid — then the way of wisdom is to follow what we take to be the Gospel way.

As a Calvinist, I am not yet convinced that the "if" clauses that I have just cited are correct. But I continue to struggle with them, with an Anabaptist-type reluctance to trust even the most "sanctified" of those moral and political intuitions that have been shaped by preincarnational patterns of righteousness. The character of this struggle is still not enough, I know, to satisfy the strictest of Anabaptist expectations. But it at least points to the possibility of a Calvinism in which the politics of creation is open to the real possibility of being transformed by the politics of Jesus.

Klaas Schilder as Public Theologian

Klaas Schilder's little book *Christ and Culture* was first published just over a half-century ago. Even though it has been available in English translation for a quarter-century,[1] the book is little known in North America, except for a small circle of Reformed Christians in the Dutch immigrant community. This neglect is unfortunate. Schilder's views on "Christ and culture" are quite pertinent to present-day discussions in North America regarding the proper mode of Christian involvement in public life. My purpose here, then, is to explore the contemporary relevance of Schilder's thought for the North American context.

The Scope of "Public"

The phrase "public theology" has come to denote, in recent decades, a rather vital area of discussion in North American theology. To be sure, the agenda of public theology is not composed of entirely new subject matter. North American Christian thinkers have long been concerned with issues that have fallen within the scope of "Christian social ethics," and they have also addressed topics of political theology, as well as those matters associated with the "church and society" projects of the World Council of

1. K. Schilder, *Christ and Culture*, trans. G. van Rongen and W. Helder (Winnipeg: Premier Printing, 1977).

This essay previously appeared in *Calvin Theological Journal* 28 (November 2003). It is printed here with permission.

Churches. Of course, these other subdisciplines, especially social ethics, are still very much alive. But even these discussions have begun to be conducted with an awareness that there are broader questions about "public" life that are not adequately addressed simply by focusing on ethical, political, or church-and-state topics.

This expanded theological focus parallels — and is to some degree influenced by — an emphasis that has taken hold in the broader American academic community in recent decades. Already in the 1970s the well-known sociologist Peter Berger was complaining that people concerned about normative issues of societal life tended to give too much attention to the relationship of individuals to the political order. In doing so, he said, they failed to recognize the important role of what he called "mediating structures." If we are to avoid the twin evils of individualism on the one hand and statism on the other, he argued, we must pay attention to the ways we can strengthen a whole variety of associational patterns — neighborhood organizations, youth clubs, service groups, churches, and families themselves — that can provide a buffer zone between the state and the individual, thus providing crucial resources for character formation.[2]

Since the 1970s, an important group of scholars has taken up, with similar concerns, the cause of "civil society." A recent prominent case in point is the work of Harvard political scientist Robert Putnam. In a much discussed 1993 essay, "Bowling Alone," and in a 2001 book with the same title,[3] he bemoaned the decline of participation in "voluntary societies" in North American culture. His title, for example, is a reference to the fact that while more Americans are bowling than ever before, fewer people are joining bowling leagues than in the past. When people "bowl alone," they do not sit around and eat together during their bowling activities, and there is a significant loss, Putnam argues, in the "social capital" associated with camaraderie and team spirit. The decline in these types of social bonds means that individuals do not develop the qualities of public character that are the preconditions for a healthy participation in civil society. When this pattern prevails, the dangers posed by Berger's individualism-or-statism alternatives are acute.

These same concerns are very much on the minds of the Christian

2. Peter Berger, *Facing Up to Modernity: Excursions in Society, Politics, and Religion* (New York: Basic Books, 1977), 140.

3. Robert Putnam, "Bowling Alone," *Journal of Democracy* 6, no. 1 (January 1995): 65-78; for the book version, see Robert Putnam, *Bowling Alone: The Collapse and Revival of American Community* (New York: Simon and Schuster, 2001).

participants in the public theology discussions. By choosing to focus on "public" life, they are recognizing that there is a vast and complex territory that lies between the individual and the state. They want to emphasize the importance of those contexts for human association that extend beyond the realm of kinship, but are not yet — or at least they ought *not* to be — swallowed up by the "political." And they are especially interested in how the Christian community can effectively address this broader public agenda.

An Important Debate

These public theology discussions have given rise to significant disagreements. An intense debate, for example, has been waged over the question of the kind of language Christians may use in addressing issues of public life. One thinker who has stirred up much controversy is Duke University's Stanley Hauerwas, who has drawn on the Anabaptist tradition to insist on the importance of "radical discipleship" communities that stand over against the status quo of public culture. Hauerwas has been especially outspoken in his criticisms of the notion that Christians can employ a "neutral" public language, on the assumption that terms like "justice" and "peace" are understandable from a variety of worldview perspectives. That assumption, Hauerwas insists, is fundamentally misguided. How can we as Christians give meaning to such terms, he asks, "apart from the life and death of Jesus of Nazareth"? Only the biblical witness to Jesus' ministry "gives content to our faith, judges any institutional embodiment of our faith, and teaches us to be suspicious of any political slogan that does not need God to make itself credible."[4]

Hauerwas's critics have responded by charging him with a much too narrow theological framework. James Gustafson, for example, has accused Hauerwas and his sympathizers of succumbing to "the sectarian temptation," a pattern of thinking that fails to acknowledge a robust theology of creation.[5] A similar critique has been set forth by Max Stackhouse, who defends a common public discourse by arguing that from a Christian per-

---

4. Stanley Hauerwas and William Willimon, *Resident Aliens: Life in the Christian Colony* (Nashville: Abingdon, 1989), 23.

5. James M. Gustafson, "The Sectarian Temptation: Reflections on Theology, the Church and the University," *Catholic Theological Society of America Proceedings* 40 (1985): 88.

spective "human life has, at its root, a very profound *logos,* rooted in *theos,* that makes it possible for Jews, Christians, Hindus, Muslims and humanists to talk reasonably with one another and to live together in a society governed by a modicum of justice. Further, we can, in some measure, talk across boundaries and more or less discern what is valid and not valid in what others say. And we expect others to understand us and to challenge us when we do not make sense."[6]

More recently, though, Hauerwas has actually been criticized from the other end of the spectrum for *conceding* too much to the possibility of a common language. Robert W. Brimlow highlights some comments in Hauerwas's writings where he seems to allow for some sort of "translation" of particularistic Christian language into terms that make sense to non-Christians. These concessions, argues Brimlow, blunt the force of Hauerwas's emphasis on radical discipleship.[7] Christians, Brimlow insists, "are called to the margins; we are called to be weak and separate and to view ourselves as such. We therefore must turn our back on all that is incompatible with the Gospel."[8]

This brief sketch does not do justice to the complexities of this important debate. But it should be sufficient to demonstrate that these contemporary American Christian thinkers are exploring issues that have long been argued about — indeed, often with quite divisive consequences — within the Dutch Reformed community. Those long-standing debates were much on Schilder's mind as he wrote *Christ and Culture.* And the perspective he spells out in that short book deserves careful consideration in our present context.

The Relevance of Reformed Thought

Little attention has been paid in these recent American debates to the nuances of classical Reformed thought. To be sure, some of the key figures — Gustafson and Stackhouse are important cases in point — see themselves as appropriating specifically Reformed themes in rejecting the perspective

6. Max L. Stackhouse, "Liberalism Dispatched vs. Liberalism Engaged," *Christian Century* 112, no. 29 (October 18, 1995): 963.

7. Robert W. Brimlow, "Solomon's Porch: The Church as Sectarian Ghetto," in *The Church as Counterculture,* ed. Michael L. Budde and Robert W. Brimlow (Albany: State University of New York Press, 2000), 115.

8. Brimlow, "Solomon's Porch," 123.

of Hauerwas and others. But in offering their critiques of "the sectarian temptation," Gustafson and Stackhouse choose to make their case with reference to what they see as a venerable tradition of Christian political thought that they associate with a broad range of thinkers, a group that includes, but is by no means limited to, the Reformed contribution. For example, in responding to Hauerwas's sustained attack on the "liberal" tradition of Christian political thought, Max Stackhouse offers this brief account of the sort of liberal perspective that he wants to defend:

> Such liberal views are rooted in the Bible and have been embraced by Augustine, Thomas, Luther, Calvin, Wesley and Edwards — and, for that matter, by Locke, Kant, Weber, Troeltsch, Whitehead and the Niebuhrs. This kind of liberal Christian believes that Christianity offers the best account of why it is that all humans can come to this table of conversation ("general revelation," *justitia originalis,* the gift of reason in the *imago dei,* all distorted but not erased by sin). And this kind of liberal Christian also believes that one of the key tasks of the church is to continually rediscover, extend and thereby refine our understanding of this capacity so that it may help sort through the religious stories, principles and actions that people use to see which are most adequate to God and for holy living.[9]

While I will not go further into the details of this particular debate about the appropriateness of Christians employing a neutral public discourse, enough has been said, I think, to see that the differences come down, in rough terms, to this set of alternatives: the reformulation of a classic Anabaptist-type perspective for application to contemporary pluralist democracy, on the one hand, and, on the other, a broad "common ground" framework that draws on a variety of resources in the Christian tradition to reinforce an active liberal Protestant engagement in the public arena.

What does a confessionally Reformed outlook have to say by way of assessing the issues at stake in this debate? That is the question I will be wrestling with in what follows, with a special focus on the case that Schilder makes in *Christ and Culture.* But before I look at the specifics of Schilder's perspective, I must lay out the limits I have set for myself in pursuing this exploration.

9. Stackhouse, "Liberalism Dispatched," 963.

First, it will be very clear here that I am discussing these issues as a *North American* Reformed Christian. While I have a keen interest in the various theological perspectives that have emerged within the Reformed community in the Netherlands, I still view the interactions between those diverse schools of thought from a considerable distance. I spend most of my time in a theological and spiritual environment that is best described as broadly evangelical, and there are very few people in my day-to-day world who have even the faintest grasp of some of the issues that have been debated with great passion on Dutch soil. In such a context, I am forced to be very selective in applying lessons that I have learned from studying the Dutch scene to my North American context.

Second, I do take a *sympathetic* approach to the American debate that I have just briefly described; I am convinced, for example, that important and helpful points have been made on both sides of the argument. In this regard I know that I am assessing the issues in a spirit quite different from Schilder in discussing the options presented. I think it quite likely that he would have rather quickly found reasons simply to dismiss both options as deeply defective. But I am convinced that it is possible both to approach the North American debate with sympathy while at the same time insisting that some key insights offered by Schilder point to an alternative way of seeing the situation — a perspective that should be taken seriously by public theologians in North America.

Third, I am drawing on these insights from Schilder as an American *Kuyperian.* Abraham Kuyper is one person from the Dutch Calvinist context who is familiar to the larger Christian community in North America. But the awareness is of a very general sort. For example, in October 2000 the well-known sociologist Alan Wolfe — himself a secularist thinker — published a much discussed essay in the mass circulation magazine *Atlantic Monthly,* in which he discussed the emergence of a strong evangelical scholarship, especially at places like Calvin College, Wheaton College, and Fuller Theological Seminary.[10] Wolfe singled out Abraham Kuyper's influence as an important factor in this development. But Kuyper's thought was described only in very general terms, as encouraging serious Christian intellectual activity in pietist environs where the life of the mind has often been neglected.

While there are Christians in North America outside of the Dutch-

---

10. Wolfe's article can be found on the Web at http://www.theatlantic.com/issues/2000/10/wolfe.htm.

American subculture who do know some of the more specific details about Kuyper's perspective, they certainly are quite ignorant of many of the aspects of Kuyper's thought that have been much debated in the Netherlands. Even most of the American scholars who would happily identify themselves as Kuyperians would be hard put to give an account of what Kuyper thought about such matters as ecclesiastical hierarchicalism and presumptive regeneration. "Kuyperianism" in the American context is a label that has come to stand for some very general themes; it is associated with such things as an appreciation for the "not-one-square-inch" manifesto regarding the kingship of Jesus, a broad acceptance of the idea of sphere sovereignty, and a commitment to the integration of faith and learning.

Indeed, one of the ironies about this situation is that some of the specific formulations that American Christians associate with Kuyper's influence may actually be closer to Schilder's thought than to Kuyper's. I must confess, for example, that after many years of employing the notion of the *cultural mandate* in my own writings, with the confident sense that in doing so I was propagating an important Kuyperian theme, I was quite surprised to discover N. H. Gootjes's observation that this term "was in all probability coined by Schilder."[11] And I was even more surprised to learn from Gootjes's discussion that another view that I had long attributed to Kuyper, namely, that the Christian community is called to produce its own uniquely God-honoring patterns of culture, is actually a position developed by Schilder as an alternative to Kuyper's perspective. Since culture was for Kuyper, as Gootjes points out, intimately linked to common grace, Kuyper was not inclined to see special grace as producing a distinctive *culture* as such.[12]

Schilder and Kuyper

While Schilder was frequently quite critical of Kuyper, it seems clear that he often meant to be appropriating some Kuyperian themes against others in Kuyper's thought. For example, in a 1951 speech to a young women's

11. N. H. Gootjes, "Schilder on Christ and Culture," in *Always Obedient: Essays on the Teachings of Dr. Klaas Schilder*, ed. J. Geertsema (Phillipsburg, N.J.: Presbyterian and Reformed, 1995), 35.
12. Gootjes, "Schilder," 39.

convention Schilder encouraged his *vrijgemaakt* hearers not to worry if they found themselves isolated, because of their convictions, from the general trends in Dutch culture. Indeed, he insisted, Reformed Christians should see that sort of marginalization as a sign of faithfulness. "If our numbers do not shrink over the whole world," he observed, "we should ask ourselves whether we have ever really comprehended Christ's eschatological discourses and properly understood the Revelation of John."[13] It is interesting that Schilder backed his own words here by appealing to Kuyper's authority. Kuyper rightly recognized, said Schilder, that only when the antithesis between belief and unbelief is stated as clearly as possible can we "see to it that the half-hearted hybrid hangers-on leave as soon as possible, shaking their heads."[14]

Most important, though, are the words Schilder used to conclude these observations: "Thus Kuyper in 1878."[15] What Schilder obviously wanted to signal here was that he was invoking the authority of the "earlier" Kuyper. The need to think about "earlier" versus "later" in assessing Kuyper's various comments about church-world relationships is explained by the Calvin College historian James Bratt:

> Significantly, Kuyper's appeal to the antithesis peaked in the first half of his career, the period of institutional formation, and declined in his later years, when Calvinists had to take their share of managing public life. The concept served [in the earlier phase of his career] a crucial strategic purpose: besides showing Reformed skeptics that cultural activity did not endanger purity of faith, it fortified group identity during a potentially threatening transition. Certainly it must have mobilized many Seceders, living as they did under the memory of separation.[16]

In the later stages of Kuyper's public leadership he was less inclined to emphasize the radical antithesis between belief and unbelief. It is clear that Schilder saw this as a sign of a weakening in Kuyper's commitment to Reformed orthodoxy. Bratt, on the other hand, seems to applaud the devel-

13. Klaas Schilder, "Your Ecumenical Task," in Rudolf Van Reest, *Schilder's Struggle for the Unity of the Church*, trans. Theodore Plantinga (Neerlandia, Alberta: Inheritance Publications, 1990), appendix III, p. 452.

14. Schilder, "Your Ecumenical Task," 453-54.

15. Schilder, "Your Ecumenical Task," 454.

16. James D. Bratt, *Dutch Calvinism in Modern America: A History of a Conservative Subculture* (Grand Rapids: Eerdmans, 1984), 19.

opment. He insists that the strong antithetical thinking of the earlier Kuyper, while important for gaining the Reformed community's trust in Kuyper's cultural leadership, also had connections to Calvinism's "darker legacy," for "few doctrines could match the antithesis at fostering spiritual arrogance or abusing principial analysis."[17]

I agree with Bratt that there are some dangers associated with a Reformed perspective on culture that leans heavily on the idea of the antithesis. But I also worry much about the dangers posed by the emphases of the later Kuyper — not the least of them being a triumphalist spirit and a too-easy accommodation to the patterns of non-Christian thought and action. Schilder was very aware of these dangers. And the case he makes in spelling out his own alternative perspective seems at times — as I read his writings within the contemporary North American context — to have some important similarities to the Anabaptist-type thinking of Stanley Hauerwas and others. This factor alone makes it interesting to consider what Schilder might have to say to Reformed Christians in America who take the "public theology" debates seriously.

Schilder's *Christ and Culture* is well under one hundred pages in length, but even so I will not touch on all the matters he treats. Schilder's tone is terse, and it is clear that he has many controversies on his mind as he develops his case. And before he actually gets around to discussing cultural activity as such, he covers much theological territory, especially issues of Christology. This is not the sort of book that is designed to appeal to American readers, especially those who are unfamiliar with Schilder's theological context. Schilder needs an American "translator-interpreter," someone capable of the difficult task of recontextualizing his thoughts for a new situation. My effort here will not fulfill that purpose. But I hope I can at least provide some hints as to how the larger task might be accomplished.

My modest effort here will treat only two basic themes in his discussion. First, I will look at the ways in which his views give some support — more than most American thinkers with Reformed sympathies, including American Kuyperians, would be inclined to offer — to the Anabaptist-type cultural strategy proposed by Hauerwas and others. But then I will look at how such emphases for Schilder fit into a larger perspective in which there are at least some hints toward a theological rationale for a broader cultural task.

---

17. Bratt, *Dutch Calvinism*, 19.

The "Anabaptist" Corrective

I begin with a provocative observation that Schilder makes in the last three sentences of his book: "Blessed is my *wise* ward-elder," he writes, "who does his home visiting in the right way. He is a *cultural* force, although he may not be aware of it. Let them mock him: they do not know what they are doing, those cultural gadabouts of the other side!"[18]

The implication here is clear. The ordinary work of the local congregation, conducted without conscious attention to any mandate to engage in cultural transformation, is in fact a crucial cultural activity — more important from a Christian perspective than the efforts of those who want directly to shape the larger culture in its many dimensions.

In the recent North American debates Stanley Hauerwas has made claims that are very similar to the one Schilder is setting forth in this comment. In one of his many provocative formulations, Hauerwas has argued that the church does not *have* a social ethic, the church *is* a social ethic. "Put starkly," says Hauerwas, "the first social ethical task of the church is to be the church."[19] And then he explains further, using examples that parallel Schilder's reference to his faithful elder, that the church best serves the larger culture when it "sets its own agenda. It does this first by having the patience amid the injustice and violence of this world to care for the widow, the poor, and the orphan. Such care, from the world's perspective, may seem to contribute little to the cause of justice, yet it is our conviction that unless we take the time for such care neither we nor the world can know what justice looks like."[20]

The fact that Schilder's views so closely parallel a contemporary American perspective that claims inspiration from the Anabaptist tradition leads us to ask about the relationship between Schilder's perspective and an Anabaptist one. Needless to say, Schilder would not likely appreciate the comparison. Calvinists have harbored a long-standing hostility toward Anabaptist life and thought — so much so that the accusation of Anabaptist leanings has been one of the more serious insults Calvinists have used in debating with each other.

My own conviction is that this deep-seated animosity toward Anabap-

18. Schilder, *Christ and Culture*, 86.
19. Stanley Hauerwas, *The Peaceable Kingdom: A Primer in Social Ethics* (Notre Dame, Ind.: University of Notre Dame Press, 1983), 99.
20. Hauerwas, *The Peaceable Kingdom*, 100.

tists on the part of Calvinists has to be understood as an "intrafamily" matter. I have argued this at some length elsewhere,[21] so I will not repeat the details of my case here. But to briefly summarize: it seems clear to me that the Reformed community's frustrations with the Anabaptists — beginning with John Calvin's experience in Switzerland — had much to do with the ways in which the Anabaptists have accused Calvinists of inconsistency on two important points.[22] The first matter has to do with the Reformed emphasis on church discipline. Noting that Calvin and his followers accused the Lutherans and Catholics of laxity on this matter, the Anabaptists boasted that they took discipline far more seriously than the Reformed.

The second issue is the church's relationship to the larger culture. Here too the Anabaptists ridiculed the Calvinists for claiming to believe in total depravity while regularly finding patterns of accommodation with sinful culture. They especially singled out for criticism the Calvinists' willingness to endorse, and even to encourage an active involvement in, the political system of the larger culture. Obviously, the Anabaptists were most upset by the Calvinists' willingness to use the "sword" in their political and military involvements. But even apart from the concern about overt violence, there is a very basic Anabaptist objection to what they saw as a Calvinist eagerness to compromise with the political patterns of a sinful culture.

These Anabaptist-type criticisms of Calvinism as such can be found in Schilder's writings when *as* a Calvinist he criticizes other Reformed Christians for their understanding of the proper strategies for Christian cultural involvement. If my analysis of the "intrafamilial" character of Reformed-Anabaptist polemics is correct, then this should not surprise us. Schilder is attempting to avoid the very inconsistencies that the Anabaptists have pointed to in much Calvinist practice: he insists on rigorous discipline within the church, in order that the people of God can live out their obedient patterns of cultural life; and he wants to do full justice to the reality of the antithesis between believing and unbelieving cultural activity.

I noted earlier that Stanley Hauerwas himself has been criticized for toning down some of his own antitheticalist comments with his suggestion that the particularist language of Christian discipleship can be "translated"

---

21. Cf. my *He Shines in All That's Fair: Culture and Common Grace* (Grand Rapids: Eerdmans, 2001), 20-24.

22. For much evidence for what I am suggesting here, see Willem Balke, *Calvin and the Anabaptist Radicals*, trans. William Heynen (Grand Rapids: Eerdmans, 1981).

into a less overtly Christian public discourse. Hauerwas's motive here is laudable. He obviously senses an obligation to contribute directly to the well-being of the larger human community. The problem, however, is that he does not provide a clear theological basis for fulfilling this obligation — a defect that leaves him open, as we noted earlier, to the charge by other Anabaptists that he is being inconsistent with his basic premises. From a Reformed perspective, Hauerwas's problems are endemic to Anabaptist thought, where there is a reluctance to acknowledge the cultural importance of the doctrine of creation. It is a significant benefit of Schilder's thought that while he too senses the larger cultural obligation, he also provides a nuanced creational basis for taking the obligation seriously.

The "Abstinence" Option

Schilder has little use for Christians who choose simply to ignore the problems that plague the larger human community. He has very harsh words for that kind of "Christian [cultural] abstinence" that "originates in resentment, laziness, diffidence, slackness, or narrow-mindedness"; such, he says, "is sin before God."[23] But he also insists that there is a "heroic" abstinence, and this is the strategy he commends. The right kind of cultural abstinence happens, he argues, when "Christian people [are] maintaining their colleges, supporting their missionaries, and caring for the needy who were left them by Christ, . . . [and] are doing a thousand other works of divine obligation" that make it difficult for them to perform those highly visible works of "cultural transformation" for which Kuyper and others have called. Schilder does not question the legitimacy of a broader cultural calling, but other urgent[24] needs in the present situation it "finds its limits and legitimation in, e.g., Matthew 19:12, where Christ speaks about those 'that make themselves eunuchs for the Kingdom of heaven's sake' and not in order to avoid this Kingdom."[25] This self-limiting pattern is not anticulture as such, but it does restrict the territory in which we carry out our cultural activity.

23. My comments in this section closely follow my treatment of Schilder's views in *He Shines in All That's Fair*, 78-80.

24. The English translation of Schilder's text is misleading here. It has him citing the present "emergency," whereas he is actually pointing to the urgency *(nood)* of other pressing concerns in the life and mission of the church.

25. Schilder, *Christ and Culture*, 69-70.

There is much to be said in favor of this vow-of-abstinence approach to cultural involvement. It certainly can be quite legitimate for a specific Calvinist community — or an Anabaptist one for that matter — to restrict its cultural tasks to the maintenance of its own "internal" life. Just as individuals have specific callings, so do particular Christian communities. Schilder's use of the image of eunuchs for the sake of the kingdom in this regard, then, is a helpful one.

We must ask, though, whether this particular vow of cultural abstinence is required of *all* Christian churches. Once we admit that the decision to abstain from a broader cultural involvement is a special vow — the acceptance of a vocation to do without something that is in other circumstances, and for other Christians, a worthy thing to pursue — then we must ask what it is about our own present circumstances that calls for this pattern of abstinence. It is clear, for example, that the Lord called his people in Old Testament times to work for the well-being of the larger Babylonian society in which he had placed them during the time of their exile: "But seek the welfare of the city where I have sent you into exile, and pray to the LORD on its behalf, for in its welfare you will find your welfare" (Jer. 29:7).

Was the larger cultural calling more urgent in those ancient times than it is in our present situation? Is there something unique about our contemporary context that requires all of us to be cultural eunuchs? We can understand how, for example, Schilder's wartime experiences, where he hid for months at a time from the Nazis, might have led him to think in terms of a temporary reordering of the church's priorities. But it is difficult to know why his specific recommendations ought to apply to the whole Christian community under present cultural conditions, or even to the whole *Calvinist* community.

The "Restraint" Promise

I do not want to make too much, however, of this abstinence theme in Schilder's discussion. If he means to be suggesting that the church of the present age, both in Europe and in North America, must pledge abstinence until the Lord's return, then I believe he is simply wrong. But I do not see this as the main thrust of his account. At the very least, it is not the main thrust of what we can reappropriate from his reflections as we seek to be faithful to the Lord's cultural call in our present situation.

A recognition of the possibility of an abstinence vow can be a helpful thing to keep in mind, though, for our contemporary context. I have already observed that many present-day "public theology" discussants seem to give the impression that the Anabaptist perspective, with its strong antitheticalist tones, is the only plausible alternative to a liberal perspective that, selectively drawing on Reformed and other sources, emphasizes commonness and a neutral public discourse in the larger public arena. In arguing for the abstinence vow, Schilder is not insisting that cultural withdrawal is a matter of nonnegotiable principle. He gives full expression to the cultural mandate in his discussion — indeed, at points he does so in a way that exceeds the eloquence that many of us associate with Kuyper's manifestos on this subject. Much of what he says seems designed to inspire the Christian community to move into the larger cultural arena with great enthusiasm. But when he suddenly endorses the abstinence strategy, it is not because he is convinced that a larger cultural program is illegitimate as such, but rather because of his gloomy assessment of the historical circumstances in which he finds himself.

Actually, Schilder's cultural pessimism is shaped at least in part by the acceptance of an apocalyptic reading of the contemporary scene. Schilder observes, for example, that during the course of history God restrains Satan, so that the proclaiming of the gospel can on occasion "penetrate very deeply even into the circles of the unbelievers." But while "[t]his restraint is never completely lacking in this world," neither "will it be of a constant measure" throughout the course of time. Indeed, we can be sure, he says, that it "will decrease to a minimum at the end of time," when "any *status quo* existing between the Church and the world will be denounced — from both sides — also in cultural life, even precisely there. Then the whole world — except God's elect — will crowd together around the Antichrist."[26]

I have no quarrel with Schilder's eschatology as he states it here. But I do think it is risky to base our overall counsel to the church on cultural matters on firm assessments regarding where we are in relationship to the end-time events. My own strong inclination is to rely on the "restraint" promise, described so clearly by Schilder, in the hope that by our efforts God's Word can indeed in our own day — to repeat his words — "penetrate very deeply even into the circles of the unbelievers." At the same time, of course, we must pray for the discernment to know when the time actu-

26. Schilder, *Christ and Culture*, 57.

ally arrives when we, the Lord's people, must resist with all our strength the power of the Antichrist. And we best arm ourselves against this day, I am convinced, by looking for special signs of lawlessness, of rebellion — overt or subtle — against God's creating and redeeming purposes in the world. These signs include the broader patterns of lawlessness that show a disregard for that which God deeply cares about: racial justice, the plight of the poor, fidelity in human relationships, the dignity of the nonhuman created order. As long as we prepare ourselves to oppose this lawlessness wherever and whenever it appears, a sensitivity to warnings about the future can serve to strengthen us for faithfulness to the gospel.

Our Human "Being-Together"

Not only does Schilder hold out the hope that we can, in at least some historical situations, proclaim the Word in such a way that it will "penetrate very deeply even into the circles of the unbelievers" — he also gives us a helpful way of thinking about the cultural goals we are hoping to promote in such proclamation. There does exist, he tells us, "a *sunousia*, a being-together, among all men." This is not to be confused, of course, with "cultural *koinonia*," which is a bond that "can only be achieved wherever the same nature is directed towards a common goal through love for the same basic principles and wherever the same interests are promoted in common faith and hope and love."[27] But neither can we ignore *sunousia* by insisting that *koinonia* is our exclusive Christian concern.

Schilder's *sunousia* is roughly equivalent to the "public" or "civil society" themes in the recent American discussions. His comments about the importance of sustaining *sunousia,* the being-together of Christians with members of the larger human community, are scattered and few in number, and they are always closely paired with warnings against conformity to the cultural patterns of the sinful age. But for all of that, he does make these comments, and when he makes them it is clear that he sees the sustaining of *sunousia* as an important Christian obligation. We can wish he had said more on the subject, and in the absence of further amplification by him we have to work a bit to tease out his meaning. But in doing so, we can be confident that we are spelling out ideas that — however reluctant he was to treat them at length — are clearly implied by what he says.

27. Schilder, *Christ and Culture,* 55.

Schilder's warnings against cultural compromise typically draw on the Bible's apocalyptic writings. For example, he argues, citing Revelation 18:4, that the church is called by the Lord to come out of Babylon. But he is quick to add that this does not mean that Christians are "to go out of the world" as such. Continuing with the imagery of Revelation 18, he observes that refusing to associate with Babylon-as-harlot "does not mean to condemn womanhood, to renounce nature." Here Schilder places "Ezekiel 16" in parentheses, alluding to the way in which the Lord, while condemning Israel for her harlotry, nonetheless remembers in mercy her original created womanhood — her underlying "nature." And then he offers this summary statement about our relationship to Babylon: "Not to be partakers of her sins does not mean: along with her creaturehood to deny or abdicate the *sunousia*."[28] Thus "the tension between our lot of being in contact with men *(sunousia)* and our daily duty to fellowship *(koinonia)*."[29]

These comments provide the framework for understanding Schilder's highly nuanced assessment of the cultural achievements of unredeemed humanity — at points he even speaks of their "contributions" in this regard. In making these assessments, he has no use for the Kuyperian conception of common grace. For Schilder, grace is always a saving power, and the only sense in which it is "common" is that it is shared by all who truly belong to Christ.[30]

There is, however, a "common tempering" in God's dealing with the human race as a whole. This means that "[l]ife is not yet split up into the forms of hell and heaven. The godless are still prevented in their cultural labour from ecstatically raging against God in the paroxysm of satanism, although this is in direct line with their hidden desire." At the same time, the elect are also being tempered by God, in that they are presently being "prevented from doing adequately what is in their line," in order that the Lord might pursue "the goals of the history of salvation and revelation."[31] In our present situation, "nothing is fully developed and consummated, nothing is mature as yet."[32]

In this "interim-of-the-interim" time,[33] there are still "small remnants" of the original createdness that can be discerned in the cultural ac-

28. Schilder, *Christ and Culture*, 82.

29. Schilder, *Christ and Culture*, 83.

30. Schilder, *Christ and Culture*, 47.

31. Schilder, *Christ and Culture*, 57.

32. Schilder, *Christ and Culture*, 56.

33. Schilder, *Christ and Culture*, 58.

tivities of unredeemed humanity. Schilder's concession here is obviously grudging. He is not inclined to speak, for example, in the sorts of glowing terms that Calvin used when he wrote of an unredeemed humankind who, "though fallen and perverted from its wholeness, is nevertheless clothed and ornamented with God's excellent gifts."[34] But Schilder does allow that "these residues . . . are still able, according to the scheme of development and restraint that Christ's Sender maintains in the Christological progress of all history, to instigate new cultural contributions as it pleases Him. This is an instigation the possibility of which was already given in the paradisal world, and which has its *kairos* only because Christ has His own aim and intention with the world and reserved it unto the fires of judgment day."[35]

The case that Schilder is articulating here — admittedly, only in broad outline — provides important correctives to most of the existing options in contemporary public theology. Unlike the liberal appropriation of creational and Logos motifs in support of a Christian public involvement that makes much of our human commonness, Schilder insists on the radical sinfulness of the cultural patterns in our fallen world. But unlike the recontextualized Anabaptist perspective of the contemporary defenders of a radical Christian communal identity, Schilder attempts to do justice to the continuing display of God's creating purposes, acknowledging the vestiges of "nature" even in the midst of Babylonian corruption. The church must work diligently at developing its own "internal" cultural life, but it must at the same time recognize its cultural obligations to the larger human community. Schilder's strong — and decidedly un-Anabaptist — creational emphasis is clear, even if he expresses it somewhat reluctantly: "The *koinonia* is given us by Christ, the *sunousia* comes from God the Creator."[36]

I am convinced that there is much here that is helpful, even crucial, for contemporary Reformed thinkers to consider. But the perspective also must be developed further, spelling out implications for the purpose of addressing contemporary issues of public life. I am confident that this can be done, and I will illustrate this conviction briefly by offering one important example where I believe we can extend Schilder's thought by drawing on some hints that are present in his discussion.

---

34. John Calvin, *Institutes of the Christian Religion,* ed. John T. McNeill, trans. Ford Lewis Battles (Philadelphia: Westminster, 1960), 2.2.15, p. 273.

35. Schilder, *Christ and Culture,* 59.

36. Schilder, *Christ and Culture,* 55.

Public Piety

Not too long after the destruction of the World Trade Center by Muslim terrorists, three Michigan congregations of the Protestant Reformed Churches cosponsored a service in response to the tragic events that had occurred in New York City. According to the brief report on this service in the Protestant Reformed magazine the *Standard Bearer,* the pastors who led the service reflected on these "three areas of concern for the Christian. How do we show concern for God's people who may have suffered directly from the tragedy? How do Christians put those events into the broad picture of our Lord's return? And how do we deal with the feelings of fear we see in ourselves as well as in our children?"[37]

What is obviously absent in this list of concerns is anything having to do with the *non-Christians* whose lives were profoundly affected by the terrible events that had occurred. To be sure, this is a brief news report, and it may not tell us all the subjects that were addressed in this service. And it may well be that other Protestant Reformed gatherings dealt with other sorts of concerns relating to the September 11 tragedy. If so, though, these other matters were not reported in the *Standard Bearer* — and my own perusal of subsequent issues of that magazine revealed no other significant references to the September 11 events. It is not mere quibbling, then, at least to point to the fact that in this brief news report the sole emphasis is on the concerns of believers: those elect persons who suffered because of these events; the ways in which God's people should interpret these events in relation to the end-times; and the fearfulness of Christian families who viewed the destruction from a distance.

The Protestant Reformed Churches were established, under the leadership of Herman Hoeksema, because of their refusal to accept the Kuyperian understanding of common grace as it was adopted by the Christian Reformed synod's doctrinal statement on the subject in 1924. Hoeksema and his followers have consistently resisted any notion of an attitude of divine favor toward nonelect people. What other Calvinists interpret as gracious divine gifts to the reprobate, the Protestant Reformed view as providing opportunities for the unredeemed to extend their rebellion against God.[38]

37. http://www.prca.org/standard_bearer/2001oct15.html#NewsChurches.
38. A detailed exposition of the Protestant Reformed dissent from the Kuyperian perspective can be found in Herman Hoeksema, *The Protestant Reformed Churches in America:*

Schilder adopts a similar viewpoint. The appearance of a common cultural giftedness, he insists, is due to the fact that believer and nonbeliever alike are working within the same creational context. The similarity of their cultural labors "is not caused by the similarity of their diverging minds but by that of the stiff, recalcitrant material"; using this same material, they create very different products: one a building for worship and the other a place for revelry, "but both of them go for their clay to the same pit and for their marble to the same quarry."[39]

I have no fundamental quarrel with Schilder's account here. Even though I have argued in my own writings that there are significant benefits to be found in common grace theology, I have also expressed sympathy for Henry Van Til's proposal that it is best "to place the term 'common grace' in quotation marks," on the grounds that, as Van Til insists, it seems risky to equate the very real "beneficent goodness of God to the non-elect sinners" with the redemptive "blessings which God bestows upon elect sinners in and through Jesus Christ, the Mediator."[40] Van Til's worries about a straightforward endorsement of the idea of common *grace* are grounded in genuine worries — ones that I share — about some dangerous tendencies in common grace theology.

But for all that, I also worry about tendencies that I see in the straightforward *denial* of common grace. And these tendencies are displayed clearly in the limited agenda addressed by the Protestant Reformed pastors in their worship service. Most Reformed Christians, when they witness the horrors of human suffering, experience a deep sadness on behalf of the victims and their families, *regardless of whether those victims are Christian or not.* And when they witness the bravery of firefighters, police, military, and ordinary citizens, in their efforts to rescue the wounded and the dying in situations of that sort, most Reformed Christians admire those efforts and thank God for these displays of human goodness, *regardless of whether those performing the heroic acts are Christians or not.*

What should we make theologically of these Christian responses? Are we being confused in experiencing sadness and admiration for what hap-

---

Their Origin, Early History, and Doctrine (Grand Rapids: First Protestant Reformed Church, 1936); for a more recent account, see Herman Hanko, *For Thy Truth's Sake: A Doctrinal History of the Protestant Reformed Churches* (Grandville, Mich.: Reformed Free Publishing Association, 2000).

39. Schilder, *Christ and Culture*, 56.

40. Henry R. Van Til, *The Calvinistic Concept of Culture* (Grand Rapids: Baker, 1959), 244.

pens in the lives of nonredeemed people? Does God *disapprove* of what we experience? I believe that these are extremely important questions. They have to do with the kinds of character traits — the spiritual dispositions, if you wish — that we should cultivate as people who are called to be holy in our thoughts, conduct, and desires (see 1 Pet. 1:13-16).

Kuyper does seem to be aware of the need for developing what we might think of as a theology of *public piety*. The "interior" mode of common grace "is operative," he argues, "wherever civic virtue, a sense of domesticity, natural love, the practice of human virtue, the improvement of the public conscience, integrity, mutual loyalty among people, and a feeling for piety leaven life."[41] Kuyper clearly means to encourage the cultivation of these qualities in the redeemed as well as the unredeemed. And it is precisely these traits that I am saying ought to characterize our Christian responses to tragic events like the New York City attack.

Schilder does not address such concerns in his discussion. But he drops phrases on occasion that could be developed for what might be called a theology of public piety. In a passage, for example, where he is emphasizing the central role of the church for cultural formation, he observes that the church is "the mother of believers" who gives birth to a renewed humanity that is called to "bear the burdens of the whole world."[42] This church, he further explains, "can in a national community proclaim the norms of God in the language of the time and place concerned and so make known to that community what riches can, according to its own nature, be developed in its life, and how this can and should be done."[43]

Again, these are at best hints. But they are worth exploring. What does it mean for us to "bear the burdens of the whole world"? How can we as believers, especially in times of a national crisis, speak to the larger human community "in the language of the time and place" about "riches" that are associated with the "nature" of that larger community?

John Calvin's advice to civil magistrates is provocative in this regard. When a nation's leaders are thinking about going to war, he says, not only should they take great care "not to be carried away with headlong anger, or be seized with hatred, or burn with implacable severity," but they should also "have pity on the common nature in the one whose special fault they

---

41. Abraham Kuyper, "Common Grace," in *Abraham Kuyper: A Centennial Reader,* ed. James D. Bratt (Grand Rapids: Eerdmans, 1998), 181.

42. Schilder, *Christ and Culture,* 79.

43. Schilder, *Christ and Culture,* 80.

are punishing."[44] If this "pity on the common nature" is an appropriate attitude to cultivate toward the kind of person whom Calvin describes in this context as an "armed robber," should we not be even *more* diligent in cultivating kindly feelings toward those who are *victims* of various sorts of oppression?

Schilder's strong emphasis on God's creating purposes, and on the power of these purposes at work even where they are not acknowledged by sinful humanity, should encourage us to explore his hints — muted as they might be — in the direction of a theology of public piety. For Reformed Christians who take seriously the reality of the antithesis between belief and unbelief, the theological rationale for positive and holy feelings toward the larger human community does not come easily. Yet many of us experience these feelings stirring in our souls — and sometimes even raging there — in spite of the lack of any theological encouragement from our antitheticalist teachers. Given the larger strengths of the antitheticalist Reformed perspective, we ought diligently to explore any resources that this perspective offers — even in the form of phrases that seem to be dropped gratuitously in the middle of otherwise rather harsh warnings against worldly alliances.

The apostle counsels us to refuse to conform to the world's patterns in this way: "Do not fear what they fear, and do not be intimidated, but in your hearts sanctify Christ as Lord." And we are, he says, to provide to anyone who asks of us "an accounting for the hope" that resides within us. But he also adds a mandate that speaks to the "character" dimension of our relationships with other human beings: "yet do it with gentleness and reverence" (1 Pet. 3:13-16). To cultivate these dispositions — key components of a public piety for our own day — is a mandate to all who seek the patterns of holiness that are pleasing to the Lord.

In *Christ and Culture,* Schilder does not give explicit attention to the cultivation of this particular dimension of holiness. Indeed, he seems reluctant to move in that direction. But in spite of his reluctance, he does offer an important framework — and even a few helpful hints — for those who are willing today to take up that task.

---

44. Calvin, *Institutes* 4.20.12, p. 1500.

Learning from the Dutch Calvinist "Splits"

In 1795 a bolt of lightning struck the steeple of the Dutch Reformed Church of Hackensack, New Jersey. The stone above the church door was dislodged and fell to the ground, breaking into several pieces. Carved in that stone had been the Dutch Reformed motto, *Eendracht Maakt Macht* — "Unity Makes Strength." The lightning bolt had now divided the sentence, with *Eendracht* on one piece and *Maakt Macht* on another.

William O. Van Eyck, who tells this story, informs us that this event came to be interpreted in two very different ways in the Reformed community. Some saw it as an ominous warning against a spirit of divisiveness. Others took it as a sign of encouragement to those who felt it important to be strong in their convictions, even when that meant destroying Dutch Reformed *eendracht*.[1]

It was this latter propensity for divisive theological controversy among many Dutch Calvinists that the novelist Peter DeVries poked some fun at in a semi-autobiographical reference in one of his novels: "'One Dutchman, a Christian; two Dutchmen, a congregation; three Dutchmen, heresy' was the charge leveled at us by more Americanized people, who boasted, for instance, of belonging to denominations that hadn't had a schism in a hundred years. To these my father always tersely replied, 'Rotten wood you can't split.'"[2]

---

1. William O. Van Eyck, *Landmarks of the Reformed Fathers; or, What Dr. Van Raalte's People Believed* (Grand Rapids: Reformed Press, 1922), 176-77.

2. Peter DeVries, *The Mackerel Plaza* (New York: Penguin Books, 1958), 32.

This essay previously appeared in *Calvin Theological Journal* 31 (April 1996). It is printed here with permission.

DeVries is right about these "splitting" tendencies. Despite their size, the Dutch communities in the Netherlands and North America have created a rather remarkable variety of Calvinist church groups. (I would say a variety of *denominations,* but disagreement about that term has itself caused at least one split, with one group insisting, as we will see, that "federation" is the theologically correct label.) Some of the differences in North America have been imported from the religious scene in the Netherlands. But the North American Dutch have also introduced their own unique variations.

How are we to understand this Dutch Calvinist diversity? DeVries' humorous comments seem to suggest that the answer lies in ethnicity as such: the Dutch simply have a fondness for "splitting." This is not an uncommon way of viewing the phenomenon, although it is usually put — à la DeVries — in a joking, or half-joking, manner. Another way to answer the question is to look for those theological motifs in Reformed thought that might foster a schismatic spirit: What is it in Reformed theology that reinforces an "us versus them" mentality in ecclesiastical life?[3] Yet another approach would be to find an answer that links theology to culture, as in James Bratt's persuasive argument that the Christian Reformed Church's doctrinal controversy in the 1920s over "common grace" had much to do with the very practical challenges of cultural assimilation.[4]

These are plausible options to pursue in attempting to understand why Dutch Calvinists are given to the kinds of theological controversies that have resulted in their "splits." In this discussion, however, I will follow a slightly different path. I will take a brief look at some of the actual theological content at stake in Dutch Calvinist diversity. I will note three doctrinal themes that regularly show up in Dutch Calvinist debates, asking why these theological topics loom large in controversies among the Dutch Reformed. The first is an ecclesiastical governance issue, the second a concern about the Reformed understanding of regeneration, and the third the tensions over the church's relationship to the larger culture. After briefly looking at these items, I will suggest that what is at stake here is a tension among some quite different and long-standing patterns of configuring Reformed thought. An awareness of the issues involved in assessing these

3. See, for example, the comments on this topic by I. John Hesselink, *On Being Reformed: Distinctive Characteristics and Common Misunderstandings* (Ann Arbor, Mich.: Servant, 1983), 57-62 and 85-92.

4. James D. Bratt, *Dutch Calvinism in Modern America: A History of a Conservative Subculture* (Grand Rapids: Eerdmans, 1984), 111-19.

configurations is, I am convinced, important for a proper understanding of Reformed identity.

While I will take my time exploring some of these differences, I will eventually get around to a constructive task. My own views about the nature of the church, and the church's relationship to the larger culture, are greatly influenced by the theological perspective set forth by Abraham Kuyper. But I also think that Kuyper's views on these matters need some serious nuancing, in the light of contemporary realities as well as in dialogue with people who have lodged some important criticisms of some of Kuyper's teachings. Thus, I will get around to articulating a "neo-Calvinist" perspective that draws heavily on Kuyper, while also reworking some of his views in interaction with some of his critics. In this chapter, however, I will attend to Kuyper's views only insofar as they fit into the account I will offer of the more general "splitting" patterns among Dutch Calvinists.

Church Governance

In an introductory essay to *Paradigms of Polity,* a book of readings about ecclesiastical governance in the Presbyterian and Reformed tradition, one of the editors characterizes what he takes to be the consensus view, as follows: "The main principles of the presbyterian form of government derived from Scripture are these: the rule by a plurality of elders in the local church, the submission of the local governing body to a higher governing body, and the unity of churches finding its most concrete representation in the connection of the churches and their elders in regional and transregional bodies, sometimes called 'courts' when discipline is undertaken."[5]

Most Presbyterian and Reformed readers would consider this an unexceptionable description of presbyterian polity. But the wording would make many Dutch Calvinists very nervous. The most crucial point of concern would be the way in which the authority of ecclesiastical assemblies is portrayed in this brief account. The notion that a regional or national synod is a "higher governing body" requiring "submission" on the part of "the local governing body" would be rejected outright by many

5. Joseph H. Hall, "History and Character of Church Government," in *Paradigms of Polity: Classic Readings in Reformed and Presbyterian Church Government,* ed. David W. Hall and Joseph H. Hall (Grand Rapids: Eerdmans, 1994), 5.

Dutch Calvinists. The concern about this kind of portrayal is fed by two important convictions. One is that regional and national synods are properly thought of as "broader" rather than "higher" assemblies. And the second conviction is that the decision-making group in the local church is a "governing body" in a very different sense than a classis/presbytery or a synod/assembly.

While the editors of *Paradigms of Polity* are obviously not attuned to Dutch Reformed sensitivities on this subject, they do publish major excerpts from the 1619 Church Order of Dordrecht in their anthology, including article 31, whose meaning has been much discussed in the Dutch Calvinist tradition: "If anyone complains that he has been wronged by the decision of a minor assembly, he shall have the right of appeal to a major ecclesiastical assembly, and whatever may be agreed upon by a majority vote shall be considered settled and binding, unless it be proved to conflict with the Word of God or with the Articles formulated in this General Synod, as long as they are not changed by another General Synod."[6]

The mainstream of the Presbyterian and Reformed tradition has treated this article as an endorsement of the view that local assemblies must be in "submission" to "higher" assemblies. But many Dutch Calvinists passionately oppose the language of "higher" and "lower," noting that the Synod of Dordrecht itself avoided such terminology. They insist on the autonomous authority of the local elders; under no conditions, they argue, may the local church transfer its obligation to promote fidelity to the Scriptures, and the correlative authority to do so, to a broader assembly.

The ecclesiological basis for this interpretation of Reformed polity has been worked out in great detail by the "liberated" *(vrijgemaakt)* churches in the Netherlands, a group that departed in 1944 from the large Reformed *(Gereformeerd)* denomination that had been formed in 1892 by a merger of Kuyper's *Doleantie* (Grieving) group and the majority of the older *Afscheiding* (Seceding) congregations. The theologians of the "liberated" churches claim Kuyper's authority for their perspective on this particular issue. And Kuyper is quite quotable on the subject, as in this pithy formulation: "the Synod does not stand above the Churches; rather, the

---

6. Hall and Hall, *Paradigms of Polity,* 180; I have eliminated a bracketed alternative phrasing that the editors include here from the Christian Reformed revision of Dordrecht's formulation; for a complete and unrevised version of the Church Order of Dordrecht, see *The Doctrinal Standards, Liturgy, and Church Order of the Netherlands Reformed Congregations* (Sioux Center, Iowa: Netherlands Reformed Book and Publishing Committee, 1991), 179-89.

Churches stand above the Synod. And over both is God's Word."[7] On this view, the authority of broader assemblies is "fundamentally different from the authority the consistory has over the congregation — which is an 'official' kind of authority, by virtue of the office of the office-bearers. . . . The major assemblies are not 'higher authorities.' A major assembly is just an assembly of delegates from a larger number of churches. But this does not cause their authority to accumulate."[8]

This last sentence captures the "federationist" character of the ecclesiology at work here. Indeed, in *vrijgemaakt* (liberated) ecclesiology, this is thought of as an expression of "the great 'Reformed principle'" that

> the federation of churches is a matter of a voluntary act of free churches in accordance with what Holy Scripture states concerning the unity of the Spirit to be maintained. They have agreed to do things in the same way; to support each other in several respects; to have mutual supervision over each other in order that they may continue to be true and faithful churches of the Lord Jesus Christ; to create a certain form of jurisdiction in their midst; and to undertake a number of common activities, e.g. regarding the training for the Ministry of the Word.[9]

It is not uncommon for this pattern of thought to be labeled by its Reformed critics as "congregationalist." "Localist," however, would be a better term, since on this view ecclesial authority is not invested first of all in the congregation as such, but in the ministry of the elected elders of the local church. This localist impulse runs deep among the Dutch Reformed. As Alastair Duke has observed, "the Calvinist churches in the Low Countries, as in France, came into existence as individual congregations: the presbyterian or synodal framework followed"[10] — a pattern that is somewhat dif-

7. Quoted in Cornelis Veenhof, "Church Polity in 1886 and 1944," in *Seeking Our Brothers in the Light: A Plea for Reformed Ecumenicity*, ed. Theodore Plantinga (Neerlandia, Alberta: Inheritance Publications, 1992), 126.

8. *Decently and in Good Order: The Church Order of the Canadian and American Reformed Churches*, commented on by G. Van Rongen and K. Deddens (Winnipeg: Premier Publishing, 1986), 68.

9. *Decently and in Good Order*, 12.

10. Alastair Duke, "The Ambivalent Face of Calvinism in the Netherlands, 1561-1618," in *International Calvinism, 1541-1715*, ed. Menna Prestwich (Oxford: Clarendon, 1985), 126; see also Peter Y. De Jong, "The Rise of the Reformed Churches in the Netherlands," in *Crisis in the Reformed Churches: Essays in Commemoration of the Great Synod of Dort, 1618-1619*, ed. Peter Y. De Jong (Grand Rapids: Reformed Fellowship, 1968), 15-16.

ferent from, say, what Michael Lynch has described as Scotland's "parish-based reformation,"[11] where the idea of a strong "national church" was present from the beginning.[12]

Regeneration

At three evening gatherings in Ancaster, Ontario, in October 1992, representatives of various smaller Reformed groups met to discuss their differences. The groups were composed of persons from the Free Reformed Churches, who have ties to the Dutch *Christelijke Gereformeerde* (Christian Reformed) *Kerken;* the Canadian Reformed Churches, who are linked to the Dutch "liberated" churches; and an assortment of churches that have Christian Reformed roots and have either stayed in that denomination as "concerned" churches, or have left it to form the Orthodox Christian Reformed Churches, or have declared an "independent" status.

The published record of these discussions shows that the proper understanding of regeneration was an important topic.[13] The subject was of special concern for representatives of the Free Reformed Churches, in their exchanges with the persons who defended the "liberated" perspective. The Free Reformed Church's counterpart in the Netherlands is the denomination that consists of those churches of the 1834 Secession who chose not to join the merger in 1892 between the majority of Seceded congregations and the *Doleantie* group that Abraham Kuyper had led out of the mainstream Reformed *(Hervormde)* Church in 1886; it was that merged denomination from which the "liberated" churches had departed in 1944. In the Burlington discussions, the Free Reformed theologians insisted that the *Doleantie-Afscheiding* merger had been a mistake from the start — a perspective not endorsed by the 1944 dissenters — and that a key factor in the mismatch was Kuyper's views on infant baptism.

Kuyper was a vocal defender of the notion of "presumptive regeneration," as informed by his professed adherence to a supralapsarian

11. Michael Lynch, "Calvinism in Scotland, 1559-1638," in *International Calvinism, 1541-1715*, 232.

12. Cf. James Kirk's discussion of the influences on Scottish Reformation polity in his *Patterns of Reform: Continuity and Change in the Reformation Kirk* (Edinburgh: T. & T. Clark, 1989), 77-95.

13. Cornelis Van Dam, ed., *The Challenge of Church Union: Speeches and Discussions on Reformed Identity and Ecumenicity* (Winnipeg: Premier Publishing, 1993).

soteriology. On this view, since regeneration is God's secret planting of the seeds of a new redeemed orientation in an individual heart, it can occur long before there is any discernible manifestation of spiritual renewal in the person's life. Kuyper's critics take special offense, for example, at "his teaching that Paul was regenerated while still an enemy of Christ and His people."[14] On such a view, the children of believers, even though they had not yet consciously embraced God's covenantal promises, can be presumed to be regenerated until such a time as that presumption is either confirmed or challenged by the pattern of life they choose to follow.

This perspective fosters a false sense of security in the church, the critics argue.[15] For one thing, it has very bad consequences for the preaching of the Word. This charge was put bluntly in 1904 by Foppe Ten Hoor, one of Kuyper's harshest critics during the debates over these issues around the turn of the twentieth century. Kuyper's perspective, Ten Hoor insisted, promotes a mood in the church where

> the seriousness of life is weakened and gradually forgotten. Sinners are no longer driven to Christ by the terrors of the Lord and by the awareness of their miserable condition and the fear of perishing forever. Imagine what it will be for that teacher when he will stand before the judgment seat with his congregation, both old and young, and if there will be some — who knows how many — who expect to enter but will not be able, and if these will then say to their teacher: you have deceived us. You have taught us that we should proceed from the assumption that we were born again. We believed you, and now we are lost forever! You have misled us![16]

---

14. Cornelis Pronk, "The Union of 1892: A Free Reformed Evaluation," in *The Challenge of Church Union,* 31.

15. As noted, in the Burlington discussions it was the Free Reformed thinkers who focused especially on Kuyper's views on this subject. But the "presumptive regeneration" issue also figured prominently in debates that led to the formation of the "liberated" churches in 1944. For a summary of *vrijgemaakt* opposition to Kuyper's views on this subject, see D. De Jong, "The Significance of the Liberation of 1944 for the Gathering of the Church Today," in J. Faber, D. De Jong, and J. Mulder, *Secession and Liberation for Today: Commemorative Lectures on the Secession of 1834 and the Liberation of 1944* (London, Ontario: Inter League Publication Board, 1986), 19-38.

16. Quoted in Cornelis Pronk, "F. M. Ten Hoor: Defender of Secession Principles against Abraham Kuyper's Doleantie Views" (Th.M. thesis, Calvin Theological Seminary, 1987), 110.

For the Free Reformed, this situation can only be remedied by a strong endorsement of the kind of "experiential" preaching associated with the "Second Reformation" *(nadere Reformatie)*.[17] Thus they lodge serious criticisms of both the doctrinalist and "redemptive-historical" preaching styles of other Reformed groups.[18]

Church and World

In a speech he gave to a convention of young women of the "liberated" Reformed Churches in 1951, Klaas Schilder, who had led the "liberated" group in their 1944 departure from the *Gereformeerde* churches, warned his charges that while they should not simply choose to be isolated from other church groups and the larger culture, neither should they reject that marginal status if it is thrust upon them. Indeed, the "liberated" leader proclaimed, "[i]f our numbers do not shrink over the whole world, we should ask ourselves whether we have ever really comprehended Christ's eschatological discourses and properly understood the Revelation of John."[19] Schilder immediately went on to quote Abraham Kuyper to the effect that Christian people must set their uniquely Christian principles in as sharp a contrast as possible to the perspectives of other groups. This is because Kuyper recognized, Schilder argued, that only when "the antithesis" between belief and unbelief is stated as clearly as possible can we "see to it that the half-hearted hybrid hangers-on leave as soon as possible, shaking their heads." And then Schilder added: "Thus Kuyper in 1878."[20]

The date of Kuyper's comment here is important. Schilder was deliberately calling attention to the fact that he was appealing to the authority of the early Kuyper. James Bratt explains the importance of the "early-late" distinction in Kuyper's thought with this interesting commentary:

17. The best account in English of this movement is Joel R. Beeke's essay "The Dutch Second Reformation *(Nadere Reformatie)*," published as an appendix to his *Assurance of Faith: Calvin, English Puritanism, and the Dutch Second Reformation* (New York: Peter Lang, 1991), 383-413; Beeke's essay also appeared in *Calvin Theological Journal* 28, no. 2 (November 1993): 298-327.

18. Cf. "Response of Rev. C. Pronk," in *The Challenge of Church Union*, 63-71.

19. Klaas Schilder, "Your Ecumenical Task," in Rudolf Van Reest, *Schilder's Struggle for the Unity of the Church*, trans. Theodore Plantinga (Neerlandia, Alberta: Inheritance Publications, 1990), appendix III, p. 452.

20. Schilder, "Your Ecumenical Task," 453-54.

Significantly, Kuyper's appeal to the antithesis peaked in the first half of his career, the period of institutional formation, and declined in his later years, when Calvinists had to take their share of managing public life. The concept served a crucial strategic purpose: besides showing Reformed skeptics that cultural activity did not endanger purity of faith, it fortified group identity during a potentially threatening transition. Certainly it must have mobilized many Seceders, living as they did under the memory of separation. But its darker legacy was equally apparent: few doctrines could match the antithesis at fostering spiritual arrogance or abusing principial analysis.[21]

Both Schilder and Bratt recognize that as Kuyper's public career evolved, he increasingly downplayed the notion of a radical "antithesis" between belief and unbelief. But while Schilder concentrates on what he sees as Kuyper's departure from pure orthodoxy, Bratt attends to the relationship of Kuyper's theological emphases to his role as a cultural leader. The early Kuyper appealed to the antithesis, Bratt argues, in order to reassure conservative Calvinists that they could maintain a clear sense of "group identity" as they moved from a sense of cultural marginalization to active involvement in broad programs of cultural reform.

Bratt's discussion of Kuyper's career is quite nuanced and illuminating. He certainly intends no unqualified endorsement of Kuyper's later thought; indeed, he notes "problems of internal logic" in Kuyper's theology of common grace.[22] But for all that, Bratt seems to have little patience with the separatist Calvinism of Kuyper's early constituents. Kuyper was attempting to move these folks, he insists, away from a "darker legacy" of "spiritual arrogance" that afflicts Calvinists who find the prospect of taking "their share of managing public life" to be "threatening."

There is a more charitable, and I think more plausible, way of treating the antithetical origins of Kuyper's thought. On this interpretation the early Kuyper saw the idea of a radical antithesis as a central motif in a coherent pattern of Calvinist thought, an outlook to which Schilder was giving expression in the comments quoted above. From this perspective, Calvinists should be willing to live as a minority presence on the margins of the cultural status quo, consistently avoiding compromise with principles that are different from their own.

21. Bratt, *Dutch Calvinism*, 19.
22. Bratt, *Dutch Calvinism*, 20.

Furthermore, there is reason to think that the early Kuyper actually found this outlook quite attractive. It was the perspective held by the rural Calvinists whose persistent prayers for his conversion had been, as he once put it, the occasion for "the rise of the morning star in my life."[23] In his earlier efforts, Kuyper made a sincere effort to develop the cultural implications of an antithesis-centered theology. As his career unfolded, however, and as he experienced considerable success as a political leader, he departed significantly from this perspective, blending some of its elements with themes from other patterns of Reformed thought. Thus, the move from earlier to later Kuyper was from an internally coherent understanding of Reformed discipleship to a more eclectic mix of Calvinist emphases.

The "Darker Legacy"

Bratt's depiction of antithesis-centered Calvinism as embodying a "darker legacy" of "spiritual arrogance" has a familiar Calvinist ring. Reformed leaders have typically used this kind of language to signal their refusal to deal theologically with the issues being posed by "extreme" elements. The most obvious case in point for this rhetorical ploy is the Reformed portrayal of the Anabaptists.

Calvinist thinkers have been eager to portray Anabaptist thought and practice as unworthy of serious theological engagement, as in article 36 of the Belgic Confession, where the Anabaptist views on political authority and "community of goods" are condemned as "detestable." But Willem Balke's careful study shows that John Calvin's own frustrations with the Anabaptists[24] had to do with the fact that the Anabaptists "out-Calvinisted" the Reformed community on at least two important points. The first was church discipline. The Calvinists were very critical of Catholics and Lutherans for their lack of attention to the role of discipline in the Christian community. The Anabaptists, however, took discipline even further than the Calvinists, insisting on very tight patterns of communal control. The Calvinists responded by labeling the Anabaptists as "perfectionist."

23. Quoted in Louis Praamsma, *Let Christ Be King: Reflections on the Life and Times of Abraham Kuyper* (Jordan Station, Ontario: Paideia Press, 1985), 49.

24. Cf. Willem Balke, *Calvin and the Anabaptist Radicals,* trans. William Heynen (Grand Rapids: Eerdmans, 1981).

The second point had to do with church-world relations. Calvinism has been well known for its stark portrayal of human depravity. But Reformed thinkers, having started with this strong emphasis on human sinfulness, regularly introduced modifications — of the sort associated with "common grace" teachings — that allowed them to endorse some of the things going on in the larger culture (especially the workings of civil government). On this point too the Anabaptists chided them for their inconsistency, insisting that a negative assessment of unregenerate human nature required a strict posture of separation from the world. Here the Calvinist response featured the kind of condemnatory language echoed in Bratt's reference to the "spiritual arrogance" of a "darker legacy" of Calvinist separatism.

John Howard Yoder and I have joined forces from both sides of the Reformed-Anabaptist divide to argue that the arguments between Calvinists and Anabaptists are not disputes between radically different theological types.[25] They are elements in intrafamily argument. These disputes reach a high intensity because the differences between the two groups are of a more intimate character than either of their arguments with, say, the Lutherans or the Catholics.

It should not surprise us, then, if some of the most passionate debates within the Reformed community address an agenda similar to that of the Reformed-Anabaptist arguments. Indeed, one important feature of intra-Reformed controversies is that there frequently comes a point in the heat of the argument when one of the parties will reach into the Calvinist arsenal and toss out the accusation that the other side is "Anabaptist" or "Labadist."[26] The frustration experienced by Calvinists whose views were treated in this manner is given poignant expression by Herman Hoeksema in his description of the Christian Reformed leadership's rejection of his views in the 1920s: "And all that opposed them and refused to believe and

25. Cf. John H. Yoder, "Reformed versus Anabaptist Social Strategies: An Inadequate Typology," and Richard J. Mouw, "Abandoning the Typology: A Reformed Assist," *TSF Bulletin* 8, no. 5 (May-June 1985): 2-10.

26. "Labadist" refers to the teachings of Jean de Labadie, a seventeenth-century Jesuit-turned-Calvinist who established Anabaptist-type Reformed conventicles as an alternative to the "worldliness" of the mainstream Reformed congregations. For some examples of the use of these labels in Reformed controversies, see Van Eyck's account of the Hackensack secession of 1822, in Van Eyck, *Landmarks,* chapter 12, and Bratt's discussion of Christian Reformed controversies in the early twentieth century, in Bratt, *Dutch Calvinism,* chapters 7 and 8.

proclaim this theory of common grace, they proudly and disdainfully branded as Anabaptist!"[27]

What I am arguing here is that the "Anabaptist" charge should not be taken as an insult; neither should it be allowed to be used as a move to close off theological discussion. The three topics I have identified as looming large in Dutch Calvinist "splits" are in fact also prominent on the Anabaptist agenda. If we insist, as I want to do here, that these topics, whether in their Anabaptist or their Calvinist "split" formulations, arise naturally within a Reformed context — even if they are dealt with very differently by different groups — then it seems to me that there are important lessons to be learned from all this about Calvinist identity.

The Benefits of Calvinist Diversity

In the spring of 1866 Albertus Van Raalte returned to the Netherlands from Holland, Michigan,[28] to address the Secessionists' synod. Van Raalte, one of the original leaders of the Dutch Secession of 1834, was greeted warmly. But his admirers were also curious about the fact that Van Raalte himself had experienced a secession from his ranks, with the 1857 departure of the group that was to become the Christian Reformed Church. In his remarks Van Raalte was charitable toward his North American opponents. The difficulties were due, he said, to "diverse elements which had moved from here [the Netherlands] to North America and to various other reasons, though not to heterodoxy."[29]

Van Raalte's wise comment highlights two important observations. One is that Dutch Calvinism is indeed an entity containing "diverse elements." And the second is that we do well not to think of the theological differences that characterize this diversity as stemming from "heterodoxy."

We can benefit from Calvinist pluralism by celebrating the fact of Reformed diversity. To have a coherent pattern of Reformed thought and

27. Herman Hoeksema, *The Protestant Reformed Churches in America: Their Origin, Early History, and Doctrine* (Grand Rapids: First Protestant Reformed Church, 1936), 16.

28. Van Raalte had led a group of emigrants from the Netherlands in 1846, and established the town of Holland, Michigan, in 1847.

29. Quoted by Willem van't Spijker, "The Christian Reformed Church and the Christelijke Gereformeerde Kerken in Nederland," in *Perspectives on the Christian Reformed Church: Studies in Its History, Theology, and Ecumenicity,* ed. Peter De Klerk and Richard R. De Ridder (Grand Rapids: Baker, 1983), 368.

practice requires the integration of a variety of important themes: God's supreme Lordship, divine providence, election, human fallenness, sovereign grace, covenant community, the security of the believer, and so on. These themes can be put together in different "mixes" and with different emphases. For example, the advocacy of a strong pattern of Christian separation from the world is based on a properly Calvinist recognition of the fallenness of unredeemed cultural activity. But the competing view, that God is secretly at work accomplishing good things in secular culture, is also based on a very Reformed appeal to the reality of God's providential governance of all things.

To reflect on the diversity of various Calvinist configurations can be highly instructive. We will not be properly instructed, though, if we simply declare some of the ways of "mixing" Reformed themes as altogether out of bounds, as has been the case with our anti–Anabaptist/Labadist rhetoric. It does no good to set important questions aside by tossing out charges of "perfectionism" and "spiritual arrogance." Leonard Verduin has pointed out, for example, that the "believers' church" emphasis of the Anabaptists resurfaces within the Dutch "experiential" strain of Calvinism: Mennonites will only baptize people who have had an experience of conversion; experiential Calvinists will only baptize the children of *parents* who have had an experience of conversion.[30] Along similar lines, the strong preference of Dutch Calvinist pietists for a "gathered" church versus a "territorial" church[31] parallels an important feature of Anabaptist ecclesiology.

Given that the "diverse elements" in the Reformed community all intend to be drawing on Calvinist themes, and that they are all involved in the necessary task of integrating these themes into a coherent pattern of Reformed thought and practice, the debates among the various groups can be an extremely helpful exercise in examining the contours of Reformed identity. I am convinced that we can best pursue this examination by focusing on the implications of Calvinist diversity for pastoral theology. The pastoral motif is clearly evident in the challenges posed by the Calvinist

---

30. Leonard Verduin, *Honor Your Mother: Christian Reformed Church Roots in the 1834 Separation* (Grand Rapids: CRC Publications, 1988), 21.

31. Cf. F. Ernest Stoeffler's now-classic account of Dutch Reformed pietist thought in chapter 3 of his *Rise of Evangelical Pietism* (Leiden: Brill, 1965). For an account of how the tensions between these two understandings of the church were played out within the leadership of the 1834 Secession, see Willem van't Spijker, "Catholicity of the Church in the Secession (1834) and the Doleantie (1886)," in *Catholicity and Secession: A Dilemma?* ed. Paul Schrotenboer (Kampen: J. H. Kok, 1992), 82-89.

"splits." Nelson Kloosterman captures this theme nicely when he insists that the Dutch 1834 Secession was a recovery of "the pastoral application of the church's confessional heritage."[32]

The three themes I have discussed — a localist ecclesiology, an emphasis on experiential preaching, and a deep desire to draw sharp boundaries between church and world — can certainly be construed along these lines. If church discipline, as an integral mark of the church, is to be exercised in a vibrant pastoral manner, then the authority of the local church must be carefully guarded. And it does seem to follow from this that the pastoral task must be conjoined to a preaching ministry that calls for the people of God to seek a strong experiential basis for their common faith. This communal commitment, in turn, requires a clear sense of how the church's patterns of thought and practice differ from those of the larger culture.

Whatever the proposed solutions to the questions being dealt with here, the questions themselves are of crucial importance for maintaining a vital Calvinist pastoral ministry. If the ongoing debates about these matters can be given a pastoral focus, looking at the ways in which the Reformed community has generated diverse patterns of spiritual formation and pastoral care, perhaps some new lessons can be learned about the rich spiritual resources of the Reformed tradition.

To be sure, the debates will not always be easy to sustain, since certain ways of configuring Calvinist themes permit less openness than others to theological dialogue, even with opponents who profess a sincere commitment to the Reformed faith. Perhaps a new call to pursue the discussion with a focus on pastoral theology can create new possibilities for dialogue. But even where a lively interchange of ideas among actual representatives of these various configurations is not a realistic possibility, those of us in the Reformed "mainstream" must wrestle seriously with the issues that have been raised in the "splits." Indeed, we ignore them at our theological and spiritual peril.

32. Nelson Kloosterman, "The Doctrinal Significance of the Secession of 1834," in *The Reformation of 1834: Essays in Commemoration of the "Act of Secession and Return,"* ed. Peter Y. De Jong and Nelson D. Kloosterman (Orange City, Iowa: Pluim Publishing, 1984), 37-40.

True Church and True Christians:
Some Reflections on Calvinist Discernment

In an important little book, published in 2001 by the World Council of Churches, two theologians, one Orthodox and the other Lutheran, explored with admirable candor some difficult questions about ecclesiology. Peter Bouteneff, the Orthodox representative, pointed out that while ecumenical declarations about the nature of the church typically give the impression that their formulations are neutral, they actually exclude the basic convictions embodied in Orthodox ecclesiology. The drafters of these declarations seem to have no difficulty acknowledging the existence of a variety of genuine Christian churches, each of them possessing — to one degree or another — legitimacy as an ecclesial entity. Whatever tensions they might see between this endorsement of ecclesiological pluralism and the creedal confessions regarding the one holy and catholic church are usually explained in terms of the "visible" versus the "invisible" church. Thus, the primary mission of the ecumenical movement is to work at giving visible expression to the invisible unity that we possess in Christ.

This ecclesiological perspective, Bouteneff observed, does not sit well with the Orthodox. Like it or not, he argued, Orthodoxy "identifies *itself* with the one, holy, catholic and apostolic Church." On this self-understanding there cannot really be any divisions *within* the true church — all other groups claiming churchly identity in fact exist in separation

---

This essay previously appeared in *That the World May Believe: Essays on Mission and Unity in Honour of George Vandervelde*, ed. Michael W. Goheen and Margaret O'Gara (Lanham, Md.: University Press of America, 2006). It is printed here with permission.

from the one true church. The very notion, then, of a council of diverse "churches" is problematic from an Orthodox perspective, according to which Christian unity can only occur when all these separated individuals and groups return to the Orthodox fold.[1]

Bouteneff's Lutheran coauthor, Anna Marie Aagaard, responded to his reflections by registering her concern about Orthodoxy's inability to give any precise account of the positive ecclesial status of Christian groups outside of Orthodoxy. But she also found some glimmers of hope in several of Bouteneff's probings, especially in his insistence that Orthodoxy has to find a "space" in its ecclesiology for those non-Orthodox who, while not belonging to churches, properly understood, still obviously "share in the life of Christ."[2] Bouteneff responded to her challenges by acknowledging that there is more work to be done in developing an Orthodox ecclesiology that takes ecumenical realities into account. But he also urged the non-Orthodox to be clear about the fact that "we Orthodox . . . are clear and unapologetic about the content of our theology"; this means, Bouteneff insisted, that others would do well to "stop being surprised and offended" every time the Orthodox state their understanding of the church.[3]

Calvinist Exclusivity

In his review of the Aagaard-Bouteneff book, published in the *Calvin Theological Journal*, George Vandervelde made it clear that he has, as a Reformed Christian, much sympathy for the Orthodox position. Indeed, he noted, in setting forth the Orthodox case with such candor, Bouteneff had identified "the central issue facing the ecumenical movement today."[4] We do not serve the cause of unity, said Vandervelde, when we fail to state our real differences clearly. Indeed, he suggested, the frank expression of dissenting views is a necessary phase of the ecumenical journey, for "[w]here two or three representatives, even of exclusionary communities, pray together, Christ's promised presence opens up a new road of, and toward,

---

1. Anna Marie Aagaard and Peter Bouteneff, *Beyond the East-West Divide: The World Council of Churches and "The Orthodox Problem"* (Geneva: WCC Publications, 2001), 35.

2. Aagaard and Bouteneff, *Beyond*, 108.

3. Aagaard and Bouteneff, *Beyond*, 116.

4. George Vandervelde, review of *Beyond the East-West Divide: The World Council of Churches and "The Orthodox Problem,"* by Anna Marie Aagaard and Peter Bouteneff, *Calvin Theological Journal* 38, no. 2 (2003): 356.

church unity."[5] When Vandervelde refers to a plurality of "exclusionary communities," he knows of what he speaks. He himself stands in a tradition that has long defended an exclusionary ecclesiology in a manner strikingly similar to Bouteneff's formulations. For the past few decades Vandervelde has represented the Christian Reformed Church (CRC) in a variety of conciliar ecumenical organizations. While he has been an active participant in these dialogues, his official status has been as an appointed representative of a "nonmember" denomination — the CRC has been reluctant to be fully involved in the more inclusive manifestations of conciliar ecumenism.

The CRC's nervousness about ecclesiological inclusivity has a long history, beginning with John Calvin's writings. Indeed, Calvin's struggles to explain the ecclesial status of the Roman Catholic Church are not that far from Bouteneff's attempts to identify a "space" within Orthodox ecclesiology for non-Orthodox denominations.

Even though Calvin saw the Roman authorities as having done much to destroy the proper patterns of the church's life and mission, Calvin nonetheless insisted that he could not bring himself to "deprive the papists of those traces of the church which the Lord willed should among them survive the destruction." Thus "the Lord wonderfully preserves" within the Catholic Church, he argued, "a remnant of his people, however woefully dispersed and scattered." This remnant preserves "those marks whose effectiveness neither the devil's wiles nor human depravity can destroy." But these marks are not enough to grant legitimate churchly status to the Roman Church as such. Since some of the most important marks of proper church-ness "have been erased" in that body, Calvin was forced to conclude "that every one of their congregations and their whole body lack the lawful form of the church."[6]

Calvin was obviously ambivalent as he tried to sort out these matters. On the one hand he wanted to draw some clear boundaries between churches that remain faithful to the gospel and those that are Christian churches only in name. But he was not prepared simply to write off all members of the latter category as infidels. So he was left with a distinction not unlike the one drawn by Bouteneff: there are Christians who belong to that body that is properly thought of as being *church,* and there are others

5. Vandervelde, review of *Beyond,* 359-60.

6. John Calvin, *Institutes of the Christian Religion,* trans. Ford Lewis Battles, ed. John T. McNeill, 2 vols. (Philadelphia: Westminster, 1960), book 2, chapters 11 and 12, pp. 1051-52.

who, while belonging to entities that lack legitimate ecclesial status, must nonetheless be viewed as a preserved "remnant" (Calvin) who still "share in the life of Christ" (Bouteneff).

Two Reformed Confessions

The Reformation-era churches that were shaped by Calvin's thought also wrestled with these issues, and their key confessional documents share his ambivalence, wanting to maintain a clear notion of the necessary marks for proper church-ness while also acknowledging the presence of genuine Christian faith in settings where those marks are not present. As Henk Weijland has observed,[7] there is a discernible difference in tone and emphasis, if not in substance, in the way this ambivalence is handled in the Westminster Confession and the Belgic Confession. While the Westminster document, unlike the Belgic, explicitly condemns the pope as "the AntiChrist,"[8] it quickly shifts its focus to the ways in which even "[t]he purest churches under heaven are subject both to mixture and error," calling on Calvinists to nurture a "communion [which], as God offereth opportunity, is to be extended unto all those who, in every place, call upon the name of the Lord Jesus."[9] The Belgic Confession, on the other hand, makes much of the distinction between the "true church" and the "false church," insisting that every Christian must be united with the former while staying separate from the latter at all costs.[10]

As a Dutch Calvinist denomination, the CRC defines its commitment to Reformed orthodoxy in terms of subscription to the Belgic Confession, along with the Heidelberg Catechism and the Canons of Dort. This means that the "true church/false church" distinction has been an important part of its confessional vocabulary. More importantly, this distinction has played an important role in divisive historical events that have deeply influenced the CRC, in both the Netherlands and North America. It is not necessary here to provide details about all these "splits."[11] But it is impor-

7. Henk B. Weijland, "Is Secession Allowed?" in *Catholicity and Secession: A Dilemma?* ed. Paul Schrotenboer (Kampen: J. H. Kok, 1992), 112.

8. Westminster Confession, chapter 25, section 5, at http://www.creeds.net/Westminster/wstmnstr.htm.

9. Westminster Confession, chapter 26, section 2.

10. Belgic Confession, article 28, at http//www.creeds.net/belgic/index.htm.

11. For details of the Netherlands, see W. W. J. Van Oene, *Patrimony Profile: Our Re-*

tant to note that more often than not the intra-Calvinist debates focused on whether a given Reformed body possessed what the Belgic Confession stipulated as "the marks of the true church": the faithful preaching of the Word, the proper ministry of the sacraments, and careful church discipline (article 29).

It is difficult to avoid the conclusion that the Belgic Confession's formulations, like those of Orthodoxy described earlier, provide little ecclesiological "space" for legitimate ecclesial entities that do not manifest "the marks of the true church" as understood in a Reformed context. And this restrictive space has often been celebrated in more conservative Dutch Calvinist environs, where the Belgic Confession's insistence that "[t]hese two Churches" — true and false — "are easily known and distinguished from each other" has been taken as a clear warning against the sort of compromise permitted by relying, for example, on a distinction between the visible and the invisible church.

Kuyperian "Multiformity"

The Dutch statesman-theologian Abraham Kuyper was himself a leader in one of the major splits that occurred in the nineteenth-century Dutch Reformed community. Nonetheless, the Belgic Confession's restrictive ecclesiological perspective was deeply troubling to Kuyper. While on most other matters Kuyper insisted upon strict adherence to the Confession's doctrinal formulations, he was convinced that on this subject the Belgic Confession was wrong. He saw its exclusivist declarations as typical of the Reformation-era thinking, where Calvinists were firmly convinced "that their own confession bore an absolute and exclusive character." Anything that conflicted with some item in the Calvinists' confessional documents "was a falsification of the truth," with the result that their "own Church was held to be the purest, not merely by way of comparison, but so as to be actually looked upon as the only lawful continuance of *the* Church of the apostles."[12]

---

formed Heritage Retraced, 1795-1946 (Winnipeg: Premier, 1999), and for North America, James D. Bratt, *Dutch Calvinism in Modern America: A History of a Conservative Subculture* (Grand Rapids: Eerdmans, 1984).

12. Abraham Kuyper, *Principles of Sacred Theology,* trans. J. Hendrik DeVries (Grand Rapids: Eerdmans, 1954), 659.

In rejecting this restrictive ecclesiology, Kuyper argued for a legitimate "multiformity," or "pluriformity," of the church. Kuyper wanted to see in a positive light "differences of climate and of nation, of historical past, and of disposition of mind" — thus acknowledging a reality that "annihilates the absolute character of every visible church, and places them all side by side, as differing in degrees of purity, but always remaining in some way or other a manifestation of one holy and catholic Church of Christ in Heaven."[13] This multiformity was, for Kuyper, an instance of a larger pattern. He saw our diverse perspectives on the truth as a result of God's creating designs. God loves multiformity, and he built it into the very fabric of the created order. Even if the fall into sin had not occurred, human history would have produced much pluriformity. It was to be expected, then, that the providential unfolding of church life would produce a healthy dose of perspectival diversity.

While Kuyper was clear about the fact that his defense of ecclesial multiformity contradicted key tenets of Reformation-era Calvinism, he also insisted that in a deeper sense his positive assessment of ecclesial multiformity was a legitimate extension of developments set in motion by the Reformation. For one thing, he saw in Calvinism's increasing endorsement of the idea of religious freedom — the advocacy of the rights of diverse churches to pursue their various patterns of life and worship — a recognition of at least a de facto ecclesial multiformity: this encouragement of churchly pluralism gradually led to an appreciation for "national differences of morals, differences of disposition and of emotions, [and] different degrees in depth of life and insight, [which] necessarily resulted in emphasizing first one, and then another side of the same truth."[14]

More importantly, though, Kuyper argued that even in some of its earliest confessional statements Calvinism implicitly endorsed a more inclusive viewpoint: "Without attracting at once attention to itself as such," he argued, "this multiformity was sealed confessionally in the dogma of the visible Church as the revelation of the invisible Church."[15] In this regard Kuyper quoted chapter 25, article 1 of the Westminster Confession: "The Catholic or Universal Church which is invisible, consists of the whole number of the elect that have been, are or shall be, gathered into one, under Christ the Head, thereof; and is the spouse, the body, the fulness of

13. Abraham Kuyper, *Lectures on Calvinism* (Grand Rapids: Eerdmans, 1931), 63-64.
14. Kuyper, *Lectures on Calvinism*, 64.
15. Kuyper, *Principles of Sacred Theology*, 663.

Him that filleth all in all."[16] This article, he said, "beautifully sets forth [the] heavenly all-embracing nature of the church."[17]

Contra Kuyper

Kuyper's views on this subject have not been very popular in conservative Dutch Calvinist circles, even where he has had considerable influence on other theological matters. One of his critics, Professor Jelle Faber of the Theological College of the Canadian Reformed Churches, has argued, for example, that Kuyper's notion of multiformity, "which is taught neither by the Scriptures nor by the Reformed confessions, . . . has proved to be an undermining factor in the fight against the sins of the church and for its reformation." Faber warns against "the danger of what I call a polarization of the so-called 'invisible' and the so-called 'visible' church," which "results in a low esteem for what is called the visible church, a weakening of church-consciousness, [and] a lack of understanding of the seriousness of the calling to separate from the false church."[18]

In arguing that the idea of an invisible church is a dangerous one, and that the true church must be thought of as a visible entity that bears the three marks set forth in the Belgic Confession, Faber insists that he does not mean to suggest that only Reformed Christians belong to the true church:

Do not say to me: you are surely speaking about only the Reformed churches. No, I am not only speaking about the Reformed churches! I am speaking about the church of God, the church of God that He knows in His eternal decree, the church that will be gathered out of all tongues and tribes and nations. . . . So let us not speak in too static a manner about the boundaries of the church. . . . [T]hey are boundaries that are continually expanding, until the knowledge of the Lord will fill the whole earth, as God has promised through the prophet Isaiah.[19]

Nonetheless, Faber's primary emphasis is on the visible church, the "assembly of the true Christian believers washed by the blood of Christ,

16. Westminster Confession, chapter 25, article 1.
17. Kuyper, *Lectures on Calvinism*, 61.
18. Jelle Faber, *Essays in Reformed Doctrine* (Neerlandia, Alberta: Inheritance Publications, 1990), 114-15.
19. Faber, *Essays in Reformed Doctrine*, 126.

renewed by His Spirit."[20] He sees this assembly as clearly discernible, and insists — following the Belgic Confession — that all Christians are obliged to separate themselves from those gatherings that can be clearly seen to be false churches, and to join the true church, those assemblies that bear the marks of ecclesial legitimacy.

Recognizing the exclusivist character of the case he is making, Faber takes up the question of the status of those who are not members of the visible assembly of true believers. There are people, he observes, who possess a genuine faith in Christ and who diligently study the Word, but who have not joined the true assembly of believers. While they are genuine Christians, they are nonetheless "disobedient children of God" who are living in sinful separation from the assembly of true believers. "When they die, all sin will be taken away, also sin with respect to the church."[21] But for the present they are not living in full obedience to the will of God.

To account for the status of these believers who live apart from the visible church, Faber introduces "a distinction between being a member of Christ and being a member of Christ's body." All members of Christ's body are members of Christ, but not all members of Christ are members of Christ's body.[22] Although Faber does not explicitly deal with the status of those Christians who have not departed from the assemblies of false churches, it is clear that his distinction covers these cases also. Following Calvin's observations about the "remnant" that remained in the Roman Catholic Church of his day, Faber could argue that there are Christians who fail to fulfill their obligation to separate themselves from false assemblies, even though they possess a saving faith in Christ. Because of their disobedience, they are not incorporated into Christ's body, his visible church on earth. But they are nonetheless — even in their sinful separation from the true church — members of Christ.

In spelling out the exclusivist perspective that he sees mandated by the Belgic Confession, Faber has arrived at a distinction that is almost exactly parallel to the one set forth by Bouteneff in his attempts to clarify Orthodox ecclesiology. Both Bouteneff and Faber link the marks of ecclesial legitimacy to very visible practices and structures. Those groups who call themselves Christian but do not conform to these marks cannot be considered members of true "churches" in the proper sense of the term. At the

20. Faber, *Essays in Reformed Doctrine*, 128.
21. Faber, *Essays in Reformed Doctrine*, 129.
22. Faber, *Essays in Reformed Doctrine*, 129.

same time, in saying this, neither Faber nor Bouteneff is willing to deny salvific status to all who pursue their Christian callings apart from membership in the eccesially legitimate assemblies. These persons and groups are "members of Christ" (Faber); they "share in the life of Christ" (Bouteneff).

Sinful Diversity

It would seem that for a Reformed Christian who wants to honor the Dutch Calvinist confessional tradition while also pursuing friendly ecumenical relations, Kuyper's path is the more productive one to follow. Kuyper rejects what he sees as the Belgic Confession's exclusivist ecclesiology, while also insisting that Reformation-era Calvinism was in other ways promoting what would become a more adequate perspective — one that celebrates a variety of legitimate forms of ecclesial life.

But as G. C. Berkouwer — George Vandervelde's doctoral mentor at the Vrije Universiteit of Amsterdam — has pointed out, the Kuyperian path is not without its own problems. Berkouwer does see much value in the insistence that lies at "the core of Kuyper's ecclesiological epistemology," namely, that "[o]ur knowledge of the truth is always imperfect and inadequate."[23] But Berkouwer also points out that ecclesial multiformity is not always a positive phenomenon. Indeed, he argues, in our present experience of churchly diversity, what Kuyper thinks of as "the different 'forms' of the Church are anything but harmonious; they are not directed toward the well-being of all, to the equipment of the saints, to the work of ministry, or to the building up of the body of Christ (Eph. 4:12)."[24] The fact is that our present patterns of church life, with our multiple forms of belief and practice, are — in good part at least — a fragmenting of the unity that God desires for his church.

To be sure, Kuyper was clearly aware of the scandalous aspects of the fact of ecclesial multiformity — Berkouwer cites comments by Kuyper about Satan's influence on many church divisions.[25] But even so, Berkouwer worries that the net effect of Kuyper's strong endorsement of

23. G. C. Berkouwer, *The Church*, trans. James E. Davison (Grand Rapids: Eerdmans, 1976), 58.
24. Berkouwer, *The Church*, 53.
25. Berkouwer, *The Church*, 57.

multiformity is to accept divisions within the body of Christ that we should in fact be working to overcome. In this sense Berkouwer finds something that needs to be retained in the more exclusivist emphasis on "the one true church." Given the actual realities of a divided church, says Berkouwer — embodying "much more tension than is expressed in the doctrine of pluriformity" — the idea of a visibly unified "pure church" can serve as an ideal toward which we must strive.[26]

"The Marks of Christians"

Berkouwer's call to work for visible unity, even while appreciating the positive aspects of ecclesial multiformity, is an attractive option for someone who might want to modify the harsh exclusivist tones of the Belgic Confession. But it is not difficult to imagine how the defenders of strict adherence to the Belgic Confession's formulations might respond to his attempt to make his peace with the tradition in this manner. They would insist that in his eagerness to get along with his ecumenical neighbors, Berkouwer has appealed too quickly to the alleged "spirit" of his confessional tradition while ignoring its specific warnings against compromising the truth.

It is important, however, to encourage these critics to be sure that they themselves are paying attention to all the confessional specifics. When people appeal to the Belgic Confession to defend strict exclusivism, they typically focus primarily on what is said about the marks of the true *church,* without paying equal attention to what is said in that same context about the marks of true *Christian individuals.* It is important to discern who the real Christians are, the Confession says, and we can do so by attending to these "marks of Christians": that they come to God "by faith; and when they have received Jesus Christ the only Saviour, they avoid sin, follow after righteousness, love the true God and their neighbour, neither turn aside to the right or left, and crucify the flesh with the works thereof." To be sure, the Confession continues, there will "remain in them great infirmities; but they fight against them through the Spirit, all the days of their life, continually taking their refuge in the blood, death, passion and obedience of our Lord Jesus Christ."[27]

As stated here, of course, this is compatible with Faber's insistence that

26. Berkouwer, *The Church,* 71.
27. Belgic Confession, article 29.

people can be "members of Christ" without being members of that visible assembly that comprises "the true church." Unfortunately for Faber's case, however, the Confession makes it clear that it does not mean to allow for the existence of genuine Christians who have failed to join the true church. In article 28, in explaining why no one "ought to withdraw himself, to live in a separate state from" the assembly that bears the marks of the true church, it issues the unambiguous verdict that *"out of it there is no salvation"* (emphasis mine).

This does not bode well for those who want to offer a coherent account of the Confession's teaching on this subject. If there is no salvation outside of that visible church that bears the confessionally prescribed marks of ecclesial legitimacy, we have to conclude that only those who belong to that church can be thought of as genuinely sharing salvifically in the life of Christ. If, on the other hand, we want to acknowledge that people can be genuine Christians even though they live apart from assemblies that conform strictly to the marks stipulated by the Confession, we must allow for a more inclusive understanding than the Confession seems to allow of that church apart from which "there is no salvation." Either way we seem to be compelled to deny something that the Confession clearly urges us to accept.

We are left, then, with a certain degree of confessional messiness. Nor does Kuyper's strategy, of simply disagreeing with the Confession, fare much better. In his desire to put a very positive face on ecclesial multiformity, Kuyper ends up with his own messiness, running the real risk of encouraging an unholy acceptance of unnecessary, even sinful, divisions within the church.

The truth seems to be that it is impossible for us to avoid some messiness in expressing some of our key ecclesiological convictions. But that may not be a bad thing. If our confessional documents have a serious weakness, it is not in their messiness but in their failure at crucial points to be explicit about the *need* for messiness. Conservative Reformed thinkers often appeal to those documents to explain "our stand" on a given subject to persons representing other perspectives. This is an unfortunate image. As George Vandervelde put it in his review of the Bouteneff-Aagaard book, our efforts to clear the path for a close relationship with other Christians take place on "a journey together."[28] The "stand" image is not an appropriate one for Calvinist pilgrims. We are a people in motion. And while we

28. Vandervelde, review of *Beyond*, 359.

have started out on our pilgrimage with a specific set of instructions for the journey of faith, we have inevitably found ourselves conversing along the way with Christian fellow travelers who have begun the journey with somewhat different travel instructions.

As we engage in these conversations, we often find it difficult to explain to our fellow pilgrims why we take our own travel instructions with utmost seriousness — especially as we insist on talking about a very visible way of being "the true church" while also desiring to be open to people who view things from quite different perspectives. We are motivated to keep at the effort, though, because we regularly recognize in our dialogue partners those individual "marks" that the Belgic Confession tells us to look for in our efforts to identify those who are trustworthy companions on the way. We see people from many different worshiping communities who very clearly — and often very admirably — "follow after righteousness, love the true God and their neighbour, neither turn aside to the right or left, and crucify the flesh with the works thereof."[29] And even though we may disagree with them on how best to understand what it means to configure the contours of our pilgrimage together, we know that if we refuse to journey on with them we run the risk of refusing also to follow the Guide who alone can lead us to our journey's End.

29. Belgic Confession, article 29.

Baptism and the Salvific Status of Children:
An Examination of Some Intra-Reformed Debates

What does God think of children? Is it fair to say that God has a positive disposition toward children *in general?* Or are God's saving mercies directed primarily toward the infant children of *believers?* Or is it an even more restricted focus than that: Is the divine love directed exclusively toward *elect* children, that is, those children whom God knows will someday end up in heaven? And what does this mean for our understanding of the practice of infant baptism?

These questions may not seem very interesting to Christians in a variety of theological traditions. Indeed, they will likely strike many as quite impertinent. The fact is, however, that a concern about this cluster of questions has on occasion triggered considerable theological controversy in the Reformed tradition. Sometimes those debates have even resulted in denominational divisions.

It is not always clear from a quick survey of these polemics why the issues generate so much passion for Reformed people. In this chapter I want to probe beneath the surface to identify some of the underlying concerns. These arguments have often been linked to questions about baptismal practices, but they have also been a way of focusing on the relationship between two central Reformed concepts, namely, *election* and *covenant.*

This essay previously appeared in *Calvin Theological Journal* 41 (2006). It is printed here with permission.

Revising Westminster

When Benjamin Warfield wrote his 1899 essay "The Polemics of Infant Baptism," he never referred to any disagreements within the Reformed world. Instead he concentrated exclusively (after a very brief introductory distancing of his view from the Roman Catholic position) on responding to the arguments lodged by Baptist theologians against the practice of infant baptism.[1] In one sense this is odd, given Warfield's focus on baptismal polemics. Presbyterians had often argued among themselves about baptismal practice, and the debates could get quite acrimonious. When, for example, the Scottish historian James Walker described, in his 1888 Cunningham Lectures, the differences that had been aired between Samuel Rutherford and Thomas Boston on whether the children of "openly-wicked parents" should be baptized — a much-discussed topic in seventeenth- and early-eighteenth-century Scotland — he noted that when Rutherford argued for such a practice "[a]lmost with vehemence," Boston had responded by depicting Rutherford's view as "simply monstrous."[2]

But Warfield was writing in a time when many of the more traditional Calvinists in Presbyterian circles in the United States were eager to distance themselves from harsh views about God's treatment of this or that group of infants. In the final decade of the nineteenth century a movement was afoot in the northern Presbyterian denomination — led by Charles Briggs of New York's Union Seminary — to revise the Westminster Confession so as to tone down what the advocates of confessional revision saw as the harsher expressions of traditional Calvinism.[3] Warfield and his Princeton colleagues, along with their orthodox ally at Union, W. G. T. Shedd, argued against the proposed revisions, on the grounds that the revisionists' claims regarding Westminster's harshness were unfounded.

1. Benjamin B. Warfield, "The Polemics of Infant Baptism," *Presbyterian Quarterly* 13 (1899): 313-34; also available at http://www.the-highway.com/InfantBaptism_Warfield.html.

2. James Walker, *The Theology and Theologians of Scotland, Chiefly of the Seventeenth and Eighteenth Centuries* (Edinburgh: T. & T. Clark, 1888), 122-23.

3. For my comments here about the debates over confessional revision, I am relying on Lewis Bevens Schenck, *The Presbyterian Doctrine of Children in the Covenant* (New Haven: Yale University Press, 1940; Phillipsburg, N.J.: Presbyterian and Reformed, 2003), 119-47, as well as David B. Calhoun, "Old Princeton and the Westminster Standards," in J. Ligon Duncan III, *The Westminster Confession into the 21st Century: Essays in Remembrance of the 350th Anniversary of the Westminster Assembly*, vol. 2 (Ross-shire, U.K.: Christian Focus Publications, 2004), 33-61, and David B. Calhoun, *Princeton Seminary*, vol. 2, *The Majestic Testimony, 1869-1929* (Carlisle, Pa.: Banner of Truth Trust, 1996), 121-24, 187-94.

One of the passages that triggered the calls for revision was a section in the Westminster Confession's chapter "Of Effectual Calling," in which the salvific status of infants was addressed: "Elect infants, dying in infancy, are regenerated and saved by Christ through the Spirit, who worketh when and where, and how he pleaseth. So also are all other elect persons who are incapable of being outwardly called by the ministry of the Word."[4] The revisionists saw this passage as clearly teaching that only a small subgroup of children receive saving mercies, thus reinforcing the widespread impression of a Calvinist God who is both arbitrary and stingy in dispensing grace.

The antirevisionists refused to own this interpretation, however. Shedd made their case forcefully in a book published in 1893. How we understand the confession's reference to "elect infants," he observed, depends on what we take the antithesis of that category of persons to be. And here, he insisted, there were two options: "One makes the antithesis to be, 'non-elect infants dying in infancy'; the other makes it to be, 'elect infants not dying in infancy.'" The first interpretation means to contrast elect and nonelect infants, while the second posits two classes of elect infants: those who die in infancy and those who do not. Shedd set out a detailed case for the second interpretation, according to which "[t]here are no non-elect dying infants"; all children who die in infancy are saved, he insisted. Indeed, in the final analysis it comes down to a simple matter of exegesis, turning "upon the point whether the Saviour's declaration, 'Of such is the kingdom of God,' means, 'Of *all* such,' or, 'Of *some* such.'" Shedd had no doubt that the former reading was the correct one.[5]

Shedd did not deny that earlier writers who were revered by him and his fellow antirevisionists taught the damnation of some infants. But in their own way, he argued, these theologians were actually providing a basis for a "widening of the circle of infant election."[6] Shedd used Augustine as a case in point. Like Calvin and his followers, Augustine adamantly opposed any watering down of the doctrine of original sin. All human beings under fallen conditions are born with "a corrupt disposition" and are thus deserving of eternal death.[7] Augustine was right to refuse any minimizing of

4. Westminster Confession of Faith, chapter 10, section 3, in Philip Schaff, ed., *The Creeds of Christendom, with a History and Critical Notes*, vol. 3 (Grand Rapids: Baker, 1996), 625.

5. William G. T. Shedd, *Calvinism: Pure and Mixed, a Defence of the Westminster Standards* (Carlisle, Pa.: Banner of Truth Trust, 1986), 113.

6. Shedd, *Calvinism*, 109.

7. Shedd, *Calvinism*, 107.

the punishment due to our sinful nature. What he failed to see, however, was the possibility that he might "have magnified the divine mercy" by allowing that God might save, not just a subset of dying infants, but all of them as a decision of sovereign grace: "Justice cannot give two decisions as to whether original sin *deserves* eternal death; but mercy can give two decisions as to whether it will or will not *pardon* it. Augustine might therefore have affirmed the exact and full retribution due to original sin in the case of infants as in that of adults, and then have affirmed with the later Calvinist that the infinite compassion of God frees all of them from the dreadful guilt and penalty by the blood of atonement."[8]

Whether Shedd's interpretation of this section of the confession captured the exact intentions of the Westminster divines is probably open to debate. But there is no question that he was giving expression to a fairly solid consensus of most of the key leaders of the orthodox party of his own day. And when the church adopted a "Declaratory Statement" on these matters in 1903, both Shedd and the Princeton theologians were content with the way the question of infant election was treated. The declaration stipulated, "[w]ith reference to Chapter X, Section 3, of the Confession of Faith, that it is not to be regarded as teaching that any who die in infancy are lost. We believe that all dying in infancy are included in the election of grace, and are regenerated and saved by Christ through the Spirit, who works when and where and how He pleases."[9] Warfield, for one, was actually quite enthusiastic in his endorsement of the declaration. It not only "reaffirms" the meaning of the confession, he announced, but it does so in a manner as "to protect this text from false inferences and to strengthen it by explication."[10]

Not all Presbyterians were as confident as Warfield was that this explication of the confession's views regarding the election of infants was a step forward. Those conservatives who were, a few decades later, to leave the northern Presbyterian church to form the Orthodox Presbyterian Church had serious doubts about the 1903 declaration. Professor John Murray, who taught for many years at Westminster Theological Seminary, strongly defended the *un*-"explicated" words of the original confession. In

8. Shedd, *Calvinism,* 109-10.

9. Declaratory Statement (1903) of the Presbyterian Church in the United States of America, in Schaff, *The Creeds of Christendom,* 3:920-21.

10. Benjamin B. Warfield, "The Confession of Faith as Revised in 1903," in *Selected Shorter Writings,* vol. 2, ed. John E. Meeter (Phillipsburg, N.J.: Presbyterian and Reformed, 1973), 373.

claiming to clarify the Reformed understanding of the election of infants, Murray argued, the Declaration of 1903 had spoken with too much certainty on a matter about which the Scriptures themselves were unclear. He refused to adopt the view that "all who die in infancy are the recipients of the saving grace of God," choosing rather to "leave that question in the realm where it belongs, namely, the unrevealed counsel of God."[11] On this point, then, Murray and others in the Orthodox Presbyterian Church preferred to align themselves with the views of Calvin and many early Calvinists rather than to embrace the more inclusive emphases of the Old Princeton theologians.[12]

It is important to keep in mind, however, that the disagreement between, say, a Warfield and a Murray on this question of the salvation of persons dying in infancy is in fact a very Calvinist disagreement. Both sides saw themselves as jealously guarding a primary emphasis on divine sovereignty and human unworthiness. One group made their point by insisting — without any effort to soften the point — that God is free to choose whom he will save while consigning others, including guilty dying infants, to the eternal punishment they fully deserve. The other group, in arguing for the salvation of all dying infants, saw themselves as being equally protective of the prerogatives of a sovereign God who, precisely because he is sovereign, can dispense his saving mercies, in the words of the Westminster Confession's brief comment on elect infants, "when and where, and how he pleaseth."

Why Baptize Children?

While questions about the salvific status of children who die in infancy have been important for Reformed theologians, much more attention has been given to questions about the status of those infant children of believers who do *not* die in their early years. Specifically, much attention has been given to the standing of *baptized* children in the eyes of God. What does the baptism of a child mean in terms of the child's relationship to God?

11. John Murray, "Why We Baptise Infants," excerpted from the *Presbyterian Guardian* 5 (1938), at http://www.datarat.net/DR/baptism.html.

12. For an account of the rejection by the Orthodox Presbyterian Church of the 1903 Declaration, see Edwin H. Rian, "The Beginnings of Unbelief," at http://www.american presbyterianchurch.org/unbelief.htm.

A typical response by Reformed theologians begins with a denial of the theology of baptismal regeneration. There is nothing about the rite of baptism itself that somehow guarantees the salvation of the person being baptized. Warfield's case is the standard one for many in the tradition. Baptism itself cannot be taken as effecting salvation. "All baptism," he says, "is inevitably administered on the basis not of knowledge but of presumption. And if we must baptize on presumption, the whole principle is yielded; and it would seem that we must baptize all whom we may fairly presume to be members of Christ's body." This means that "it is inevitable that we shall baptize all those for whom we may, on any grounds, fairly cherish a good presumption that they belong to God's people — and this surely includes the infant children of believers, concerning the favor of God to whom there exist many precious promises."[13]

In those brief comments, Warfield uses a form of the word "presume" four times. This same term with its variation was used quite freely by other Reformed thinkers in America at the time — numerous examples of which are provided by Lewis Bevens Schenck in his detailed account of the discussions that took place during this period.[14]

Presuming Regeneration

While Presbyterian theologians could toss out the term "presume" and its variants in a fairly unself-conscious manner, it was not so among the Dutch Calvinists, for whom, both in the Netherlands and in North America, the term as applied to baptized children has occasioned bitter controversies.

The central reference point in these controversies was Abraham Kuyper's defense of "presumptive regeneration," a perspective he outlined for an American audience in an 1891 essay. While Calvinists know they can never "pronounce absolutely on the presence or absence of spiritual life in infants," he argued, they do have grounds, given the covenant promises recorded in the Scriptures, for affirming that God would have believers presume that their infant children are the "recipients of efficacious grace, in whom the work of regeneration proper has already begun" by the divine implanting of the "seed of faith." Thus, according to Calvinist teaching, "this consideration based on the divine Word made it imperative [for be-

---

13. Warfield, "Polemics of Infant Baptism," 313.
14. Schenck, *The Presbyterian Doctrine*, 104-47.

lievers] to look on their infant children as elect and saved and to treat them accordingly."[15] Such, he insisted, was "the import of all Calvinistic confessions, where they treat of the sacraments." And there can be no room, Kuyper stipulated, for disagreement on the subject within the boundaries of Reformed orthodoxy: "It amounts to a total subversion of the Calvinist view therefore: 1. To deny that the seed of regeneration can be produced by God in a new-born babe. 2. Not to assume this in the case of children of believers. 3. To administer Baptism to them on any other supposition. 4. Not to consider them in bringing them up as potentially regenerated, and not to make this the basis of the demand for conversion."[16]

There is no debating that at least part of what Kuyper argues on this subject has much precedent in Reformed thought. For example, in his lengthy defense of infant baptism in the *Institutes,* John Calvin answers his opponents by pointing to John the Baptist whom, he says, God "sanctified in his mother's womb." So "let us not attempt, then," he continues, "to impose a law upon God to keep him from sanctifying whom he pleases, just as he sanctified this child, inasmuch as his power is not lessened."[17] After all, he observes later, God "keeps his own timetable of regeneration."[18]

This insistence on God's sovereign power to regenerate infants when and where God pleases was repeated by many early Reformed scholars, as was demonstrated by Geerhardus Vos, who translated the above-mentioned essay by Kuyper, and who addressed some of the same issues in his 1891 rectoral address at the Christian Reformed Church's Theological School in Grand Rapids, Michigan.[19] Vos — who would soon move to Princeton Seminary where he would teach for many decades — assembled numerous examples of Calvinist theologians who used the kind of point

15. Abraham Kuyper, "Calvinism and Confessional Revision," trans. Geerhardus Vos, *Presbyterian and Reformed Review* 2, no. 7 (July 1891): 388.

16. Kuyper, "Calvinism and Confessional Revision," 390.

17. John Calvin, *Institutes of the Christian Religion,* ed. John T. McNeill, trans. Ford Lewis Battles, Library of Christian Classics, vols. 20 and 21 (Philadelphia: Westminster, 1960), 4.16.17, pp. 1340-41.

18. Calvin, *Institutes* 4.16.31, p. 1357.

19. Geerhardus Vos, "The Doctrine of the Covenant in Reformed Theology," in *Redemptive History and Biblical Interpretation: The Shorter Writings of Geerhardus Vos,* ed. Richard B. Gaffin (Phillipsburg, N.J.: Presbyterian and Reformed, 1980). This address was delivered in Dutch, under the original title, *De verbondsleer in de Gereformeerde theologie,* and published locally in Grand Rapids; an English translation by S. Voorwinde and W. Van Generen was printed privately in 1971; this version was used for the Gaffin volume with some editing by Gaffin.

made by Calvin as support for the doctrine of presumptive regeneration. Vos cites, for example, Beza's statement that while "the hidden judgment must be left to God," we can assume that *"normally, by virtue of the promise, all* who have been born of believing parents, or if one of the parents believes, *are sanctified,"* and Peter Martyr's verdict that "we assume that the children of believers are holy, as long as in growing up they do not demonstrate themselves to be estranged from Christ."[20]

Unlike Kuyper, however, Vos pays careful attention to the disagreements among key Reformed thinkers in spelling out their views about the regeneration of infants. Especially helpful is his sorting out of the nuances among three schools of thought on "the time when the promises of the covenant are usually realized by regeneration in the children of the covenant."[21] The first school holds that all children of believers, and not only those who die in their infancy, "possess the Holy Spirit from their earliest childhood and so are born again and united to Christ."[22] The second school, while refusing to be dogmatic about when regeneration takes place, sees the administration of infant baptism as the most likely occasion when many children receive regenerating grace. One of the theologians Vos cites here is William Ames, who suggests that "God infuses the habitus or principle of grace in some at the time of their baptism," while conceding that "God can communicate this same grace both before and after baptism."[23] A third school, however, insists on positing a special relationship between regeneration and the conscious reception of the promises of the gospel. Vos notes that those who argue for this perspective see "the preaching of the Word [as] the usual means by which regeneration takes place," and "that God does not depart from this rule without necessity." The act of regeneration, then, typically "bides its time," in the children of believers, "until they can be brought to a conscious possession of the sealed blessings of the covenant."[24]

It is the third view that seems to comport with the description offered in the Canons of the Synod of Dort (1618-19) of how the elect are brought to faith: "[W]hen God carries out this good pleasure in his chosen ones, or works true conversion in them, he not only sees to it that the gospel is proclaimed to them outwardly, and enlightens their minds powerfully by the Holy Spirit so that they may rightly understand and discern the things of

---

20. Vos, "Doctrine of the Covenant," 263-64.
21. Vos, "Doctrine of the Covenant," 264.
22. Vos, "Doctrine of the Covenant," 264.
23. Vos, "Doctrine of the Covenant," 266.
24. Vos, "Doctrine of the Covenant," 266-67.

the Spirit of God, but by the effective operation of the same regenerating Spirit, he also penetrates into the inmost being of man, opens the closed heart, softens the hard heart, and circumcises the heart that is uncircumcised."[25] To be sure, this does not settle the issue, even when all parties agree to take the canons as their benchmark for questions of Reformed orthodoxy. Advocates for the other two views could argue that the account given here in the canons applies primarily to those who come into the covenant community as adults — or even that the account is a highly compacted description of stages that need not take place in a certain order within a limited period of time.

In any event, it is important to be clear about the points of agreement among these parties. None of them wants to deny the mysteries of the regenerating work of the Spirit; regeneration can take place wherever and whenever God chooses to dispense sovereign grace. Nor does any of them want to see the baptismal ceremony as — in the manner they would attribute to their Catholic opponents — somehow "automatically" or "mechanically" dispensing regenerating grace.

How, then, are we to understand the issues under dispute among these parties, especially since, as we shall see, the issues among them have been debated on occasion with much zeal and with church-dividing effects? At least two factors are at work in these debates, one pastoral and the other strictly theological. The pastoral factor has to do with what sorts of spiritual expectations we can legitimately encourage within a Reformed community. This factor is most clearly seen in the discussions of the salvific status of children who die in infancy. Given the Calvinist teaching regarding the natural "depravity" of every human being, including tiny babies, as well as the teaching that the salvation of any individual is decided only on the basis of divine election — where it is also taken for granted that not all human beings are numbered among the elect — what comfort can be offered to parents whose young child has died? It should not surprise us that Reformed theologians would engage in significant speculation on this pastoral matter, even though there were not resources in their theology for a decisive resolution of the issues. The simple fact that a child had been baptized, for example, cannot be a basis for certainty regarding its eternal destiny, since Calvinists are at pains to oppose any assumptions about an "automatic" dispensing of grace in baptism.

25. The Canons of Dort, Third and Fourth Points of Main Doctrine, Article 11, *Ecumenical Creeds and Reformed Confessions* (Grand Rapids: CRC Publications, 1988), 134-35.

The theological factor has to do with the Calvinist insistence that the act of regeneration cannot be repealed — "once saved, always saved" — a teaching that raises interesting theological challenges for understanding the character of infant baptism. In the Dutch Reformed tradition, for example, the historic Form for the Administration of Baptism of Children states that "baptism witnesses and seals unto us the washing away of our sins through Jesus Christ," with these results: "the Son seals unto us that He washes us in His blood from all our sins, incorporating us into the fellowship of His death and resurrection, so that we are freed from our sins and accounted righteous before God."[26] This seems to state quite unambiguously that by virtue of baptism a child is salvifically quite secure. Yet it seems also clear that some baptized children will depart from the path of discipleship. How are we to understand what their baptism means, especially if we hold to the Calvinist teaching that the salvation that comes to us when Christ "washes us in His blood from all our sins" can never be taken away from us?

As we have seen already, this question gets answered in various ways within the Reformed community. And even in spelling out his typology of three schools of thought on the regeneration of the infant children of believers, Geerhardus Vos acknowledges nuances and shifting formulations among the thinkers within a given school.

In a more fundamental sense, however, the real issue comes down to choice over how one is to handle a tension between two theological themes that loom large in Reformed thought: *election* and *covenant*. When the tension is resolved by placing a primary stress on divine election, there is a corresponding insistence that the covenant promises set forth in the baptismal form really apply only to the children who are numbered among the elect. The baptized children who eventually depart from the paths of godliness are not, strictly speaking, parties to the covenant. When, on the other hand, the tension is resolved with a primary emphasis on the covenant, then the covenant promises are seen as genuinely applied to all baptized children, whether or not they are predestined for salvation. On this view, the doctrine of election — while firmly endorsed — is relegated to the realm of mystery. It is the church's task, the argument goes, not only to proclaim the promises of the covenant, but also to set forth the conditions according to which those promises will be fulfilled. When children do not, during their lives,

---

26. *Psalter Hymnal: Centennial Edition* (Grand Rapids: Publication Committee of the Christian Reformed Church, 1959), liturgy section, 85.

satisfy the conditions of the covenant, they must be considered covenant-breakers. And one cannot break a covenant to which one is not subject.

The Dutch Reformed community has long been conscious of the differences between these two perspectives, and at times it has been willing to tolerate the differences within its acknowledged boundaries of orthodoxy. For example, in 1892 the group of churches that Abraham Kuyper had led out of the larger Reformed denomination united with a group that had seceded from that larger body in 1834. The negotiations that led to this ecclesiastical union were complicated ones, not the least reason for which was their different views on the relationship between election and covenant. Herman Hanko has provided a concise summary of the two perspectives:

> The Kuyperians taught the following concerning the covenant: (1) it is unilateral, that is, one-sided in its establishment and in its maintenance; (2) it is unconditional; (3) only the elect are in the covenant; (4) baptism signifies that the elect children of the covenant are incorporated into it from infancy, as a general rule.
>
> The people who traced their ecclesiastical origins to the Separation of 1834 taught: (1) a bilateral covenant, that is, one which took on the form of an agreement between two parties; (2) a conditional covenant in which man had to fulfill conditions in order to enter the covenant; (3) all who are baptized are included in the covenant in an objective sense; (4) baptism signifies that the promise of God is signified and sealed objectively to every baptized child.[27]

The two parties did argue about these matters, but for the most part the differences between them came to expression in subsequent debates over the merits of Kuyper's teachings regarding presumptive regeneration. In an important sense, that was somewhat of a diversion, since Kuyper's views on that subject were in fact a way of spelling out what he saw as the implications of the insistence that only elect children are parties to the covenant. If we say — so the Kuyperian argument goes — that in baptism the child is in fact redeemed by Christ, then we must presume, once that baptism has taken place, that the child is one of the elect. Only if that child later departs significantly from the standards of godliness can we relinquish that presumption.

27. Herman Hanko, *For Thy Truth's Sake: A Doctrinal History of the Protestant Reformed Churches* (Grandville, Mich.: Reformed Free Publishing Association, 2000), 264-65.

In 1905 the synod of the church that had been formed by the 1892 merger addressed the question of presumptive regeneration, in a decision known in Dutch Reformed circles as "the Conclusions of Utrecht." The decision included what was basically a straightforward endorsement of Kuyper's view: "According to the confession of our churches, the seed of the covenant is to be considered regenerated and sanctified in Christ according to God's promises, until the opposite becomes clear in their lives and in the ideas they hold when they grow up." It did add, though, a gentle correction to the way the Kuyperians typically talked about the "ground" for administering baptism: "However, it is less accurate to say that baptism is administered to the children of believers on the ground of their presumed regeneration, because the ground for baptism is God's promise and ordinance."[28]

In offering this slight amendment the synod was acknowledging here a point of theology that was later made forcefully by Herman Hoeksema:

> The ground for infant baptism cannot and may not be sought in the presupposition that those infants are regenerated. For, in the first place, nothing more than a presupposition can rest upon a presupposition. And for infant baptism we must certainly have a firmer basis than a mere presupposition. Besides, we know for a certainty that not all the fleshly children are, or become, regenerated, while nevertheless *all* the children of believers must be baptized. . . . [T]he firm ground for the baptism of the little children of the church lies only herein, that God causes His covenant to run in the line of continued generations. . . . And since God establishes His covenant with believers and their seed in their generations, therefore it follows that also those generations of believers must receive the sign of God's covenant.[29]

Hoeksema's critique of Kuyper on this issue of the "ground" of baptism is especially significant in that Hoeksema was — as we shall see — a strong supporter of the Kuyperian idea that the covenant promises can only be legitimately addressed to children who are elect. But Hoeksema saw clearly

---

28. "Conclusies van Utrecht, 1905," English translation, in the Christian Reformed Church's *Acts of Synod*, 1942 (Grand Rapids: Christian Reformed Publishing House, 1942), 352. The document is reprinted in Hanko, *For Thy Truth's Sake*, 427-31.

29. Herman Hoeksema, *Believers and Their Seed: Children in the Covenant*, rev. ed. (Grandville, Mich.: Reformed Free Publishing Association, 2000), 95-96.

that *that* doctrine did not have to be linked to an endorsement of pre-sumptive regeneration.

The 1905 synod was widely interpreted as having attempted to formu-late a compromise view: endorsing a pragmatic justification of presump-tive regeneration, while also gently chiding Kuyper for treating presump-tive regeneration as a theological "ground" for infant baptism. But as Hoeksema's critique shows, the effect of the synodical declaration was to give much ammunition to the defenders of the more basic Kuyperian no-tion that the covenant must be subordinated to election. They received from the synod permission to keep talking about presumptive regenera-tion — albeit in more modest tones — if they chose to do so; but more im-portantly, the way was now clear for those who were so inclined to mount a strong theological defense of the for-the-elect-only understanding of the baptismal promises, without having to link that to an energetic defense of presumptive regeneration.

The theological tensions over the question of presumptive regenera-tion were not laid to rest by the 1905 decision. They finally surfaced as open conflict in the 1930s, when the pastor-theologian Klaas Schilder led a theo-logical charge against some key aspects of the covenant theology associ-ated with the Utrecht Conclusions. The debates continued into the 1940s, unrestrained even by the German occupation of the Netherlands. Schilder was imprisoned for a while by the Nazis for his participation in the Dutch resistance movement, and after his release he went into hiding. During this period he continued to write against the theology of the Utrecht synod's declarations, and his opponents took steps to censure him for his theologi-cal resistance. Even though Schilder was unable to appear before ecclesial assemblies to respond to his opponents, he and several other like-minded pastors and professors were suspended from their official duties, and then deposed from their offices in 1944. Schilder and his allies responded by de-claring themselves "liberated" from an ecclesiastical "hierarchicalism" that chose to impose "extrabiblical" doctrines upon the believing community. They established a "federation" (a term they much preferred over "denom-ination") that came to be known as the Reformed Churches in the Nether-lands (Liberated) — in Dutch, *de Gereformeerde Kerken in Nederland (vrijgemaakt)* — which became the third largest of the country's dozen or so Reformed denominations.[30]

---

30. The history of this conflict, and the subsequent developments in the churches es-tablished by Schilder and his sympathizers, is told in detail, from the Hoeksema perspective,

When many members of these Liberated congregations emigrated from the Netherlands to Canada during the years immediately following World War II, they were faced with the dilemma of where to seek church affiliation in North America. Schilder warned these followers against joining Christian Reformed congregations, since that denomination had endorsed the Utrecht Conclusions. Instead, he encouraged them to affiliate with the Protestant Reformed churches — the denomination that had been founded by Herman Hoeksema and his colleagues after they had been deposed from the Christian Reformed ministry in the 1920s because of their opposition to the Christian Reformed Church's 1924 declarations in support of the theology of "common grace."

But soon the disagreements about covenant theology that had caused so much turmoil in the Netherlands also divided the new immigrants from the Protestant Reformed leadership. What is especially instructive about this version of the debate is that it was carried on primarily by two gifted thinkers, Hoeksema and Schilder, who had once been friends but who were not afraid to draw the lines very sharply in delineating the differences between them on this subject. It would be difficult to find a clearer confrontation between two very different Reformed understandings of the nature of the promises made in baptism, with Hoeksema arguing for a direct link between covenant and election, and Schilder insisting that the promises of the covenant must be offered without attempting to understand the mysteries of electing grace.

Herman Hoeksema gave much attention throughout his career to the nature of the promises given to children in baptism. One significant issue at stake in his protests against the Christian Reformed Church's synodically endorsed theology of "common grace" was the way in which that outlook encouraged, on Hoeksema's reading, a "free offer" of salvation to the nonelect. His strong convictions on this matter led him in turn to oppose any hint that this sincere offer of salvation might be extended to nonelect children in the baptismal ceremony. For this reason he was worried that Schilder's immigrant followers in Canada might import that same theology into the Protestant Reformed Churches. And, even though his denomination dealt rather quickly with the Schilderian incursion in the local Canadian context — resulting in the establishing of the Schilder-oriented Cana-

---

in Hanko, *For Thy Truth's Sake,* 297-315, and, from the Schilder perspective, in W. W. J. Van Oene, *Inheritance Preserved: The Canadian Reformed and Free Reformed Churches of Australia in Historical Perspctive* (Winnipeg: Premier, 1975), 277-96, 65-80.

dian Reformed Churches — the debate did not die off within the Protestant Reformed ranks, resulting in a major schism not long afterward, in 1953.[31]

Hoeksema's extensive writings on the debated issues[32] were summarized nicely in a 1950 synodical decision, "A Brief Declaration of Principles of the Protestant Reformed Churches."[33] Appealing to passages from the Scriptures and the historical Dutch Reformed confessions, the statement declares:

1. That all the covenant blessings are for the elect alone.
2. That God's promise is unconditionally for them only: for God cannot promise what was not objectively merited by Christ.
3. That the promise of God bestows the objective right of salvation not upon all the children that are born under the historical dispensation of the covenant, that is, not upon all that are baptized, but only upon the spiritual seed.

When the traditional baptismal form states, then, that while "our young children do not understand these things, we may not therefore exclude them from baptism" and that they are thereby "received unto grace in Christ," this has to be taken as teaching, the Protestant Reformed synod stipulated, "[t]hat here none other than the elect children of the covenant are meant and they are unconditionally, without their knowledge, received unto grace in Christ." Since it "is very evident," said the synod, any suggestion "[t]hat the promise of the covenant is conditional and for all that are baptized" is to be firmly repudiated. God does not promise or offer anything to persons he does not intend to redeem.

Schilder responded to Hoeksema with the insistence that we do in fact offer the covenant promises sincerely to all baptized children. And when we make the offer, he added, we do well also to leave aside questions about the mysteries of divine election:

31. The debate that led to the split of 1953 is chronicled in Hanko, *For Thy Truth's Sake*, 297-315.

32. Cf. his book-length discussion in *Believers and Their Seed*, as well as the discussion at many points in his *Reformed Dogmatics* (Grand Rapids: Reformed Free Publishing, 1966).

33. For the text of this document, see Hanko, *For Thy Truth's Sake*, 434-60; it is also reprinted, without the original's many citations from historical confessions, in Jelle Faber, *American Secession Theologians on Covenant and Baptism*, and Klaas Schilder, *Extra-Scriptural Binding — a New Danger*, one volume containing both works (Neerlandia, Alberta: Inheritance Publications, 1996), 58-71.

Our thoughts must be led by the fact that promise and demand are two parts of every covenant. The covenant is established with the believers and their seed; that is according to God's own word! There are those who do not say "yes" to those words and by that become manifest as falling away, and there are others who do say "yes" (Yes, LORD, here I am). God has thought differently about them, according to what Calvin calls the awe-inspiring decree of election and reprobation, but what He thinks to Himself is for Him, what He says is for me! Only the latter is the covenant and that is why all believers with their children are real covenant children, and they are really baptized; only if we accept that we can throw out the anchor into the river which is navigable for the church and have it catch in the firm bottom of God's spoken word. If a believer thinks "I am baptized, but of what use is that to me; it could have been a mistake, and not a real baptism (only some drops of water)," then he will never have rest. But what is promised and demanded you may consider as something that you have coming to you, as a right, and that gives certainty.[34]

Baptismal Promises

There is no question that Schilder's perspective represents the actual majority view in the Reformed tradition. But, again, the debate between Schilder and Hoeksema points to a deep tension within the Reformed understanding of these things. It must be said in Hoeksema's favor that he rightly calls our attention to themes in the traditional forms for administering infant baptism that do not square easily with the doctrine of election when taken as applying to all baptized children. Schilder may be correct in insisting that we set aside all thoughts about the mysteries of God's electing purposes when we witness an actual baptism of a child. But surely there will be very urgent circumstances in the hearts of parents when questions about the meaning of the traditional baptismal formulations become poignant. What *does* it mean for Reformed believers, for example, when the pastor says, in applying the waters of baptism to the foreheads of their children, that with this water Christ also "doth wash us in His blood from

34. Klaas Schilder, "The Main Points of the Doctrine of the Covenant," trans. T. van-Laar (1992) (an address given on August 31, 1944), available at http://spindleworks.com/library/schilder/covenant.htm.

all our sins, incorporating us into the fellowship of His death and resurrection, so that we are freed from all our sins, and accounted righteous before God"?

When the oldest Dutch Reformed baptismal form was written, the authors likely did not have the concerns of anxious parents primarily in mind. The liturgical formulations emerged in contexts where open rejection of church affiliation by those who had been baptized as children was less common than it has become in recent centuries. Thus the problem of rejection of the baptismal promises looms larger now than it did in the past. And it is clear that in attempting to address this problem, we cannot simply lump the rejecters in with all those people in the world who have never shown any interest in, and who lack any knowledge of, the Christian faith. As one mid-twentieth-century Christian Reformed leader put it — likely with Hoeksema's perspective in mind — if we think of the covenant as "a vital relationship," then it makes sense to say that only those who are regenerated are truly in it. But there is also the sense in which it is "a legal relationship," a framework in the context of which a person can be thought of as *violating* the covenantal obligations — the person "who is in no sense within the covenant can hardly break it."[35]

To be sure, it was an option for Hoeksema simply to deny this. He wanted to pay very explicit attention at every point in his theology to a sharp distinction between those who were "in" — people who had been elected to salvation from all eternity — and those who were "out" — a group he did not shrink from regularly characterizing as "reprobates." Given this insistence, he could have simply held to a view that says that the only *genuine* baptisms are those administered to elect children, and that all other human beings — those who are raised in the Christian community as well as those who have no contact with the life of the faithful — are simply to be classified as reprobates.

But Hoeksema cannot bring himself to settle for such a stark portrayal. While "[s]trictly speaking," he affirms, "no one can maintain that anyone who has been reprobated by God can really belong to the covenant of grace," it is also the case that "this people of the covenant reveals itself historically as intertwined with and connected with an evil and reprobate shell, carnal Israel." And it is clear biblically that it is the entirety of this peoplehood, elect and reprobate alike, who are "addressed and treated as

---

35. R. B. Kuiper, *To Be or Not to Be Reformed: Whither the Christian Reformed Church* (Grand Rapids: Zondervan, 1959), 68-69.

God's people" — even though God's real "purpose is the salvation of the elect kernel."[36]

Still, says Hoeksema, these nonelect children of the church are not simply "to be placed on a par with the heathen, with those who never come into contact with God's covenant." In their lives "there is indeed a certain influence of God's covenant." As branches of the vine that are cut off, it is not the case that they "stand in no living connection with the vine whatsoever. No, the distinction is between the branches which *do* bear fruit and other branches which *do not* bear fruit." In this sense, we can think of a certain way of belonging to the covenant that does not result in bringing forth those results that can only result from the gift of saving grace.[37] These non-fruit-bearing members of the church are "children of the kingdom in the outward sense of the word"; they "live very close to the stream of grace, so close that they understand and taste something — or sometimes even much — of it, but always with a natural understanding and an impenitent heart."[38]

To be sure, Hoeksema quickly adds that these people *"receive no grace."*[39] Indeed, these "children of the kingdom who are cast out shall certainly be beaten with double stripes, precisely because they despised and trampled upon that which they once tasted."[40] What is interesting here, however, is not so much that he sees these unfruitful branches as especially worthy of divine wrath, but that he does feel compelled to create a third class of people who do not fit, without significant explanation, into the class of either the elect or the reprobate. Basic to Hoeksema's theology is the distinction between two radically different subgroups within the human race: those who are damned and those who through no merit of their own have been drawn by the Spirit into a covenantal fellowship with God. But he must also admit to another group: they are damned, to be sure; but unlike the vast majority of the other reprobates, they are not able to "entirely escape the vibrations of the Holy Spirit as these operate and reveal themselves in the church."[41]

---

36. Hoeksema, *Believers and Their Seed*, 137.
37. Hoeksema, *Believers and Their Seed*, 140-41.
38. Hoeksema, *Believers and Their Seed*, 142-43.
39. Hoeksema, *Believers and Their Seed*, 144, emphasis Hoeksema's.
40. Hoeksema, *Believers and Their Seed*, 148.
41. Hoeksema, *Believers and Their Seed*, 147.

"The Secret Things"

No Calvinist should simply dismiss Hoeksema's perspective as totally wrongheaded. He is making use of categories that are basic to the theology set forth in the Calvinist Reformation. The proper response for those who accept the importance of those categories is the one given by Charles Spurgeon to those fellow Calvinists who in his day made their case in terms similar to Hoeksema's: "I do not think I differ from any of my Hyper-Calvinistic brethren in what I do believe, but I differ from them in what they do not believe. I do not hold any less than they do, but I hold a little more, and, I think, a little more of the truth revealed in the Scriptures."[42] And the truth is surely that the Scriptures do not focus exclusively, or even primarily, on the categories associated with the doctrine of election when expressing the promises and expectations associated with God's covenant with the believing community.

Schilder deals with the covenantal promises in a manner akin to Spurgeon's spirit, and it is good to heed his counsel in our Reformed understanding of what happens when the covenant promises are uttered at a baptismal ceremony:

> Promise and demand are, in the service of God, very closely connected together. God does not say "I promise you" as a special decree, but He speaks to me with a concrete condition: immediately the demand of faith is put forward. Promise and demand belong together; the two are one. Therefore God chooses the form of speaking with a condition; not that I earn salvation with my faith. No, God is silent about the question whether a specific person shall receive faith through election, and about the question whether that specific person shall appear later to have been elected. Totally silent about the question whether I am elected, He speaks to me with a living voice about promise and demand: the goods lay in the promise; if you accept the promise then it is for you.[43]

The tone and spirit of Schilder's thoughts here are a good indication of why so many of John Calvin's followers, when someone among them has

---

42. Charles Spurgeon, "A Defence of Calvinism," available at http://www.spurgeon.org/calvinis.htm.
43. Schilder, "The Main Points of the Doctrine of the Covenant."

lingered too long in reflecting on the doctrine of election, have issued the reminder set forth in Deuteronomy 29:29: "The secret things belong to the LORD our God, but the revealed things belong to us and to our children forever, to observe the words of this law."

The Seminary, the Church, and the Academy

What *kind* of entity is a theological school? What is its location in the overall scheme of things? These may seem to be very abstruse questions to pose. But I am convinced they are important ones. Questions about the "ontology" of the theological school are regularly lurking just below the surface when people talk about whether theological schools are doing a good job or how we can best measure their effectiveness.

I put the word "ontology" in quotes here to indicate that I am employing it in a somewhat loose sense. But I use the term because I also want to signal the fact that the questions I am posing are rather basic ones. I am interested in getting clear about where we are to place the theological school on the cultural map. More specifically, I am interested in how we are to understand the "being" of a theological school in relationship to the academy on the one hand and the church on the other. Is the theological school, in the most basic sense, a part of the academic world or is it best thought of as an ecclesial entity? Or is it — again, in the most basic sense — a hybrid type?

My own view is that it is indeed a hybrid, combining characteristics of both academy and church. Further on I will explain and defend this conception. I will also discuss the ways in which the issues involved here have special meaning for the contemporary evangelical movement. But first I want to lay out some of the issues by looking at a historical argument about the "being" of the theological school.

This essay previously appeared in *Calvin Theological Journal* 33 (November 1998). It is printed here with permission.

Church, Academy, and Theological School

The basic issues I want to address here were given much attention during a debate that occurred in the early 1890s as two Dutch Reformed groups in the Netherlands were involved in intense merger negotiations. One group, the Christian Reformed Church *(Christelijke Gereformeerde Kerk)*, had broken from the larger Dutch Reformed Church *(Nederlandse Hervormde Kerk)* in 1834. The other was a group of dissenting congregations that had departed from the Dutch Reformed Church in 1886, describing themselves as the *Doleantie* (the "grieving" ones). Both groups were devoted to Calvinist orthodoxy, and there was much interest on both sides in joining forces as one denominational body.

In the course of their negotiations, however, several important differences emerged. Not the least of these points of contention was the question of the proper context for theological education. The Christian Reformed Church had established a theological school at Kampen in 1854, an institution dedicated to the purpose of ministerial education. The *Doleantie,* on the other hand, had broader educational interests. The leader of the *Doleantie* was Abraham Kuyper, who had founded the Free University *(Vrije Universiteit)* in 1882. Kuyper's followers saw this university, which included a faculty of theology, as an appropriate setting for the academic preparation for ministry.

Neither side was happy with the other group's program of theological education. And the obvious fervor that characterized their discussions of this topic suggests that more was at stake than a mere fondness for a specific institution. The differences had to do with different *models* of ministerial preparation. Each side cherished something in its program for training pastors that it felt could not be accomplished adequately by the other group's chosen means of theological education.

Two Models

Kuyper's model of theological education is embodied in a perspective whose character is revealed in the very name he gave to the university he founded in Amsterdam in the 1880s. He insisted that this university, including the theological faculty that was so important to its life, had to be independent of both ecclesiastical and state control. In its life and mission it was accountable to a voluntary association of Reformed Christians who shared a common understanding of what Christian higher education — and more particularly theological education — was meant to be.

This independence was not, for Kuyper, merely an accident of historical circumstance. It followed from the very idea of a university, properly understood. His conception of the nature of the university was an application of a larger theory of human association — his doctrine of "sphere sovereignty." The details of this theory need not detain us here,[1] so I will sketch only some of the highlights. According to Kuyper, the original creation was rich with cultural potential. The Garden was from the very beginning a City that was not yet actualized. The Creator had built into the world a diversity of cultural spheres — political, scientific, artistic, familial, cultic, economic, etc. — that were meant to take concrete shape under the supervision of human beings, to whom the "cultural mandate" to "fill the earth" was given by God. The entrance of sin into the world meant that these cultural patterns developed along very distorted lines. The task of redeemed humanity, then, is to reclaim all spheres of life for the glory of God — not necessarily by imposing an "official" theocratic control on human cultural explorations, but by establishing God-honoring cultural projects and institutions (Christian political parties, Christian art guilds, Christian patterns of family life) alongside the corrupt manifestations of sinful cultural formation. "Sphere sovereignty" means that we must respect the integrity of these various cultural domains: art is not economics; the university is not a family; the state is not a church. Each sphere of cultural interaction is ordained by God with its own proper aims and its own unique patterns of authority.

Kuyper's intention was to oppose two very basic patterns of cultural hegemony: the kind of ecclesiasticism that typified, in his mind, much of medieval life, where the church went beyond its proper authority by imposing its influence on family life, art, business, and politics; and statism, which tried to invest political government with the right to direct all of cultural life to its own purposes.

For our present purposes, Kuyper's anti-ecclesiasticist impulse is most important. We can detect this impulse in these comments by the Princeton theologian Geerhardus Vos, a Dutch Calvinist who was influenced by Kuyper:

1. For the best presentation by Kuyper in English of his idea of "sphere sovereignty," see his 1898 Stone Lectures, published as *Lectures on Calvinism* (Grand Rapids: Eerdmans, 1931); for a good overview of this perspective, see Gordon Spykman, "Sphere-Sovereignty in Calvin and the Calvinist Tradition," in *Exploring the Heritage of John Calvin*, ed. David E. Holwerda (Grand Rapids: Baker, 1976), 163-208.

There is a sphere of science, a sphere of art, a sphere of family life and of the state, a sphere of commerce and industry. Whenever one of these spheres comes under the controlling influence of the principle of divine supremacy and glory, and this outwardly reveals itself, there we can truly say that the kingdom of God has become manifest. . . . [Jesus'] doctrine of the kingdom was founded on such a profound and broad conviction of the absolute supremacy of God in all things, that he could not but look upon every normal and legitimate province of human life as intended to form part of God's kingdom. . . . [But] it was not his intention that this result should be reached by making human life in all its spheres subject to the visible church. . . . [W]hat is true of the relation between church and state, may also be applied to the relation between the visible church and the various other branches into which the organic life of humanity divides itself.[2]

As applied specifically to academic life, scholars in this Kuyperian tradition are strongly inclined to see this same anti-ecclesiasticism at work in John Calvin's own thought and practice. One Dutch historian argues, for example, that while the clergy in Calvin's Geneva cooperated with the government in appointing professors to the Genevan Academy, and while those professors were subject to church discipline in their academic roles, "[i]t would be inaccurate . . . to interpret this relationship as placing the Academy, and thereby science, under the church. Church and school were meant to be two institutions in society standing side by side."[3]

Theological education, however, poses an interesting puzzle for advocates of sphere sovereignty. Is the theological school properly thought of as a part of the university, so that its primary cultural location is in what Kuyper thought of as the domain of "science"? Or is it in fact a function of the church? Kuyper's "sphere sovereignty" perspective allows for the fact that education is not restricted to schools. Educational activity takes place in various spheres: parents teach manners to their children; electricians instruct their apprentices in the skills and information necessary for their work; coaches educate their team members in how to attain new levels of athletic prowess. And churches too educate: they engage in programs of

2. Geerhardus Vos, *The Kingdom and the Church* (Grand Rapids: Eerdmans, 1951), 87-89, quoted in Spykman, "Sphere-Sovereignty in Calvin," 176-77.

3. D. Nauta, "Calvijn en zijn Academie in 1559," in *Vier Redevoeringen over Calvijn* (Kampen: J. H. Kok, 1959), translated and quoted in Spykman, "Sphere-Sovereignty in Calvin," 206-7.

catechesis. Is, then, training for ministry an extension of the church's catechetical function? Or must it be placed within that "scientific" sphere for which the university is the primary institutional expression?

Kuyper and his followers clearly opted for this latter viewpoint as they debated the topic during the 1880s. In the initial stages of the merger discussions they seemed unshakable in their demand that the Christian Reformed group transfer their "Theological School to Amsterdam, where it is to be merged with the Free University in such a way that only the practical training of future ministers is left to the original Theological School."[4] Thus, while the Kuyperians were willing to have some "practical" courses taught outside the university context, the "scientific" study of theology must take place in a uniquely academic setting.

The Christian Reformed leaders were equally adamant in arguing for ecclesiastical control of the process of theological education. They regularly quoted the apostle Paul's advice to Timothy in support of their position: "and what you have heard from me through many witnesses entrust to faithful people who will be able to teach others as well" (2 Tim. 2:2). The same Holy Spirit who is the active teacher of the local church must be explicitly acknowledged, they argued, as the authoritative presider over the processes of theological education. This can happen only if the church monitors the patterns of ministerial formation diligently and closely.[5]

To insist on close ecclesiastical monitoring was not the same, though, as demanding that proper theological education take place only in a Kampen-type institution, and many Christian Reformed delegates were willing to concede this point. The way to achieving a compromise was suggested by the final statement of the Christian Reformed bargaining position on theological education: it articulated "the principle that the Church is called to maintain its own institution for the education of its ministers, at least as regards the theological component." The Kuyper group accepted this formulation.

At first glance this way of putting it may not seem to be a compromise position. But it did in fact allow for a pluralistic settlement. In the new united church that was formed in 1892, two different institutional forms were accepted: both the Theological Faculty of the Free University and the

---

4. From correspondence between the two groups, quoted in Hendrik Bouma, *Secession, Doleantie, and Union: 1834-1892*, trans. Theodore Plantinga (Neerlandia, Alberta: Inheritance Publications, 1995), 119.

5. Bouma, *Secession*, 151.

Theological School at Kampen continued to provide programs in theological education.

The compromise character of the settlement can be seen in the way each group was allowed by the other to maintain its preferred mode of ministerial preparation. Not only did they agree to keep the two modes of theological education in operation, but they also instituted measures to influence each other's institutional arrangements: the Christian Reformed party introduced measures for the ecclesiastical monitoring of the course of theological studies at the Free University, and the Kuyper group insisted on strict scholarly standards at Kampen.[6]

Necessary Tensions

This settlement did not eliminate tensions between the two models. It wasn't long, for example, before the Kuyper party claimed that the settlement had been intended only as a temporary expedience, designed to allow the two churches to set aside their differences about theological education so that the union could take shape. But all efforts to impose a one-model system failed, and the basic terms of the settlement have held until the present.[7]

I am convinced that the tensions are healthy ones. Each model highlights an important feature of the "being" of the theological school. A healthy theological school will embody both academic integrity and ecclesial accountability. And what is significant about the 1892 compromise for our purposes is that it sends a clear signal that neither side in the dispute was wedded, when the issues were clarified, to a single institutional arrangement. The espousal of an institutional model was in each case a way of calling attention to a much desired feature of theological education.

For the position represented by Kuyper, for example, the fundamental issue is not whether a theological school is attached to a university or is maintained directly by an ecclesiastical body. What does matter is that the theological educational enterprise have its own integrity; that must be respected by all who care about the health of theological institutions.

6. Bouma, *Secession*, 168-70.

7. The question of maintaining both programs has once again been raised in recent years, although for different reasons than those discussed in the nineteenth century. The contemporary discussion focuses on dwindling numbers of theological students, scarce economic resources, and the future of specific theological schools in new merger schemes.

Whether or not a theological school is officially "sponsored" by an ecclesial body, its aims and purposes can never be simply subsumed under the aims and purposes of the church in such a way that its academic character is compromised.

But neither is it enough simply to point to the theological school's academic character. It is also accountable to the church. And this accountability is not contingent upon any actual ecclesiastical arrangement in which it happens to participate. There is something about ecclesial relatedness that also belongs to the "being" of the theological school. The "ontology" of the theological school seems to me to be captured in a formula of this sort: it is *of* the academy and *for* the church.

Some Theses about Accountability

The issues that were debated in nineteenth-century Holland have continuing relevance today. Although the present-day debates often take on a different theological cast, the question of how we understand the theological school's relationship to church and academy is still an important — even, in some cases, a burning — issue. Turning now from the historical discussion, I will attempt to offer some systematic clarification of my brief formula — in the academy and for the church — by commenting on six theses relating to the character of the theological school.

Thesis One: The theological school does, in a primary sense, find itself in the academy. A theological school *is* academic in the most straightforward sense.

As Mark R. Schwehn rightly observes: "the two constitutive functions of academies are teaching and learning"; all the other things that happen in academic settings, "reading, writing, computing, memorizing," are directed toward the expediting of these two primary activities.[8] This is true of seminaries as well. At the center of all that they do are the "constitutive functions" of teaching and learning. Therefore, the most fundamental norms and patterns of discourse appropriate to the theological school are those of academic life.

I must make it clear that when I say that the academy is the theological school's proper home I am engaging in cultural and not geographical

8. Mark R. Schwehn, *Exiles from Eden: Religion and the Academic Vocation in America* (New York: Oxford University Press, 1993), 33.

mapping. It is not wrong for churches directly to sponsor seminaries; indeed, there is no good reason why a theological school could not be physically located on ecclesiastical property. Consider an analogy: if a church should decide to own and operate a restaurant on its physical premises — as is the case now, for example, with some of the cathedrals of Europe — this does not mean that the restaurant has become "ecclesiastical" in any interesting sense. What makes a church-operated restaurant a good restaurant will have to be decided in the light of culinary and economic standards that are appropriate to the evaluation of commercial eating establishments in general; to the degree, for example, that ecclesiastical connectedness may be relevant to the rating of a specific restaurant, the general evaluative standard in question — probably, in this case, something like "ambience" — will be one relevant to the assessment of all restaurants. Similarly, the sense in which location within churchly territory is relevant to the rating of a theological school does not mean that the school is to be evaluated with reference to how good it is at *being* "church."

Thesis Two: As a Christian academic institution, the theological school is meant to be an academic manifestation of the kingdom of Christ. The theological school must model how the rule of Christ can be actualized and transformed *as* an academic manifestation of that rule. Here I mean to draw on Kuyper's "sphere sovereignty" perspective. The church is only one manifestation of the kingdom of Christ. There are other spheres of interaction — families, liberal arts colleges, parachurch organizations, even friendships — that are very much a part of Christian community, but are not contained within the sphere of ecclesial life. What makes them overtly kingdom manifestations is not that they are "churchly" but that they conform to those principles and norms that are God-honoring for the kinds of interactions they embody.

Those responsible for theological education, then, have a very basic obligation to account for how the theological school functions as a kingdom institution. And this is not the same as simply explaining how the school serves a given church body. It also necessitates showing how it pursues its academic activities in a kingdom-honoring way, as well as how it facilitates its responsibilities to other manifestations of the kingdom of Christ.

Thesis Three: The theological school's general pattern of accountability to church bodies arises out of the calling that both church and theological school have to be manifestations of the kingdom of Christ. The theological school is obligated to explain to the church how it sees itself as carrying out its responsibilities as an institutional agent of Christ's rule. Of course, the theological school is also accountable to *other* manifestations of the kingdom of Christ in addition to the church: for example, to Christian colleges and universities, to Christian professional groups (organizations of, say, Christian therapists, athletes, and corporate leaders), to parachurch mission agencies, to ecumenical networks, and the like. And each of these other entities — including the church — is also accountable to seminaries for how they pursue their own unique attempts to "show forth" the divine rule.

To emphasize that the church and the theological school are together accountable to something larger than either of them is to guard against the impression that either entity exists simply to serve the other's interests. A theological school may be accountable to a specific ecclesial body, but it also has other accountability relationships — not the least being its relationships to the larger world of theological education. The tensions that can occur because of this fact become obvious when a theological school is being evaluated by academic accrediting agencies. Sometimes peer relationships in the academy impose obligations that pull in a different direction than those set by an ecclesial body. This is not to suggest that whenever such a tension exists, academic relationships always "trump" ecclesial ones. But it does suggest that the tension is generated by involvement in two very important spheres of accountability.

Thesis Four: There is also a very special and intimate pattern of accountability between theological school and church. Educating ecclesial leaders is at the heart of what theological school education is about. This does not mean that the theological school does only what the church asks it to do by way of training leaders. The theological school must, for example, respect — and it must ask the church to respect — its own integrity as an *academic* manifestation of Christ's kingdom. Furthermore, insofar as the theological school has a significant commitment to training leaders for other kingdom associations and institutions — the Christian counseling profession, for example, or Christian social action groups, or the Christian academy itself — it is also accountable to these other institutions for how it goes about its task. But these other areas of leadership training in a theological school setting presuppose a strong sense of accountability to the church in leadership education.

To expand upon my brief formula regarding the "being" of theological education: the theological school is indeed *in* the academy; but it exists there to make the benefits of academic life available *to* the church, and out of a deep love *for* the church's life and mission.

Thesis Five: The theological school should also be accountable to the church for the way ecclesial concerns shape and inform its curricular offerings. In this sense, David Kelsey is close to the truth when he proposes that a "theological school is a community of persons trying to understand God more truly by focusing its study of various subject matters within the horizon of questions about Christian congregations."[9] To be sure, Kelsey's claim is, as stated, too ecclesiocentric; seminaries can with equal legitimacy — depending on the nature of their actual constituencies — focus their study on questions about other kingdom institutions: parachurch youth ministries, relief organizations, occupation-specific laity groups, and the like. But, for all that, the struggles and challenges pertaining to congregational life ought to have a significant influence on the theological school curriculum. To insist, as I have here, that the theological school is not itself a manifestation of "church" does not mean that ecclesial topics cannot play a very visible role in shaping the curriculum for theological education.

Thesis Six: As it pursues its special obligations to the church, the theological school must think of itself as accountable for more than the purely academic content of its leadership training. Since the theological school, *as* an academic institution, exists to serve the church, it cannot be nothing more than an academic institution. And this more-than-academic character of its life is also a part of its "being." The church has every right to expect the theological school to provide activities and programs that are necessary complements and reinforcements for academic preparation for church leadership: spiritual formation, community involvement, psychological training, etc.

Indeed, in thinking about how to provide these complements and reinforcements, theological schools can give visibility to matters that desperately need to be impressed upon the larger academic world. There is a sense in which the academy as such needs to attend seriously to those aspects of its mission that are not narrowly "academic." As Mark Schwehn has argued with much eloquence, academic activities are functions, properly conceived, of academic *community.* Academic communities in the past have nurtured, and have been nurtured by, such "spiritual" virtues as humility, faith, self-denial, and love. These qualities have been sustained in past academic settings by affections, liturgical practices, and symbol systems that are intimately intertwined with religious convictions; and, as Schwehn boldly states his case, "their continued vitality would seem to be

---

9. David H. Kelsey, *To Understand God Truly: What's Theological about a Theological School* (Louisville: Westminster John Knox, 1992), 131.

in some jeopardy under wholly secular auspices."[10] In self-consciously fostering a spirituality that is appropriate to the academic calling, seminaries can perform an important service to the larger academy.

Residual Uneasiness

The views I have just set forth in the theses make many of my friends uneasy. Since the friends I am referring to here are themselves deeply committed to the cause of theological education, their uneasiness also causes a residual uneasiness on my own part about what I am arguing for here. These friends are not insensitive to the need for programs of theological teaching and scholarship that are characterized by a high degree of academic integrity. But they worry that, in arguing that the primary cultural "home" of the theological school is not the church but the academy — even with all of my attempted qualifications and clarifications — I am treading on very dangerous ground.

I sense two deep and significant concerns at work in this uneasiness. One concern is that in arguing for the academy as the theological school's primary cultural home, I am giving the academy something it does not deserve. My friends rightly point out that the secular academy is in very bad shape. In my appeals to Mark Schwehn's compelling critique of the contemporary academy, I am in effect strongly endorsing this assessment. The secular universities today hardly serve as models of what we want seminaries to be like.

I have attempted to "cover" myself on this matter, by stating explicitly at several points that I am not asking seminaries to conform to the prevailing norms of the secular academy. But it is obvious that these caveats are not sufficient to still the fears of my friends. Why? Part of the reason is, I suspect, that it is indeed dangerous to refer to an "academy" that somehow transcends the actual realities of historical development. We do not have many existing models of academic life that are free from the confusions and conflicts that permeate the actual universities and colleges and institutes of our day.

Note that I say we do not have *many* models. But we do have some. Prominent among the examples of relatively healthy academic institutions (in the Schwehnian sense of academic health) are those that can be found

10. Schwehn, *Exiles from Eden,* 50, 56-57.

in a significant network of Christian colleges, universities — and seminaries! This is for me an important matter to emphasize. It is precisely because the world of higher education desperately needs living models of academic health that I want to emphasize the calling of theological schools to occupy their academic "home" with a sense of confident security, so that they can serve as academic cities upon a hill. This makes it especially important also to emphasize the fact that it is precisely in their efforts to operate *against* many of the prevailing standards of academic life that they will most effectively fulfill their academic callings.

At the end of *After Virtue* Alasdair MacIntyre gave a very pessimistic assessment of our contemporary cultural prospects. We must prepare, he said, for "the coming ages of barbarism and darkness" that will likely come after "the new dark ages that are already upon us." These preparations require, he insisted, "the construction of new forms of community within which the moral life could be sustained." And then he concluded with this poignant confession: "We are not waiting for a Godot, but for another — doubtless very different — St. Benedict."[11]

I am not prepared to endorse MacIntyre's general assessment of contemporary culture. But I must confess that I share his mood to some degree when I focus specifically on the contemporary academy. We are living in something like the academic "dark ages," and it is incumbent upon us to foster, to paraphrase MacIntyre, those forms of community in which the academic vocation can be sustained until we are visited by better times. Here I am happy to allow my Calvinism to take on Benedictine, even Anabaptist, tones — but with the understanding that the Benedictine-Anabaptist project is appropriate, not necessarily as *the* correct way for the Christian community to relate to its surroundings under any and all pre-eschaton conditions, but as a strategy for confronting specific historical situations. In our present context it seems to me quite appropriate to advocate the creation of those communal contexts that will protect the academic vocation from the sustained attacks being launched by our academic peers.

The second deep concern that I discern in my friends' uneasiness has to do with a desire to foster a more intimate link between church and theological school than my theses seem to permit. Let me try to dispel, or at least diminish, this concern.

11. Alasdair MacIntyre, *After Virtue: A Study in Moral Theory*, 2nd ed. (Notre Dame, Ind.: University of Notre Dame Press, 1984), 245.

Here I must acknowledge that some of the misgivings expressed by my friends arise out of deeply rooted evangelical concerns. They want theological schools to serve the cause of the gospel, with a special relationship to the life and mission of the Christian church. They worry about emphasizing too much the strictly academic dimensions of theological education — not because they do not value academic pursuits, but because they sense genuine dangers in de-emphasizing some of the unique benefits of a pattern of education that is grounded in the life of the worshiping and witnessing community.

I have made it clear that in attempting to draw some discernible conceptual boundaries between church and academy I am taking my cues from Abraham Kuyper. And I am convinced that his attempt at boundary drawing was itself fed by deep evangelical impulses. Why then do my Kuyperian emphases give discomfort to so many of my evangelical friends? I think it has to do with the fact that while Kuyper's deep motivations were indeed very evangelical in character, he was advocating a strategy for expediting these motivations that did not fit the typical evangelical pattern.

Evangelicals have consistently worried about the ways in which theological education has failed to promote the causes that they hold dear: evangelism, spirituality, intimate Christian community and nurture. Historically, this has meant that evangelicals have had to "take back" theological education from ecclesial and academic bodies that have promoted schemes of ministerial formation that were dominated by either a rationalistic orthodoxy or an Enlightenment heterodoxy. For most evangelicals this has meant establishing strong ties between theological "training" and programs — whether church or parachurch — committed to the pursuit of the central evangelical values.

Kuyper traveled in a somewhat different direction. If the theological academy had become so far removed from evangelical concerns that it no longer could be supported by the faithful, then the solution was not to bring it into closer institutional connection to the practical concerns of the faithful, but to reform the theological academy as such, insisting that the theological school must maintain a kind of "sphere independence" from churchly control.

My perspective on theological education is informed in basic ways by a desire to offer a contemporary rationale for Kuyper's scheme. But here too I must acknowledge the relevance of our actual historical development. It may be important today to emphasize some of those things that Kuyper considered it necessary to de-emphasize. For one thing, it may be that in our time the properly academic character of the theological school can only be reinforced by maintaining a much more intimate relationship to the worshiping, nurturing, and evangelizing Christian community than Kuyper envisioned. If the academy itself has lost its "spiritual" support system (as Schwehn argues), then it may be that a close connection to the spiritual life of the church is an important way of reinforcing some important *academic* features of the theological school. Or, to put it another way: it may be that the theological school needs all the help it can get from the church to assist it in nurturing a sense of the importance of vocation.

"Free" Theological Education

I began by stating my desire to offer some *probings* about the relationship of the evangelical theological school to the church. Now I must repeat that characterization with regard to what I have set forth here. Evangelicalism is a movement in which a plurality of ecclesiological perspectives is represented. Other ways of construing the relationship between church and theological school ought to be formulated and debated.

There are some themes and concerns that are at work in these present probings, however, that I would want to hold out for, even if other vocabularies and nuancings are adopted. Chief among these is Kuyper's "freedom" motif. Theological education needs to be free to pursue its unique functions in the context of the kingdom of Christ. In insisting on this I am not espousing an unbridled "free inquiry." As an evangelical Calvinist I am convinced that theological education will be at its healthiest only when it is grounded in a deep commitment to biblical orthodoxy; I firmly support the maintenance of confessional boundaries that define and safeguard that commitment in evangelical institutions. Theological educators ought not to lust after a promiscuous intellectual freedom. We are bonded to the Word of God, and to the cause of the Savior whose cosmic redemptive mission is infallibly revealed in that Word. This means that our academic callings can never be pursued in a way that distances us from the church over whom the Savior reigns as Lord.

The freedom that should be cherished in a theological school is the liberty to pursue our "bonded" service in a manner that is appropriate to an institution that is called to be an academic manifestation of the rule of Christ. We experience this freedom best, I am convinced, if we *do* think of the theological school as "academy" and we do *not* think of the theological school as, strictly speaking, "church." At the same time, we must emphasize the fact that we are accountable *to* the church as a coagency in the kingdom of Christ, and that we very much need — perhaps in our time we even *desperately* need — an intimate relationship to the work of the worshiping, nurturing, and evangelizing people of God.

I am very much in favor of pursuing such a relationship. All I would ask is that in doing so we work at thinking clearly about the theological school's "being" — about its proper relationships to both academy and church. To argue that the theological school must neither be contained within a narrow construal of ecclesial reality nor subsumed under the norms of the secular academy is — or ought to be — a way of highlighting the need for theological schools to contribute their unique gifts to all who serve in the kingdom of Christ.

Dutch Calvinist Philosophical Influences in North America

James Hutton MacKay was a Scottish clergyman who spent six years, shortly after the turn of the twentieth century, serving in the Netherlands as a pastor to the English-speaking congregations at Middelburg and Flushing (Vlissingen). Soon after he returned to Scotland from his Dutch sojourn, he gave the Hastie Lectures at the University of Glasgow. These lectures, delivered in February of 1911, dealt with nineteenth-century Dutch religious thought. In the course of describing some of the more orthodox thinkers of nineteenth-century Holland, MacKay offered these observations about the mental habits of the Dutch:

> They like to see things clearly, and to see them as they are — at least, as they seem to be to men of sound understanding. "We are a people of dykes and dams," a Dutch writer said recently, "both as to our land and our mental life." And Dr. Kuyper's often-quoted saying about the danger of "blurring the boundary lines" is characteristically Dutch. It might seem that such a mind is perhaps not the best fitted to deal with such subjects as religion, but if we are to treat theology as science, and accept the old saying that *qui bene distinguit bene docet* — a favourite maxim of theirs — much, I believe, can be learned from a people who have a remarkable gift of making distinctions, wrought into their nature, possibly, by many centuries of unrelaxing toil in making and holding that

This essay originally appeared in *Calvin Theological Journal* 24 (April 1989). It is printed here with permission.

distinction between land and sea, which to them is a matter of life and death.[1]

MacKay makes it clear in these comments that he is not the first to characterize Dutch mental habits in terms of a kind of dike building. Indeed, there were Dutch thinkers in the nineteenth century who went to some lengths to account for what they viewed as the unique cognitive traits of the people of the Netherlands by analyzing the relationship between physical and mental terrains. For example, Foppe Ten Hoor, a leader of the immigrant community in western Michigan, posited an intimate relationship between the geography of the Netherlands on the one hand and Dutch religious traits and national character on the other. Since the Dutch were a people accustomed to extracting much from very small tracts of land, he argued, they had developed a religious-intellectual style in which a strong emphasis was placed on fixing clear boundaries and digging deep for underlying principles.[2]

If talk about parallels between the geographies of the land and the mind is meant to produce evidence for a thoroughgoing "geo-intellectualism," or an "environmentalist" analysis of the mental habits of a people — as seems to be the case in Ten Hoor's employment of these themes — then we are (so to speak) on shaky ground. It is not obvious, after all, that a propensity for physical dike building is either a necessary or a sufficient condition for the cultivation of a fondness for intellectual dikes.

But the dike-building image can at least serve as a metaphor (which seems to be MacKay's intended use) that points to an important phenomenon that deserves our attention. An intense interest in fixing boundaries and digging for principles may not be a trait that all Dutch people, or only Dutch people, manifest. But an interest in such matters has certainly played a prominent role in the life of at least a significant segment of Dutch Calvinism. It is not surprising, for example, that MacKay would cite Abraham Kuyper as an example of a mental dike builder. Kuyper and his fellow "neo-Calvinists" have espoused a brand of Reformed Christianity in which intellectual articulation is highly valued.

1. James H. MacKay, *Religious Thought in Holland during the Nineteenth Century* (New York: Hodder and Stoughton, 1911), 10.
2. Cf. H. Zwaanstra, *Reformed Thought and Experience in a New World: A Study of the Christian Reformed Church and Its American Environment, 1890-1918* (Kampen: J. H. Kok, 1973), 31; and James D. Bratt, *Dutch Calvinism in Modern America: A History of a Conservative Subculture* (Grand Rapids: Eerdmans, 1984), 57.

My concern in this discussion is to investigate the manner in which a penchant for discerning intellectual boundaries and explicating fundamental principles manifested itself among the neo-Calvinists in the form of a strong interest in philosophical thought. More specifically, I will focus on the continuing influence of this philosophical orientation in the Christian Reformed community in North America.

I will not expend much effort in this discussion attempting to establish the fact that there is indeed a phenomenon here worth investigating. Anyone who is familiar with the patterns of intellectual life among the *Gereformeerden,* whether in the Netherlands or in the diaspora, will acknowledge an unusually strong commitment to philosophical thought in that tradition. Kuyper and Bavinck were theologians who insisted upon the positive and important contribution that philosophy could make to the Christian community. This insistence was endorsed enthusiastically — some would say with a vengeance — in the "Reformational" philosophical movement that has had its center at the Free University.

Nor did this espousal of a Christian philosophical enterprise weaken when the *Gereformeerde* brand of Calvinism was exported to North America. The Christian Reformed people of North America have long respected the discipline of philosophy, and they have revered their philosophers. And not only has philosophy been respected within the Christian Reformed community, it has also been one of the means by which that community has gained a certain degree of "respectability" within the larger culture. Calvin College's philosophy department is sometimes touted, even in very secularized environs, as having one of the strongest undergraduate philosophy programs on the continent. This reputation has been enhanced by the large number of Calvin alumni who have entered the field of professional philosophy. Three of them — Oets Bouwsma, William Frankena, and Alvin Plantinga — have been elected to the presidency of the American Philosophical Association, a very high honor among academic philosophers.

A consideration of these facts gives rise to questions that have often been asked, both within and outside Christian circles in North America: Why has a culturally "marginalized" subculture like the one produced by nineteenth-century Dutch immigrations promoted the philosophical enterprise so vigorously? And why have the results been so impressive? Even though these questions have often been asked, little has been done by way of sustained attempts to answer them. My discussion here is meant as a beginning in that direction.

But *only* a beginning. The best I can offer here is a mixture of specific hunches and general observations. What I do have to offer along those lines is, I think, a step in the right direction. But much detail will have to be filled in if the story is to be told adequately.

Calvinism and the Philosophical Impulse

The arguments set forth by such people as MacKay and Ten Hoor notwithstanding, the Dutch are not a uniformly philosophically minded people. There always have been Dutch folk who have shown little interest in fixing intellectual boundaries or probing for deep-rooted principles.

Nor can we find an impulse to philosophical reflection simply by exploring the character of Calvinism or Reformed life and thought as such. The Scots are a very Calvinistic people, but they have not shown a strong interest specifically in the development of a "Reformed philosophy." Similarly we do not find especially strong philosophical urges among, say, Hungarian or Nigerian or Korean Calvinists.

If a natural philosophical impulse cannot be located in Dutchness as such or in a Reformed orientation as such, can we nonetheless find it at the intersection of the Dutch and the Reformed? Is it at least a peculiar feature of Dutch Calvinism as such? It would seem not. Neither the Dutch Calvinists of the *Hervormde* community in the Netherlands nor the Dutch Americans of the Reformed Church in America have pursued or applauded philosophical scholarship with the same energies as the *Gereformeerden* and their closest North American kinfolk.

The philosophical propensities of the *Gereformeerden* cannot be viewed, then, as an expression of Calvinism as such. But neither can we ignore the fact that when the more articulate of these philosophically minded Christians are asked to explain their reasons for holding philosophy in high regard, the answers will typically be self-consciously Calvinistic: "We have to bring all of life into obedience to God's will"; "Philosophy is one of the ways in which religious motives get played out"; "Christ must be Lord of our thoughts as well as of our actions and feelings."

In offering such considerations, these Reformed Christians are not claiming to express something that would characteristically be endorsed by all who profess to be Calvinists. But they do mean to be giving expression to what they consider to be a properly formed, *consistent* Calvinism. And, while their account of the necessary ingredients of a consistent Reformed perspective is a complex affair, it will be helpful here to isolate three items of belief that have regularly been emphasized in Reformed theology but have been put to special philosophical use by the neo-Calvinists. Before looking at the specifically philosophical formulation, however, we will briefly sketch out the three emphases in straightforwardly theological terms.

The first emphasis in on *divine sovereignty.* This is a dominant theme in Reformed theology. The classic "TULIP" doctrines, for example, can be construed as an elaborate account of God's sovereign role in the salvation of individual human beings: individual persons are totally incapable of initiating or even contributing anything decisive to the redemptive transaction; the beneficiaries of salvific grace are chosen solely by divine discretion; God's redemptive actions accomplish all that he intends them to, and they cannot be resisted; nor can God's redemptive grip on an individual life be broken by any human effort. In short, God maintains sovereign control over the soterial process.

The second emphasis is on the fact of *human sin.* Even our very brief comments about the Calvinist emphasis on divine sovereignty could not avoid a reference to human depravity. And rightly so, since it is impossible to devote much attention to Reformed soteriology without noting the Calvinist focus on the ravages of sin in the human condition.

A third emphasis is on the importance of *divine law* for obedient living. Calvinism has insisted on a strong pattern of continuity between the Old and the New Covenants. One way in which this insistence on continuity is manifested is in the central place of the Decalogue in the Reformed understanding of the patterns of obedience to the divine will — thus the well-known Calvinist fondness for "the third use of the law."

Again, our interest here is in these three theological emphases as themes that have been put to philosophical use by the neo-Calvinists. In noting these three theological themes, then, I am not intending to provide an adequate summary of the major concepts of Calvinism. But these particular themes surely do belong on any list that purports to display the central themes of Reformed Christianity.

Indeed, these three themes even play an important role in Reformed communities in which no attention is given to philosophical issues. Pietist Calvinists, for example, pay considerable attention to all three items. They view themselves as humbly submitting to the will of a sovereign God who has "by grace alone" drawn them into fellowship with himself in spite of the radical nature of their sinful rebellion; this divine Ruler has broken through the resistance of their depraved hearts and called them to live in loving obedience to his revealed law.

The neo-Calvinists, however, took these same themes and appropriated them for philosophical purposes (which is not to say that they ignored their uses in theology and piety). For one thing, they carried the emphasis on divine sovereignty a step beyond the soteriological context in which it always appears in Calvinism. They insisted that the process of divine election and sanctification of individual sinners must not be viewed in isolation from the larger arena in which those redeemed sinners are incorporated into a salvific community whose calling it is in the divine economy to show forth the sovereign rule of God in all spheres of human life.

The "showing forth" of divine sovereignty, which is given attention in a number of branches of Dutch Calvinism as well as in the "covenanter" strain of Scottish Presbyterianism and in segments of English and American Puritanism, is especially strong among the neo-Calvinists. And it took on a decidedly philosophical tone in their hands; they argued, more strenuously than other Reformed groups, that manifesting the divine rule necessarily includes an intellectual showing forth, a bringing of all thoughts into captivity to the rule of Christ.

We have already noted that the theological — and, more specifically, the soteriological — emphasis on the sovereignty of God on the part of Reformed Christians is closely related to an acknowledgment of human depravity. The same close relationship holds in the philosophical context. The neo-Calvinist insistence on philosophical obedience to the norms of the divine reign is intimately interwoven with a negative assessment of the noetic powers of the unredeemed human mind. Thus their understanding of sin has an epistemological as well as a soteriological significance.

Of course, all Reformed Christians operate with at least an implicit epistemology — pietist Calvinists, for example, express rather definite opinions about the worth, or lack thereof, of "worldly wisdom." But the neo-Calvinists have made epistemology a subject of systematic investigation out of a genuine desire to gain clarification concerning the relationship between "the fallen mind" and "the redeemed mind."

The issues here were already present, at least in rudimentary form, in the thought of John Calvin himself. Calvin often portrayed the epistemic condition of the unredeemed human mind in very negative terms. But as a student of the classics, well trained in the discipline of forensics, Calvin also wanted to make positive Christian use of the insights of Seneca, Cicero, Aristotle, and the like. Calvin was aware, then, of a tension between his insistence on the depravity of the unredeemed mind and his own high regard for the ancient pagan writers. His treatment of this tension is not detailed or systematic. But he did succeed in placing the topic on the Reformed agenda. These questions regarding the noetic effects of sin and grace became crucial items for debate in Dutch Calvinism. Indeed, they figured prominently in major church "splits" in the *Gereformeerde* community of both the Netherlands and the United States. It is not surprising, then, that they should also be important topics for discussion among the philosophically minded neo-Calvinists.

But these two themes — divine sovereignty and human depravity — as taken over into the realm of philosophical investigation, cannot by themselves account for the strong interest in philosophical thought that we find in neo-Calvinism. We need to acknowledge the third emphasis, on the importance of divine law in human life.

Here it is not quite adequate to say that the neo-Calvinists simply *appropriated* a theological theme. By putting it to philosophical use, they greatly expanded the range and significance of the theme of divine law in human affairs. As already mentioned, Reformed Christians have consistently given a central place to the notion of law by insisting upon the continuing relevance of the moral law of the Old Testament for New Testament Christianity. But in the neo-Calvinist tradition law comes to play a crucial role in God's relationship to the creation as such. Divine laws do not make their first appearance in Exodus or Deuteronomy. They are the very means by which God creates and sustains the cosmos.

This theme is already very strong in Abraham Kuyper's thought, as is evident in his constant references to the creation "ordinances." But it comes to full bloom in that strand of neo-Calvinism for which divine law is the organizing theme of a detailed philosophical system: *de Wijsbegeerte der Wetsidee.* Here "law" becomes a philosophical rallying point. But even where it has not functioned explicitly as an organizing idea, it has operated as a formative concept in neo-Calvinist thought.

The Law Theme

I am not concerned in this discussion with giving detailed expositions of various strands of neo-Calvinist thought in North America. But I will briefly throw light on some different groupings of North American Reformed philosophers in order to investigate the degree to which their scholarly discussions have been influenced by Dutch Calvinist ideas. But before doing that, a very general connection between the law theme and Calvinist philosophy must be noted.

Critics of Reformed Christianity have regularly raised the charge that Calvinism nurtures a strong strain of irrationality in its understanding of the Christian life. This criticism has been given prominent attention by the philosopher Alasdair MacIntyre, who argues in his much-discussed book *After Virtue* that Calvin viewed morality as grounded in commands issued by a God who is "arbitrary" and "despotic." As MacIntyre analyzes the situation, Calvin discarded the widely accepted medieval notion of a rationally discernible human *telos;* thus Calvin no longer viewed divine commands as guidelines that God offers human beings as they engage in the rational quest to realize their own proper natures. Having lost in the Fall the power to understand ultimate issues rationally, human beings have no proper alternative but to submit without questioning to a set of moral directives whose rationale, if there is any, they cannot grasp.

Whatever the value of this account as an exposition of Calvin's actual views, there can be no doubt that many Calvinists have operated with an understanding of their relationship with God that closely conforms to this picture. Indeed, for many Reformed Christians this moral irrationalism is bounded by an even more poignant soteriological irrationalism. In much of British and American Puritanism, as well as in the "experiential" strain of Dutch Calvinism, God is viewed as arbitrary and despotic not only in his moral negotiations but also in the manner in which he distributes his redemptive benefits as such. Thus the phenomenon of Calvinists who insist that they cannot be sure of their own inclusion among the elect because they view themselves as completely at the mercy of a God who dispenses his saving grace in a purely arbitrary manner.

It should be obvious that this kind of Calvinism gets much mileage out of the first two of the three theological themes I have mentioned. This is a picture of the religious divine-human encounter in which a thoroughly sovereign God stands over against a thoroughly depraved sinner. What seems to be absent from this view of the situation, of course, is any strong sense of lawfulness. Calvinists who endorse this picture of things may, to be sure, make frequent use of the *word* "law." But for them the divine "law" actually functions as a series of arbitrary, disconnected, fiat-type commands; these commands have no unifying pattern — nothing gives them rational coherence.

It is precisely in their understanding of divine law that neo-Calvinists differ radically with this kind of soteriological irrationalism. This is certainly true for the devotees of the *wetsidee* philosophy. For them, divine law extends far beyond its Decalogic manifestation. They view law as the basic mode of God's relationship to his creation. God always speaks and acts lawfully; his words and deeds always take legislative form. And, as we will see further on, a more modest version of this picture also holds for those neo-Calvinists who have followed a different path from that of the strict defenders of "the cosmonomic idea."

A belief in the lawfulness of reality is closely aligned with a positive assessment of rational inquiry. This connection could be illustrated by offering countless examples from the history of Western thought — for example, Platonism, Stoicism, Kantianism, and Hegelianism. The connection holds in a Christian context. Where God is viewed as committing himself to the lawful ordering of his creation, there is usually a high regard for rational inquiry on the part of Christians.

The point being made here can be illustrated by looking at the way in which philosophical inquiry is or is not encouraged in various confessional communities. In those traditions where divine law is thought to be transcended or abandoned or countermanded or mitigated the closer one gets to the heart of the gospel — consider here Lutheranism, Anabaptism, and dispensationalism — there is little by way of appreciation for philosophical inquiry, and certainly for *Christian* philosophical inquiry. The two confessional communities in which Christian philosophy *has* flourished are both very law-oriented in their perspectives on creation and redemption: Roman Catholicism and Calvinism.

To return to our specific focus: for the Dutch neo-Calvinists, the God of the Bible is in a very basic sense a divine legislator. He is a deity who commits himself to lawful activity. The neo-Calvinist does not need to stand in primitive fear before a divine despot whose ways are totally unfathomable to human beings. To be sure, the neo-Calvinist will insist that our relationship to God must never lose the fundamental sense of awe that is appropriate when the creature enters the presence of the Creator. But the harsher tones of that divine mystery have been eliminated by God's own publicly announced commitment to juridical fidelity. The God of the Bible — so insists the neo-Calvinist — has covenantally bound himself to act toward his creation in ways that are reasonable and reliable. He is a faithful God who redeems his people so that they may come to understand and obey his ordinances. Thus divine sovereignty is bounded by law. And the redemption of depraved sinners is expected to result in their rational discernment of that lawfulness.

Wetsidee Thinking

In what ways has Dutch neo-Calvinism influenced Christian philosophical reflection in North America? How has the Christian philosophical impulse, stimulated by a deep conviction that a sovereign God calls sinful human beings to discern and obey his lawful will, taken shape in the environs of North American life?

I will pursue these questions by briefly examining three groups of philosophers who can legitimately be asked how Dutch Calvinism has impacted their philosophical development. Each of these groups is made up of persons who are members or products of the Christian Reformed community.

Our first group is that philosophical community that has consciously identified itself with the *wetsidee* school of thought. This is not the place either to give a summary of the main doctrines or emphases of that school or to tell the story of its embodiment as a movement in North America. Those discussions are available elsewhere.[3] Suffice it to say here that the North American manifestation of the *wetsidee* philosophy has taken the form of a relatively unified intellectual movement — at least until recently.

This movemental unity in North America was somewhat different from anything realized by *wetsidee* thinkers in the Netherlands. The differences between the two contexts are due to a number of factors, two of which are worth mentioning here. First, on the technical philosophical level, the cosmonomic philosophy was propagated in North America under the tutelage of a strong intellectual leader, Professor Evan Runner of Calvin College, who chose not to emphasize the philosophical differences that existed between "Reformational" thinkers in the Netherlands. While philosophers at the Free University were openly discussing important disagreements between Dooyeweerd, Vollenhoven, Mekkes, Van Riessen, and the like, Runner stressed to students the consensus elements among these thinkers, downplaying differences and nuances. Second, the constituency to which this philosophical perspective appealed in the early stages was

---

3. For a brief account of the development of the *wetsidee* system, see J. Klapwijk's *Reformed Journal* articles "The Struggle for a Christian Philosophy: Another Look at Dooyeweerd" (February 1980) and "Dooyeweerd's Christian Philosophy: Antithesis and Critique" (March 1980); for an account of the development of a "Dooyeweerdian" movement in North America, see Bernard Zylstra, "H. Evan Runner: An Assessment of His Mission," in *Life Is Religion: Essays in Honor of H. Evan Runner,* ed. Henry Vander Goot (St. Catharines, Ontario: Paideia Press, 1981).

made up largely of students representing the Canadian minority at Calvin College and the immigrant Christian Reformed community in Canada, for whom the *wetsidee* system functioned as an ideological basis for developing and supporting a variety of Dutch-type "separate organizations." In such circumstances, where social cohesion was an important factor, the unity of an intellectual movement was a matter to be encouraged.

The movemental side of the North American endorsement of *wetsidee* philosophy was nurtured in a number of ways. The most important of the movemental activities occurred under the sponsorship of the Association for Reformed Scientific Studies, which later changed its name to the Association for the Advancement of Christian Scholarship. In 1959 this organization initiated a series of popular conferences in Unionville, Ontario (which were occasionally repeated in other parts of Canada), and in 1967 it established the Institute for Christian Studies in Toronto. Through these means the ideas of Dutch neo-Calvinism were disseminated in the Canadian immigrant community, and eventually they flowed — as we will see later on — well beyond the borders of the settlements of the Dutch in North America.

This philosophical movement gave very explicit articulation to the three themes we have already discussed. Life in general, and intellectual life in particular, must be devoted to the service of the divine Sovereign; indeed, Kuyper's *"pro rege"* became a watchword of sorts in this movement. A proper understanding of the nature and extent of human depravity must, they insisted, do full justice to the clear "antithesis" between belief and unbelief. Others in the Reformed community might view this antithesis as in some sense mitigated by the presence of "common grace" in the world. But the early North American defenders of *wetsidee* thought resisted this way of viewing the situation. As one popular writer put it,

> Common Grace . . . does not bridge the antithesis, but rather Common Grace makes the task and calling of the Kingdom of Light possible. By Common Grace (the term is neither fortunate nor biblical) God restrains the full ultimate hatred of the Kingdom of Darkness. Without the restraining power of this Common Grace, Satanic forces would make Kingdom life impossible. . . .
>
> But Common Grace has not thereby become another basis on which Christians can now stand side by side with unbelievers. Common Grace has not now produced a neutral area, where deeds suddenly have become neither good nor bad, and where believers and unbelievers share a common life. The Antithesis, the fundamental contrast between

faith and rebellion, is radical and encompasses all the fruits of man's heart, mind and hands.[4]

This emphasis on antithesis comported well with the prominence of the idea of law in this system of thought. If the contrast between believer and unbeliever must be understood in "radical" terms, then apostate accounts of reality cannot be trusted; the cosmonomic thinkers issued their warnings on this matter, even while they acknowledged — as did Cornelius Van Til, who espoused a more heavily theological version of antithesis-oriented thinking — that unbelievers continue to operate within the confines of, and are sustained by, the riches of divine creation. An antithesis that "encompasses all the fruits of man's heart, mind and hands" provides the believer with little grounds for genuine optimism in evaluating either the intellectual patterns or the institutional structures of the reprobate community. A proper discernment of the law order of creation must take place with the awareness, as Calvin Seerveld put it, that "the judgment of narcotic sleep will fall . . . upon those who are not single-minded under the grip of the Word in their studies."[5]

As we will see shortly, this strong antitheticalism became a significant point of friction between the cosmonomic thinkers and other North American Calvinist philosophers. And it is the modification of this perspective on the antithesis that has been the most visible sign of the lessening of a movemental spirit among those who once identified themselves as ardent defenders of the *wetsidee* system.

Needless to say, none of this is merely a matter of intellectual shifting. We have already noted that the early unity of this movement was due to at least two factors: the presence of a single intellectual mentor who stressed the consensual elements in *de wijsbegeerte der wetsidee* and the felt need for social cohesion in a community of recent immigrants. Change has now occurred on both of these counts. Professor Runner's active leadership has been displaced by that of younger scholars who brought with them from their studies at the Free University the very nuances and tensions that had previously been downplayed in the consensus-oriented North American movement. And much of the felt need for social cohesion has dissipated as

4. Louis Tamminga, in an editorial response to a letter from J. Vanden Bosch, *Christian Vanguard*, February 1968, 8-9.

5. Calvin Seerveld, quoted in "No Shame Anymore," a report on the first anniversary commemoration of the opening of the Institute for Christian Studies, *Perspective*, January 1969, 2.

Dutch-Canadian Calvinists have steadily moved in the direction of cultural assimilation.

Grand Rapids Kuyperianism

In the autumn of 1974, Calvin College philosopher Nicholas Wolterstorff delivered a public address in Grand Rapids in which he evaluated the role of the Association for the Advancement of Christian Scholarship (AACS) in the Reformed community in North America. Wolterstorff's speech, which he was soon invited to deliver again in Toronto and which was published in both the *Banner* and the *Reformed Journal,* took on the status of a significant "event" in Christian Reformed environs. For many months a debate had been raging in the pages of the *Banner:* editor Lester DeKoster had written nine editorials on what he called "Cosmonomia," in which he described the philosophy of Herman Dooyeweerd and the work of the AACS in harsh terms; a number of responses had been published by persons associated with the AACS. In his speech, Wolterstorff offered an assessment of the debate.

Wolterstorff placed the dispute in the larger historical context of continuing tensions among what he termed "doctrinalists," "pietists," and "Kuyperians" in the Dutch Reformed community. He also noted that Kuyperianism itself was a divided school of thought; when the *wetsidee* philosophy was introduced in the Christian Reformed community in the late 1930s, some of the Kuyperians who were already well established at Calvin College — Clarence Bouma and Henry Stob were Wolterstorff's examples — greeted this development with enthusiasm. But soon tensions, and even open hostility, developed. The formulations of the new Kuyperians regarding their conception of the Word of God and of sphere sovereignty were not acceptable to the older Kuyperians. Wolterstorff had offered his own critique of these formulations and went on to criticize the AACS for the way it granted "canonical" status to Dooyeweerd's philosophy and for its "movementism," a spirit that, Wolterstorff observed, fostered "triumphalist" attitudes and "imperialist" practices.

In developing his critical case, Wolterstorff did not mince words. He made it very clear that he had serious differences with the AACS at significant points. Nonetheless, his address was well received by many *wetsidee* adherents; indeed, it seems to have been a significant factor in the growing rapprochement between the "non-Dooyeweerdian" Calvin College philosophers and the "post-Runner" intellectual leadership of the AACS.

218

The positive reception given to Wolterstorff's remarks was probably due to at least two factors. First, his stern criticisms were tempered by a "pastoral" tone. At the end of his speech he even ventured the opinion that many of the defects he had mentioned were already in the process of being corrected. Thus the overall impact of Wolterstorff's analysis was one of encouraging the AACS to continue its program of self-improvement — surely a very different message from the harsh condemnations of DeKoster's editorials.

But, second, and more important, Wolterstorff seemed to have sensed that the time was ripe to form a new intellectual coalition between the *wetsidee* community and our second group of thinkers, the "analytic" philosophers of Calvin College. Thus he stressed the fact that many of the criticisms being lodged against the AACS in the Christian Reformed community were more or less predictable doctrinalist or pietist complaints. And he clearly lined himself up with the *wetsidee* party in this ongoing trialogue: "I myself regard pietism and doctrinalism as mistaken."[6] To many ears this had the ring of a Kennedyesque, I-am-a-Kuyperian proclamation.

In one sense, of course, Wolterstorff's use of the Kuyperian label as a means of self-identification should not have come as a surprise to anyone. Wolterstorff's Calvin College philosophical mentors William Henry Jellema and Henry Stob were both very sympathetic to Kuyperian ideals. In his foreword to the 1964 volume of essays commemorating Jellema's retirement from Calvin College, Stob described Jellema's philosophical pedagogy in terms that should please any follower of Abraham Kuyper:

> Philosophy is for him a venture that takes place within the Kingdom, and the best philosopher is for him a trained and humble servant of the Gospel. Both philosophy and the philosopher, in his view, are there to deepen understanding and to delineate the perspectives of faith. The history of philosophy is for him the progressive articulation of competing faiths seeking appropriate understandings. These total diverging perspectives he deeply knows through a combination of disciplined scholarship and vital empathy, but it is only for one of them — the Christian — that he radically chooses, and into which he insinuates his students.[7]

6. Nicholas Wolterstorff, "The AACS in the CRC," *Reformed Journal*, December 1974, 11.

7. Henry Stob, foreword to *Faith and Philosophy: Philosophical Studies in Religion and Ethics*, ed. Alvin Plantinga (Grand Rapids: Eerdmans, 1964), viii.

Stob himself has regularly displayed strong Kuyperian leanings. In a recent essay on the antithesis he gives expression to the basic perspective that has guided him throughout his career as a philosophical theologian and ethicist:

> Let it be said that I share with Kuyper, Herman Dooyeweerd, Van Til, and many other Christian thinkers the view that all knowledge is embraced at its edges by an all-encompassing *Weltanschauung*. This means that all apprehension and reflection takes place within a global perspective in terms of which the data of experience are thought-molded and fitted into a frame. I also agree that the shape of the philosophical perspective or totality-view is determined by what one regards or evaluates as crucially significant or most real. I further agree that this judgment and evaluation is made before the cognitive process properly begins. The point of view from which the world is surveyed is not theoretically determined: it is chosen. And, what is more, the choice reflects a religious decision. It is an echo of faith.[8]

Having expressed his solidarity with the Kuyperian tradition on these fundamental matters, though, Stob goes on to underscore his differences with Van Tilian epistemology and with *wetsidee* social thought. In each case he insists that the antithetical differences between believer and unbeliever are undergirded by commonality. Both are interpreting the same God-created world. And believers can work together with unbelievers in the context of organizations that are in an important sense "neutral."

It is interesting to note here that both Stob and Wolterstorff express important disagreements and agreements with the cosmonomic thinkers. But the overall impact of their respective presentations is very different in each case. Stob seems to reach out to the Dooyeweerdians only to pull back in the end with a statement of basic disagreement. Wolterstorff sets forth his differences in a larger context of making common cause with the *wetsidee* thinkers.

But there were other factors at work when Wolterstorff made his speech in 1974. Up to that point the disputes between Dooyeweerdian and non-Dooyeweerdian Kuyperians were for the most part arguments be-

---

8. Henry Stob, "Observations on the Concept of the Antithesis," in *Perspectives on the Christian Reformed Church: Studies in Its History, Theology, and Ecumenicity,* ed. Peter DeKlerk and Richard R. DeRidder (Grand Rapids: Baker, 1983), 252.

tween academic leaders whose intended spheres of influence were roughly coextensive. Runner and the Toronto thinkers, like Jellema and Stob, were influential primarily among the Dutch Calvinists, although all had gained hearings in the larger evangelical community as well. Wolterstorff and his colleague Alvin Plantinga, on the other hand, had earned important credentials in the larger world of professional philosophers. They were widely published in technical journals, and each had taught and lectured in the major centers of North American academia. When Jellema and Stob employed Kuyperian language, they could be viewed simply as competing for control of the intellectual currents of a Calvinist subculture. But when Wolterstorff and Plantinga identified with the Kuyperian cause, it could mean that Kuyperianism was now gaining an entrée into a much larger intellectual arena, one that *wetsidee* thinkers had not yet really begun to penetrate.

All this was not without its little ironies. For example, when the rapprochement between the *wetsidee* thinkers and the Calvin College philosophical "establishment" actually took place, more matters of philosophical disagreement stood between the two parties than had previously been the case. On a purely philosophical level it is difficult to find items of significant disagreement between, say, Stob and Runner. Certainly, whatever separated them philosophically was not as great as the differences between Wolterstorff and the Toronto thinkers in 1974.

If we survey the views of the people involved in the philosophical disputes we have been discussing in the light of the three philosophical-theological emphases we outlined earlier, then Wolterstorff and Plantinga have been less overtly neo-Calvinistic as philosophers than either their teachers Jellema and Stob or the members of the *wetsidee* movement. To be sure, both Wolterstorff and Plantinga have always explicitly endorsed the Reformed understanding of divine sovereignty and have insisted on its application to the philosophical enterprise. But each of them, at various points in their careers, would probably have been viewed, at least by many Kuyperians, as having rather weak views in the second area, having to do with the noetic effects of human sin.

Wolterstorff, for example, has always been more cautious than many other Kuyperians in dealing with the differences between Christian and non-Christian philosophical activity. In a 1964 essay published in the Jellema Festschrift, he went out of his way to introduce qualifiers when dealing with the relationship of faith to philosophizing. While Runner and Stob both insisted that philosophy cannot be "neutral," Wolterstorff argued that "a philosophical appeal is typically not neutral with respect to faith" — adding that he did not think that "typically not" here could legitimately be replaced with "never."[9] Similarly, in his influential 1976 book *Reason within the Bounds of Religion,* Wolterstorff was careful not to say, in arguing that Christian theorizing ought to be consciously guided by "control beliefs," that the fact that Christians possess unique control beliefs necessitates the formulation of uniquely Christian theories. Rather, he consistently speaks of the Christian "weighing and devising" of theories — implying that Christians might, after proper "weighing," employ some of the same theories as non-Christians.

Plantinga did not really address such questions explicitly in the earlier stages of his career. It might even be said with some justice that he ignored the second of our Calvinist emphases, stressing the first and third themes. Plantinga clearly believed that the biblical God is sovereign over all of life, including philosophy. And he certainly emphasized God's commitment to orderly, lawlike ways.

In his well-known statement of "the free-will defense," with reference to "the problem of evil," Plantinga argued — in a manner that is widely credited with altering the ways in which Anglo-American philosophers treat this age-old topic — that the existence of evil in the world (in the form, say, of human suffering) is not *simply* incompatible with the existence of an all-good and all-powerful God. It may be that God willed that a certain amount of evil should exist in order that certain good states of affairs could also be realized — good states of affairs that require a certain amount of evil as a prerequisite. And if these evil occurrences are indeed *logically* necessary conditions for the existence of the good states of affairs, Plantinga argued, then even God could not will the ends without also willing the necessary means.

If, as I have already suggested, philosophical Calvinists insist that God acts in lawlike, reliable ways, then Plantinga clearly fits the pattern on this score. His God cannot easily be accused of capriciousness. But when we add to this the fact that Plantinga was fascinated in the 1960s and 1970s with the arguments of natural theology, it is easy to see how some might have gotten the overall impression that he was making the ways of an orderly God all *too* discernible to human intelligence — at least for neo-Calvinist tastes.

In recent years, however, Plantinga's views seem to have shifted signifi-

9. Wolterstorff, "Faith and Philosophy," in *Faith and Philosophy,* 31.

cantly. In the 1970s he began teaching a course in "Calvinist epistemology" at the University of Notre Dame, and in his 1983 essay "Reason and Belief in God" he formulated an extensive defense of "the Reformed objection to natural theology," drawing on the writings of Calvin, Bavinck, and Kuyper in the process.[10]

When in November of 1983 Plantinga was called upon to deliver an inaugural address as the newly appointed John A. O'Brien Professor of Philosophy at Notre Dame, he described the calling of Christian philosophers in terms that have a familiar neo-Calvinist ring. Present-day intellectual life, he observed, "is for the most part profoundly nontheistic and hence non-Christian — more than that, it is anti-theistic. Most of the so-called human sciences, most of the non-human sciences, most of non-scientific intellectual endeavor and even a good bit of allegedly Christian theology is animated by a spirit wholly foreign to that of Christian theism."[11]

In such an environment, Plantinga insisted, at least three things are required of Christian philosophers. They must show "more independence of the rest of the philosophical world." They "must display more integrity — integrity in the sense of integral wholeness, or oneness, or unity, being all of one piece." And they must manifest "boldness" — they "must put on the whole armor of God" for their philosophical efforts.[12]

Plantinga did not intend his arguments to encourage Christian philosophers to "retreat into their own isolated enclave, having as little as possible to do with non-theistic philosophers. Of course not!" But neither should they ignore the fact that philosophy "is an arena for the articulation and interplay of commitments and allegiances fundamentally religious in nature."[13]

An interest in the noetic effects of sin and grace and a concern with charting out the differences between theistic and nontheistic patterns of philosophical thought have become prominent items of Plantinga's agenda. In his own investigations of these matters he does not shrink from overtly Kuyperian formulations. Plantinga and Wolterstorff have done much in recent years to introduce the thought of the Dutch Calvinist tra-

10. Alvin Plantinga, "Reason and Belief in God," in *Faith and Rationality: Reason and Belief in God,* ed. Alvin Plantinga and Nicholas Wolterstorff (Notre Dame, Ind.: University of Notre Dame Press, 1983).

11. Alvin Plantinga, "Advice to Christian Philosophers," *Faith and Philosophy,* July 1984, 253.

12. Plantinga, "Advice to Christian Philosophers," 254.

13. Plantinga, "Advice to Christian Philosophers," 270-71.

dition to a much larger Christian, and even non-Christian, philosophical audience.

Bouwsma and Frankena

The story of the influence of Dutch Calvinism on the North American philosophical scene is certainly not exhausted by the activities of the persons and institutions already mentioned. For one thing, Calvin College and the Institute for Christian Studies are not the only centers for Dutch Reformed philosophical inquiry. Of the four most recent appointments to the Calvin College philosophy faculty, for example, one person received his undergraduate philosophical training at Trinity Christian College, another at Hope College, and two others at Dordt College.

But a complete survey of the Dutch Calvinist presence in North American philosophy must also attend to the contributions of those philosophers who have devoted their professional careers to teaching and research in secular universities. We cannot devote adequate attention to such persons here. But we must at least highlight this as an area in which further elaboration is necessary and desirable.

Two of the best-known scholars in this category are Oets K. Bouwsma and William K. Frankena. Each man spent his entire career teaching at public universities, and each received a Distinguished Alumnus Award from Calvin College after retirement. Each is also highly regarded in the philosophy profession and was elected — as already mentioned — president of the American Philosophical Association.

Bouwsma spent most of his career as a professor of philosophy at the University of Nebraska — although in his later years he served as distinguished professor at the University of Texas. Throughout his life he maintained fierce loyalties to the Christian Reformed Church. While living in Lincoln, Nebraska, he belonged for a while to a local Reformed Church congregation but later transferred his membership to a Christian Reformed congregation in Omaha, sixty miles from his home. When he moved to Texas he attended Presbyterian services but maintained his Christian Reformed membership in the Omaha church.

His confessional and spiritual loyalties were well known in the academic community. In the introduction to one of the posthumously published collections of his essays, the editors, two of Bouwsma's former students, describe him in these terms: "Well known as an essayist on

Descartes, Moore, and Wittgenstein, O. K. Bouwsma was also an equally committed student of Kierkegaard, a devoted reader of Scriptures, and a lifelong lover of the reformed church."[14]

The title of the volume just mentioned is a good indicator of Bouwsma's approach to religious issues — *Without Proof or Evidence*. He may be the most thoroughgoing philosophical fideist ever produced by North American Dutch Calvinism. In an essay entitled "Faith, Evidence and Proof" he explains his fideistic convictions at some length — and in his own unique style of writing, replete with puns, stories, and literary allusions. He devotes considerable attention to, among other biblical episodes, the stories of the call of Abram and the conversion of Saul of Tarsus. Each of these is an "exemplar of faith." They hear a call from God and they obey. At no point do they receive *evidence* of God's existence. The person who needs such "evidence," Bouwsma thinks, has not yet become a religious person. And for the religious person — the person of faith in God — the question of "evidence" does not arise.

Similarly, the believer experiences reality differently than the unbeliever:

> We may say that a Christian and any man called of God have an environment which other men do not have. When a Christian, with the psalmist, looks out upon the heavens and hears them declare the glory of God in flaming red or sees the firmament declare, in the green finery of spring, God's handiwork — he sees the same setting sun and the same expanse of earth and yet he sees something different. . . . It would be better to say that he has drunk of a sacred potion, "the waters of life," and that his life has been made new and with that his new eyes have seen new hills, pastures, valleys, and floods. "The hills girded with Joy" are not evidence that they are God's creation. They are hills seen by the psalmist or as seen by the psalmist. A transfiguration of the landscape.[15]

Bouwsma does not explicitly discuss his specifically Reformed commitments in his published writings. He is very explicit, however, about his own Christian convictions. And while his philosophical approach, espe-

---

14. From the editors' introduction to *Without Proof or Evidence: Essays of O. K. Bouwsma*, ed. J. L. Craft and Ronald E. Hustwit (Lincoln: University of Nebraska Press, 1984), vii.

15. Bouwsma, in *Without Proof or Evidence*, 13-14.

cially on religious questions, might be best described as "Kierkegaardian," it certainly comports well with at least some central elements of his Calvinism — namely, a belief in a sovereign self-revealing God who encounters human creatures who are, in their sinfulness, desperately in need of a transforming vision of reality.

William Frankena is a philosophical ethicist who taught for most of his active career in the philosophy department at the University of Michigan. His little book *Ethics* is the most widely used introductory textbook of moral philosophy in the English-speaking world and is probably one of the best-selling ethics books of all time; it has also been translated into five languages, including Dutch.

Of all the philosophers we have discussed here, Frankena has been the least inclined to reveal, in any extensive manner at least, the ways in which his own religious convictions (he is a practicing Presbyterian) have affected his philosophical development. This is not to say that he has completely ignored the relationship between religion and ethics. He regularly alludes in his writings to Christian thinkers, and one of his essays, "Love and Principle in Christian Ethics" (originally published in the Jellema Festschrift), had a strong impact on subsequent developments in theological ethics.

Frankena does occasionally drop public hints concerning his own religious commitments. For example, in a postscript to a volume of his essays edited by a former student, Frankena describes the intellectual context in which some of his earliest essays were written: "I entered my graduate work (done at The University of Michigan, Harvard and Cambridge University) in 1930, with a Calvinistic background and Hegelian sympathies. Paul Henle later remarked that he could see the Calvinism in me but not the Hegelianism, and I suppose this is still true."[16]

Frankena does not elaborate on this remark, leaving his readers to guess what the Calvinistic influence amounts to.

At the very least, though, Frankena manifests the mental traits of the Calvinist as described by MacKay and Ten Hoor. He is a philosophical boundary marker par excellence: he loves to offer typologies and to chart out distinctions and subdistinctions regarding schools of ethical thought, considering arguments for and against various positions.

---

16. "Concluding More or Less Philosophical Postscript," in *Perspectives on Morality: Essays by William K. Frankena,* ed. Kenneth Goodpaster (Notre Dame, Ind.: University of Notre Dame Press, 1976), 209.

But Frankena also operates with a deep Calvinist-type respect for the moral "ought." He entitled his presidential address for the 1966 meeting of the American Philosophical Association "On Saying the Ethical Thing," a speech that he concluded by offering some wistful comments on the contemporary drift away from the use of moral categories in assessing reality:

> I have in mind cultural relativism, irrationalism, psychoanalysis, existentialism, "the new morality," "the new immorality," "adversary culture," post-modernism, the God-is-dead line, whatever that is, "the end of ideology," and many other things — including even the prevailing position among moral philosophers of "the new approach" with whom I have associated myself. I cannot help but feel that they all somehow conspire against saying the ethical thing as I have construed it. . . . Therefore, like the hero of a play set in a century to which I and those who are with me no doubt belong, I cry,
>
> > What's that you say? Hopeless? — Why very well!
> > . . . What's that? No! Surrender? No!
> > Never! — Never!
> > No! I fight on! I fight on! I fight on![17]

The perspective on morality that Frankena has long fought for is of a sort often thought of as an "Ideal Observer" view of the justification of moral judgments. Like many Anglo-American ethicists in the twentieth century, Frankena has devoted much philosophical attention to the phenomenon of moral disagreement. What is going on when two reasonable, well-informed moral persons sustain a basic disagreement on a moral issue? Can such disputes ultimately be resolved?

Frankena has insisted that they can be — but with a stress on the "ultimately." He argues that when all rational discussion seems to be to no avail in deciding a moral dispute, and yet when a person still insists that his position is the right one, what he is implicitly claiming is that his views conform to an ultimate or ideal consensus.

> The fact that moral judgments claim a consensus on the part of others does not mean that the individual thinker must bow to the judgment of the majority in his society. He is not claiming an *actual* consensus, he is

---

17. Frankena, "On Saying the Ethical Thing," in *Perspectives on Morality,* 124.

claiming that in the end — which never comes or comes only on the Day of Judgment — his position will be concurred in by those who freely and clear-headedly review the relevant facts from the moral point of view. In other words, he is claiming an *ideal* consensus that transcends majorities and actual societies. One's society and its codes and institutions may be wrong. Here enters the autonomy of the moral agent — he must take the moral point of view and must claim an eventual consensus with others who do so, but he must judge for himself. He may be mistaken, but, like Luther, he cannot do otherwise.[18]

Of course, Frankena is not the first to appeal to a hypothetical ideal consensus of this sort. Roderick Firth and others have also defended versions of an Ideal Observer theory in ethics. And this theory has important similarities to Rawls's notion of an "original position," as well as to Mannheim's depiction of the "free-floating intellectual" and Habermas's projected "ideal speech situation."

But Frankena typically resorts to very Christian language in describing his ideal consensus. In the passage quoted above, for example, he refers to the Last Judgment as a way of picturing the situation in which details of the ideal consensus might actually be known. To be sure, he does so in terms of a disjunction: the ideal consensus might never be actualized *or* it might come with the Last Judgment. What he seems to be doing here is spelling out his case in such a way that it might be acceptable in broad outline to nontheists but also suggesting how his view might be given a theistic texture. This also seems to be what he is doing in an especially poignant passage in his presidential address, as he expands on his claim that moral disputes are ultimately adjudicable:

> It has *not* been established that this claim is false; we do *not* know that
> . . . ultimate normative disagreements, if they exist, will continue to exist
> as knowledge grows from more to more among rational men who share
> the same point of view. There is even some rough evidence to the contrary; historically, religious people who have theological beliefs of certain sorts tend to adopt the ethics of love, and, today, it begins to appear
> that, as the peoples of the world come to share more and more the same
> points of view and the same factual beliefs, they also come to regard the

18. William Frankena, *Ethics*, 2nd ed. (Englewood Cliffs, N.J.: Prentice-Hall, 1973), 112-13.

same things as desirable. At any rate, so long as the case against the absolutist claim is not better established than it is, we may still make the claim; it may take some temerity, but it is not unreasonable. As for me and my house, therefore, we will continue to serve the Lord — or, as others may prefer to say, the Ideal Observer.[19]

Frankena has clearly conducted his philosophical investigations in such a way that the Calvinist God is not completely hidden in his portrayal of moral reality. If Frankena's philosophical views are less than explicit on matters that are important to Reformed Christians, it is nonetheless true that he, like Bouwsma, has contributed significantly to a philosophical climate in North America in which the cause of Christian philosophy can be promoted with integrity, and out of a desire to communicate with a broad philosophical audience.

Philosophy and Community Leadership

There is much in the story of Dutch Calvinist philosophical ideas in North America that can serve as grist for the sociologist's — or the social historian's — mill. This story is actually not so much about ideas as it is about people in communities who received and selected and shaped and discarded ideas in the course of their attempts to come to grips with reality as they experienced it in a North American context.

It is tempting, and to some degree legitimate, then, to "sociologize" about a notion like the antithesis. Isn't there, after all, a very intimate link between the theological-philosophical "we-versus-they" and the very existential "we-versus-they" experiences of an immigrant or ethnic subcultural community? Surely it is not pure coincidence that, for example, the antithesis idea should be very attractive to Dutch Calvinists at those points when they are experiencing intense cultural alienation, and that the antithetical theme should weaken whenever they come to feel less like strangers in a strange land in their relation to North American culture.

But we must be careful with such analyses, for reasons similar to that expressed by Karl Barth when he encountered the argument that Kierkegaard's philosophy was nothing more than a manifestation of his own neuroses. That can't be, Barth responded — there are too many

19. Frankena, "On Saying," 123.

nonneurotics who agree with Kierkegaard! Similarly, there is no uniform correlation between an endorsement of the antithesis notion and an experience of cultural alienation. Nonimmigrant groups have also espoused a strict understanding of "church versus world." And the antithesis idea can reemerge in a community long after cultural assimilation has taken place.

Indeed, recent events cited in this narrative provide cautionary notes of just this sort. It may be the case that AACS members de-emphasized the antithesis as their immigrant community became more "Canadianized," but it is also true that Alvin Plantinga grew *more* antithetically oriented in his thinking during this same period — even though Plantinga has been one of the most intellectually "Americanized" of the philosophers to work within the borders of the Christian Reformed community.

This is not to deny that there is a clear pattern of interaction between philosophical ideas and cultural context that can be observed in a community like that of the Dutch Calvinists in North America. One can admit to the existence of phenomena of this sort without thereby endorsing a reductionism that insists that cultural context always determines philosophy. In fact, I am inclined to argue that an important difference between the latest stage of North American Calvinist philosophical discussion and the earlier stages of that discussion has to do precisely with the *degree* to which the espousal of philosophical doctrines is directly shaped by the cultural agenda of the subcultural community.

Let me put my point in very simple terms and then briefly elaborate on it. It is my impression that in the past — even the relatively recent past — philosophy in the Christian Reformed community was viewed by many people as an important instrument for providing intellectual direction to the members of the subculture. To be sure, this was never philosophy's only role in that community; but it was an important one. Thus the philosophical differences between, say, Evan Runner and Henry Stob were never purely "abstract," even if they might seem so to the disinterested observer. In their own minds, and in the minds of many of their constituents, they were articulating alternative cultural self-images to a community that had long worried much — and the worries were intensified by each new wave of immigration — about how it ought to relate to the larger North American cultural milieu. Under such conditions a debate over how the antithesis is to be understood is in fact a dramatic confrontation between alternative cultural self-interpretations.

If my account is correct on this point, then it is very understandable that the philosophical leaders involved in these debates would view their arguments as nothing short of a struggle for the intellectual control of an ethnic subculture — a philosophical battle in which the very mind, if not the heart, of the community was at stake. And it is precisely this "cosmic" context for the doing of Calvinistic philosophy that — on my reading of the situation — has changed in recent decades. It is the dissipation of this atmosphere, in which subcultural direction setting loomed large, that made the philosophical truce of the 1970s between the Toronto school and the Calvin College philosophical establishment possible. As long as the prize was the intellectual control of the Christian Reformed community, or significant portions thereof, the battle had to be waged. But when the focus shifted toward the broader intellectual arena, the two parties could begin to work together to propagate the neo-Calvinist vision in the larger philosophical community.

Much is regrettable about this state of affairs. It means, for example, that the Christian Reformed community has begun to change in ways that make it less susceptible than in the past to intellectual leadership of *any* sort. A bureaucratization of decision making and an increase in the "organizational" management of conflict may be inevitable, but communal life is not thereby made more interesting.

Worse yet, the changed situation for philosophers means that questions about the cultural calling of the Christian Reformed community are no longer the burning issues they once were. This is not to say that they have been settled — there certainly is no formal intellectual settlement one can document. Rather, the community is simply *finding* its place in the larger cultural milieu — or it is finding its *many* places, if you wish — even if it no longer works very hard at giving intellectual articulation to the rationale that informs its cultural negotiations.

But the changed situation is not without its benefits. For one thing, Calvinist philosophers have been relieved of the pressure of that kind of *seriousness* that weighs on intellectuals whose formulations are too closely tied to intense subcultural debates. To be sure, the absence of seriousness is not necessarily a good thing. But in this case the dissolving of one kind of seriousness has generated another kind — happily, a kind that provides for an intellectual buffer zone of sorts.

Dutch American philosophers are now freer than they were in the past to address themselves to the serious business of "ecumenical" philosophical discussion. And important steps have been taken in recent years to facilitate this important activity. Members of the Calvin College philosophy department were instrumental in founding, in 1978, the Society of Christian Philosophers; this organization, which now has almost eight hundred members continent-wide, is an important forum for dialogue and cooperative scholarship among philosophers representing a broad spectrum of confessional communities: Reformed, Roman Catholic, Anglo-American evangelical, Anglo-Catholic, Lutheran, and the like.

An informal but growing coalition of Calvinists, Roman Catholics, and Anglo-American evangelicals is perhaps an especially significant — and uniquely North American — phenomenon. Philosophers from these communities have much in common. George Marsden has proposed the intriguing thesis that for Anglo-American evangelicals the transition from the nineteenth century, when they had held a position of cultural domination, to the twentieth century, with its strong secularism, was very much like an immigration experience.[20] The resultant sense of cultural alienation, which characterized the evangelical presence for several decades in this century, was not unlike the experience of Dutch Americans and Italian Americans and Polish Americans during a similar time span. It is not only Dutch Calvinists, then, who have felt the dissolution of a strong existential *sense* of cultural "antithesis" in recent decades; similar developments have occurred in post–Vatican II Catholicism and in those conservative Protestant communities that have sponsored the much-proclaimed "evangelical renaissance" of recent years. Philosophers representing these traditions have much to talk about together, and they have been busy pursuing those conversations.

None of this releases Dutch Calvinist philosophers, though, from the obligation to attempt to provide intellectual direction to their own community. In one sense, of course, pursuing a more ecumenical agenda is itself a means of giving that kind of direction, since the Dutch Calvinist community in North America very much needs to be shown how to engage in the complex task of reaching out to others while at the same time drawing on its own spiritual roots.

And the stress here must be on *spiritual* roots. This was already recognized in 1926 by Clarence Bouma, perhaps the most articulate of the "Americanizers" in his generation of Christian Reformed leaders. Bouma insisted that the important "spiritual group consciousness" that the Dutch Calvinists had brought to North America had to be "enucleated from the

---

20. See George Marsden, "From Fundamentalism to Evangelicalism: A Historical Analysis," in *The Evangelicals: What They Believe, Who They Are, Where They Are Changing*, ed. David F. Wells and John D. Woodbridge (Nashville: Abingdon, 1975), 129ff.

national, racial, Dutch setting which it inevitably has in our thinking."[21] But Bouma was also very insistent that the Dutch American Reformed community be aware of the historical confessional community in which it stands as a possessor of this "consciousness":

> This spiritual heritage is historically rooted in the Reformation move-ment of the 16th century, more particularly in its Reformed or Calvinis-tic expression. It has received the stamp and imprint of those 19th cen-tury religious movements of Holland known as the *Secession* and the *Doleantie.* It has received new articulation and fresh inspiration in re-cent decades by the revival of Reformed thought and life in Holland un-der the masterful leadership of thinkers like Kuyper and Bavinck. Such are our spiritual antecedents and present affinities. This is the soil from which to a great extent we are still drawing our spiritual nourishment and inspiration.[22]

Calvinists in North America can still be fed by these sources of nour-ishment. But the danger that Bouma described has passed, or is at least very quickly passing: the "Dutch setting" for these Reformed legacies is no longer an "inevitable" attachment. The real question is whether the spiri-tual "nucleus" that Bouma cherished can be retained in the absence of eth-nic reinforcements.

If the heritage of Calvin and Kuyper and Bavinck — or at least all that is good and worthy of our acceptance in that heritage — is to continue to be a nurturing source in North American environs, it will take more theo-logical and philosophical *effort* than it did in the past. This effort must, in turn, also be coordinated with the larger ecumenical task, as already de-scribed. North American neo-Calvinist philosophy must continue to grow as an indigenous, ecumenically enriched activity, in which the ideas and insights of nineteenth-century Holland are appropriated and recontex-tualized for appropriate philosophical service of the sovereign Lord who redeems and sanctifies rebel sinners, equipping them for obedience to his wise ordinances.

Christian philosophy can be an important instrument by which God

---

21. Clarence Bouma, "Our School and American Life," in *Semi-Centennial Volume: Theological School and Calvin College, 1876-1926* (Grand Rapids: Semi-Centennial Commit-tee, Theological School and Calvin College, 1926), 189.

22. Bouma, "Our School," 190.

liberates his elect people from enslavement to their cultural environment, whether that environment be marked off by countless dikes and dams or by purple mountains looming over fruited plains. Philosophy, if allowed the breathing space in which to flourish, can serve as one means by which Christians can, in the midst of their cultural context, gain the healthy focus described by Clarence Bouma: "As true Puritans our eyes should not be upon circumstances or environment but upon the imperishable ideal and the everlasting God, in whom all absolute truth and all absolute values ultimately find their ground."[23]

---

23. Bouma, "Our School," 221.

Dutch and Dutch American Church Groups and Movements Especially Relevant to the Development of Dutch Neo-Calvinism

In the Netherlands

Nederlandse Hervormde Kerk (NHK). The "Netherlands Reformed Church" was established in the sixteenth century as the embodiment of the teachings of the Calvinist Reformation.

The *Afscheiding* (Secession) of 1834 was led by a small group of ministers who became convinced that the teachings and ecclesiastical structure of the Netherlands Reformed Church were no longer faithful to classical Calvinist thought and practice.

The *Doleantie* (Grieving) movement was a group of pastors, led by Abraham Kuyper, who in the 1880s protested what they saw as strong liberal trends in the Netherlands Reformed Church.

Gereformeerde Kerken in Nederland (GKN). The "Reformed Churches in the Netherlands" was the union formed in 1892 of the *Doleantie* churches with a majority of the congregations established by the *Afscheiding* of 1834.

Christelijke Gereformeerde Kerken (CGK). The "Christian Reformed Churches" were the continuation of the *Afscheiding*-established congregations that chose not to join with the *Doleantie* in the union of 1892.

Gereformeerde Kerken in Nederland (Vrijegemaakt). The "Reformed Churches (liberated)" is the federation of congregations, led by Klaas

Schilder, formed in 1944, when Schilder was deposed from his ministerial office by the GKN.

Protestantse Kerk in Nederland. The "Protestant Church in the Netherlands" was formed in 2004, uniting congregations of the NHK, the GKN, and the Dutch Lutherans.

In the USA and Canada

The Reformed Church in America (RCA): established in seventeenth-century colonial America, it is the oldest Protestant denomination, with a continuing history, in the United States.

The Christian Reformed Church (CRC): the *Afscheiding*-related immigrant group who settled in Michigan in the 1840s soon decided to join the existing Dutch Reformed denomination, but some were unhappy with that union. They pulled out in 1857, resulting in the division between the RCA and the CRC.

The Protestant Reformed Churches (PRC): because they dissented from the "Three Points of Common Grace" articulated by the Christian Reformed Synod of 1923, a group of churches, led by Herman Hoeksema (who was deposed from the CRC because of his theological dissent), formed the PRC in 1924.

The Canadian Reformed Churches (CanRC): established by post–World War II immigrants who had been members of the "liberated" congregations in the Netherlands.

The Free Reformed Churches: established by post–World War II immigrants who had been members of the Christian Reformed Churches (continuing *Afscheiding*) in the Netherlands.